WAR IN THE FAR EAST

WAR IN THE FAR EAST

VOLUME 3

Asian Armageddon, 1944–1945

PETER HARMSEN

CASEMATE

Philadelphia & Oxford

Published in the United States of America and Great Britain in 2021 by
CASEMATE PUBLISHERS
1950 Lawrence Road, Havertown, PA 19083, USA
and
The Old Music Hall, 106–108 Cowley Road, Oxford OX4 1JE, UK

Copyright 2021 © Peter Harmsen

Hardcover Edition: ISBN 978-1-61200-627-7
Digital Edition: ISBN 978-1-61200-628-4

A CIP record for this book is available from the British Library

Printed and bound in United States by Sheridan

For a complete list of Casemate titles, please contact:

CASEMATE PUBLISHERS (US)
Telephone (610) 853-9131
Fax (610) 853-9146
Email: casemate@casematepublishers.com
www.casematepublishers.com

CASEMATE PUBLISHERS (UK)
Telephone (01865) 241249
Email: casemate-uk@casematepublishers.co.uk
www.casematepublishers.co.uk

Contents

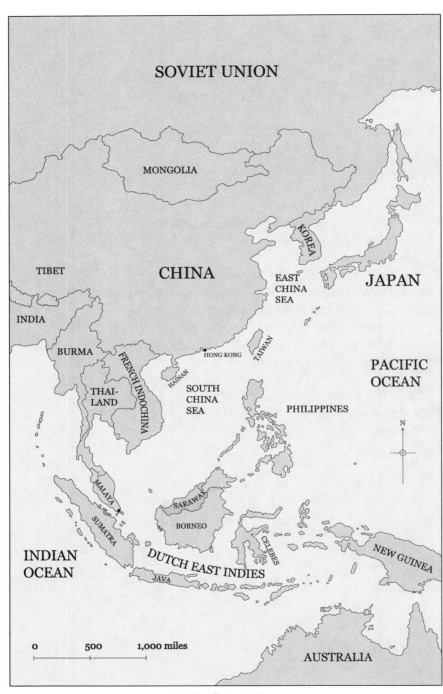

Asia Pacific in 1944.

Preface

World War II in the Asia Pacific created the modern world. While the war in Europe resulted in the ascendancy of the Soviet Union and set the stage for the Cold War, which lasted until almost the end of the 20th century, the defining event of the 21st century is arguably the emergence of a Chinese superpower, which ultimately resulted from the power constellation in Asia at the end of hostilities in 1945. Why Asia looks the way it does is impossible to fully appreciate without understanding its history during the war in the Asia Pacific. Whereas the first two volumes of the trilogy *War in the Far East* dealt with the origins and first years of that epic conflict, this volume segues into the post-war period, describing events that in some cases reverberate to this day.

That being said, the last chapter of this book is not meant as a comprehensive history of post-war Asia. That would require a whole new series of books. Instead, it is to be seen as a brief overview of how the region presented itself to the survivors of the war during the first months of "peace." Writing the word in quotation marks is not an exaggeration. For many of the societies in the Asia Pacific, there was more turmoil and more violence. History went on. By the same token, history continues in our modern world, and it colors the lenses through which we view the past. The current volume would have been written in a different way if it had appeared twenty years ago. Probably, China would have taken up less space. In this sense, history, as an academic discipline, is also in constant change.

A note on the rendering of Asian names: both for Japanese and Chinese individuals, the practice of the region is followed, and the surname is placed before the given name. For Chinese names, the modern pinyin rendering has been used, as it is now almost universally accepted. There are very few exceptions in this book, most importantly the name of the Nationalist Chinese leader at the time, who is still widely known as Chiang Kai-shek. On a somewhat different note, no attempt has been made to alter contemporary quotes using derogatory terms such as "Japs" or "Nips." While it is recognized that these terms are upsetting to a modern readership, it is necessary to keep them within their proper context, not only in the interest of historical accuracy, but also in order to better reflect the unique flavor of combat in the Pacific, characterized by the mutual hatred and contempt between the opposing forces, which, to some extent at least, set it apart from the war carried out at the same time in Western Europe. We do not learn from history by censoring it, but by confronting it squarely.

As was the case with the first two instalments of the trilogy *War in the Far East*, this volume would not have appeared in its present form but for the help of numerous individuals. Among these, I especially wish to thank the following: Chris McDougal, National Museum of the Pacific War; Janis Jorgensen, Naval Institute; Fred H. Allison and Yvette House at Oral History Section, USMC History Division; as well as staff at the Naval History and Heritage Command, National Naval Aviation Museum, and the Nunn Center for Oral History. Once again, a special thanks to my friend Jokull Gislason, who kindly read the manuscript and provided invaluable feedback. Thanks also to staff at Casemate, especially Ruth Sheppard, and to my hawk-eyed editor, Sophie MacCallum. Of course, any mistakes that may have slipped through to these pages are mine alone, just as I take sole responsibility for the interpretations that have guided my writing. Finally, and for the third time during work on this trilogy, thanks to my wife Hui-tsung and our two daughters, Lisa and Eva, for their patience.

CHAPTER ONE

Suicide Creek

January–February 1944

The first day of the year 1944 found the Marines at Cape Gloucester in the Southwest Pacific in a victorious mood. The beachhead held by members of the 1st Marine Division on the jungle-covered island of New Britain, northeast of Australia, had expanded rapidly since they had landed less than a week earlier. They had met almost no Japanese opposition and, helped by massive aerial and naval bombardment, they had carried out what one Marine described as "the perfect amphibious operation."[1] Private First Class Whitney Jacobs, who had fought with the division since the beginning of the war, noted how everything had improved compared with the operations in the Guadalcanal campaign little more than a year earlier: "We had more supplies by this time. Plenty of planes, plenty of ammunition, plenty of boats."[2]

With just a few hours to go before the old year ended, the division had achieved one of its main objectives, seizing an airfield constructed by the Japanese in the preceding months. The operation had proceeded with deceptive ease. "I don't remember anybody being really shot at actually when we got to the airfield," said Lieutenant Colonel Robert B. Luckey, an artillery officer.[3] After hoisting the Stars and Stripes on a jerry-rigged flagpole over the airfield, divisional commander William H. Rupertus proudly radioed to his superior, General Walter Krueger: "First Marine Division presents to you as an early New Year gift the complete airdrome of Cape Gloucester. Situation well in hand due to fighting spirit of troops, the usual Marine luck and the help of God."[4]

The truth was the Marines needed plenty more luck, as the battle for Cape Gloucester was only getting started. Hiding in the surrounding dense forest were thousands of Japanese, unconquered and waiting to kill the Americans. The Marines, too, were tormented by premonitions that this would be no walkover. Upon disembarking, machine gunner James W. Johnston had not taken many steps inland before he had come across a stack of dead American bodies, "muddy and bloody, mutilated and pitifully ugly." Reeling from the horrifying sight, he had run into a friend who had landed earlier and put the situation bluntly, "Man, Jim, this is the shits."[5]

Fierce as the combat was, for many Marines it was not even the worst part of Cape Gloucester. Nothing beat the rain. Indeed, they had been warned about it beforehand. "We were told in advance… it is considered to be the wettest spot on earth," said Major John P. Leonard, 1st Special Weapons Battalion. We were wet and mildewed and fungus, everything, all the time."[6] Lieutenant Colonel Lewis J. Fields, commander of 1st Battalion, 11th Marines, had similar reminiscences. "It's like a fire hose sitting over you. That's how hard it comes down. It's just like a waterfall coming down on you, and it goes on and on… Water underfoot, water above, mud. Your clothes were dirty, there was no way really to take care of yourself, because of the elements."[7]

The Japanese struck back just before dawn on January 3. Throughout the night, Marines occupying Target Hill, a 450-foot height half a mile inland from the invasion beach, could hear the ominous sound of enemy soldiers in the dark in front of them. The Japanese were cutting steps into the slope leading to their

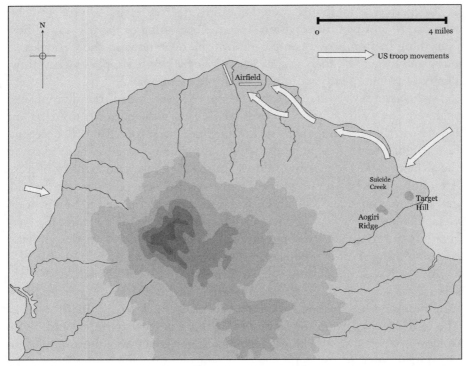

Cape Gloucester, January 1944.

positions, eventually getting within just 20 yards of the American line. Shortly before the sun was to emerge over the green tropical canopy, they launched their attack, emerging like ghosts out of the gray morning mist. The fighting was brutal. A Japanese mortar shell hit an American machine-gun position, killing two men; a third Marine was unscathed and fired the weapon into the oncoming enemy, running through belt after belt of ammunition.[8] Over the din of the battle, a loud Japanese voice could be heard. The Marines guessed it belonged to the officer leading the attack. "We located this officer's approximate position and poured heavy fire into this area," said Captain Marshall W. Moore, in command of the defense. "His screams ceased and then the attack stopped."[9]

When searching the area in front of their positions, the Marines discovered 40 dead Japanese, some of them lying in large, tangled heaps.[10] On some of the bodies, they found important information that the intelligence officers had missed during pre-invasion planning. It confirmed the existence, roughly a mile from Target Hill, of a heavily defended Japanese position named Aogiri Ridge which controlled all access to the battlefield, and also all exits away from it. The Marines had to take this for the momentum of the invasion to be sustained.[11] In order to pacify the flank ahead of an attack on the ridge, the Marines had to secure a narrow creek a few hundred yards to the west. On the face of it, it did not seem much of an obstacle, as it was just two or three feet deep and nowhere wider than 20 feet. However, its banks were steep and, more importantly, waiting beyond was a deadly foe.

Within hours, the Marines were on the move. A war correspondent described the challenge facing the men beyond the creek: "The deadly defense could not be seen, they couldn't see that the heavy growth across the creek was salted with pillboxes, machine-gun emplacements armored with dirt and logs, some of them several stories deep, all carefully spotted so they could sweep the slopes of both banks of the creek with interfacing fire."[12] The Marines repeatedly attempted to make it across, individually and in small groups, each time exposing themselves to lethal fire. One of the men was cut down by a bullet in midstream and hung over a log, calling out to his buddies, "Here I am! Here I am!" His screams continued for half an hour before he died.[13] After several futile attempts to reach the other side, the attack stalled. In the meantime, the Marines coined a name for the stream: Suicide Creek.

Following hours of tense waiting, three Sherman tanks appeared on the scene, bringing with them the promise of a breakthrough. While the sight of the steel hulls instilled new courage in the Marines, the tanks could not be deployed immediately. The steep banks prevented them from crossing the stream, so the Marines sent in an unarmored bulldozer to carve out a sloping passage to the stream's bed. The driver was killed by Japanese snipers before he was able to finish the job, and so was his replacement. A third volunteer driver, Senior Sergeant Kerry L. Lane, tried a novel approach, shielding behind the vehicle while working its controls with a shovel and an axe handle. Even though he took a sniper's bullet to the shoulder, he managed to complete the task, paving the way for the tanks.[14] "In the heat of battle, I hardly realized that I was wounded," Lane wrote in his memoirs. "I heard no noise, felt no pain, not at the moment. I was a little woozy after being hit in the left shoulder, and I was somewhat unsteady on my feet after crawling down from the bulldozer."[15]

It was now dark and too late for an attack to take place, and the Marines settled into an uneasy night on their side of the creek. In the morning of the following day, the lead Sherman tank made its way cautiously down the improved earthen ramp prepared by the bulldozer, easily negotiated the creek, and moved up the opposite bank. Two Japanese soldiers, armed only with explosives, attempted a suicide charge against the vehicle, but Marine riflemen following immediately in its tracks cut them down before they could get anywhere near the tank. After that, the tanks proceeded mercilessly and methodically, firing straight at Japanese pillboxes, crushing the defenses by their sheer weight, and machinegunning those able to escape. The battle for Suicide Creek was an American victory, won with a mixture of tactical acumen, technological prowess, and individual valor.[16]

This was at the beginning of a long, grinding struggle to wrest control of Cape Gloucester from the Japanese. It was, in fact, a series of battles for hills with names that meant nothing to people back home but would remain etched in the minds of the participants. "It was a hell of a fight," Marine Leo Magee told an Associated Press correspondent after a particularly bloody hill battle. "We had to cut our own trail and we couldn't see where the Japs were. They had caves and were dug in and we crawled on hands and knees, pulling ourselves up by grabbing trees and bushes."[17] Often, the Japanese would hit back in suicidal Banzai charges that were already becoming proverbial among the GIs. In one such assault, Marine Romus Burgin, armed with an M1 Garand rifle, ended up in hand-to-hand fighting with a Japanese soldier and found that he eventually prevailed due to his larger physique. "I had my bayonet on and I stuck him right… where the ribs join together in the breast… and just kind of flipped him right over my head," he said. At the same time, he fired his rifle into the writhing body of his enemy. "I don't know how many rounds of M1 ammunition went in him."[18]

In hand-to-hand combat, the Americans literally looked the Japanese enemy in the eye. Just as frequently, however, he was invisible, but equally lethal, as

Lieutenant Colonel Lewis J. Fields was to learn the hard way: "I organized a patrol, not ever imagining there was going to be much in the area, but there were apparently a handful of Japanese. The first guy I sent out was lieutenant Krause, who was quite a big guy and quite a football player—the report came back that he'd been shot in the head, right smack between the eyes. Gosh! Not good. So I said, 'This time we've got to send in more' So I sent Captain Moyer, who was headquarters battery CO with a much larger group from the headquarters battery, and he never came back, he was found shot between the eyes. Very accurate sniper fire, in this area, you see."[19]

It was war at its most personal, almost intimate, even when the enemy could not be seen. Often, he materialized only as an uncanny voice whispering from inside the solid green wall of jungle, "Prepare to die, Marine."[20] On other occasions, he was much more specific and revealed a surprising understanding of contemporary American culture, including baseball. "To hell with Babe Ruth!" a group of Japanese infantrymen yelled as they suddenly emerged from the dense forest to make a fatal charge against American lines, revealing that in the pre-war years the biggest star of America's favorite sport has also been a celebrity in Japan.[21]

Despite the fighting spirit displayed by the Japanese soldiers, there was a growing sense of hopelessness in their ranks. As the days of combat grew into weeks, their desperation began to show. Those falling into US hands, mostly dead already, were a pitiful sight. "The average enemy soldier fought with his stomach gnawingly empty, his clothes and shoes sodden and rotting away, and his body attacked by jungle diseases," in the words of the official US history.[22] One of the last Japanese alive was Major Komori Shinjirō, who roamed the jungle with his men, fighting the elements, disease, and hunger as much as the Americans. After his death, his diary was found by Marines. One of the last entries read, "We are very tired and without food."[23] Eventually it was obvious even to the Americans that the Japanese had worn themselves out at Cape Gloucester. "We pitied him in the end, this fleeing foe, disorganized, demoralized, crawling on hands and feet, even, in that dissolving downpour," wrote a Marine, "for in the end it was we—the soft, effete Americans—who had learned to get along in the jungle and who bore up best beneath the ordeal of the monsoon, and in these things lay our strength."[24]

The Marine spirit that won the battle at Cape Gloucester had a sinister side. It was a gung-ho attitude, which in extreme cases meant that success on the battlefield was measured not in ground taken, but in casualties sustained. A Marine lieutenant colonel visited the front line at the start of operations to capture one of the hills. He asked Henry W. Buse, the commander of 3rd

Battalion, 7th Marines, how he was doing. Buse later recreated the conversation: "I said fine. He asked, 'How many casualties you got?' And I told him, and he said, 'You better get going.' He called up several hours later, and asked me how I was doing, and I said fine. 'How many casualties have you got?' I told him they were considerably more, and he said 'Atta boy, old man.' And so he measured the success of the operation on how much blood had been spilled."[25]

★ ★ ★

Fifteen hundred miles from Cape Gloucester, in the Central Pacific, the Japanese were also on the defensive as 1943 turned into 1944. The Americans had made impressive gains in this vast ocean area during the past several months, seizing Tarawa in the Gilbert Islands, and the Marshalls were the logical next step in their advance towards Japan. All the Japanese could do was hunker behind fortified walls in their isolated outposts, waiting for the American onslaught. "I welcome the New Year at my ready station beside the gun," Mimori, a squad commander in the Japanese Army's 61st Guard Force, wrote in his diary on the atoll of Kwajalein. "This will be a year of decisive battles. I suppose the enemy... will continue on to the Marshalls, but the Kwajalein defenses are very strong."[26]

Indeed they were, but the Japanese were also hampered by the vastness of the area they had to defend. They knew the American foe was going to strike somewhere in the Marshall groups of islands, and that he would do so soon, but they did not know where. This forced them to stretch their already strained resources thinly across the map, and it prevented them from assembling any significant force in one place. "There were so many possible points of invasion in the Marshalls that we could not consider any one a strong point and consequently dispersed our strength," said Commander Nakajima Chikataka, who was on the staff of Japan's Combined Fleet, in post-war remarks.[27]

The exact same question, but put in reverse, was occupying American planners at the same time, as they pondered where in the Marshalls to land. Kwajalein, the world's largest atoll and in Japanese hands since the end of World War I, was at the center of the island group geographically, and it was also the logistical hub from which the Japanese distributed supplies to garrisons throughout the region. It was the obvious US target, except for the fact that an invasion force would have to pass by islands with known Japanese airfields. In other words, the danger was that the American vessels would have to sail through a veritable Scylla and Charybdis of enemy planes before getting onto the actual business of disembarking on Kwajalein.

Faced with these conditions, Admiral Chester W. Nimitz, the overall commander in the Central Pacific, showed his firmness of purpose and willingness to follow his instincts, even in the face of overwhelming dissent. At a planning meeting prior to the invasion, most of his immediate subordinates, all officers with enormous expertise and experience, argued in favor of a two-stage approach. Richmond Kelly Turner, the rear admiral commanding the 5th Amphibious Force, which was to head the offensive, explained how the airfields on the neighboring islands were to be taken in the first stage, and Kwajalein in the second. Nimitz listened patiently, but eventually made his decision in favor of a direct punch: "I have decided we are going to Kwajalein. The Japanese aren't going to know this, and they're going to be as surprised as you gentlemen are."[28] Turner frowned in obvious disagreement, forcing Nimitz to issue an ultimatum: "If you don't want to do it, the Department will find someone else to do it. Do you want to do it or not?" Turner's frowning face dissolved into a smile: "Sure I want to do it."[29]

Nimitz was right about surprising the Japanese by going straight for the main quarry. "There were few who thought you would go right to the heart of the Marshalls and take Kwajalein," said Commander Nakajima after the

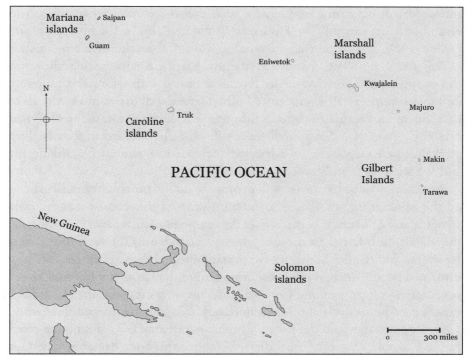

Allied advance in South Pacific, early 1944.

war.[30] This, of course, gave the Americans a tactical advantage as the element of surprise was on their side. Also on their side were meticulous planning and a willingness to face up to past mistakes and shortcomings. Turner had studied the bloody battle of Tarawa in November and prepared a detailed report on the lessons to be learned from it. His conclusion was that the Americans, already superior in material and technological terms, needed to boost that superiority even further for the attack on Kwajalein. There had to be more ships and landing craft, as well as a greater number of planes. Crucially, he insisted that he needed at least three times as much ordnance dropped in the pre-invasion bombardment. His superiors, eager to avoid a repetition of the bloodbath on Tarawa, where more than 3,000 Marines had become casualties in four days of fighting, gave him what he wanted.[31]

The operation to seize Kwajalein was divided into a northern and a southern part, which for all intents and purposes were to proceed independently of each other. The southern operation was targeting the main island in the atoll, which also bore the name of Kwajalein. It was assigned to the US Army's 7th Infantry Division, nicknamed the "Hourglass" division, which had been involved in pushing the Japanese off the Aleutians the year before. Thus, in the words of one historian, "having been the first U.S. combat division to recapture American soil, the Hourglass 7th would also be the first to capture Japanese soil."[32] The northern operation, aimed at seizing the twin islands of Roi and Namur, was handed to the 4th Marine Division. In addition to the two main invasions, a smaller force was tasked with taking Majuro atoll, 220 miles southeast of Kwajalein.[33] "[The planners] didn't want to take all of their forces into Kwajalein lagoon although it is the largest in the world," said Edwin Layton, a US Navy intelligence officer. "They wanted to seize Majuro atoll and use its lagoon as an advanced anchorage for the reserve, the supply and logistic vessels and for a refueling anchorage."[34]

As recommended by Turner, and in order to nullify the risk from the airfields on the adjacent islands, American aircraft, some of them based on the newly seized island of Tarawa, began a relentless campaign on Japanese positions in the Marshalls. It lasted for most of January and met only limited resistance, as Japanese Commander Matsuura Goro, staff officer at the Central Pacific Fleet, explained later: "The best pilots had been sent to the Northern Solomons or to new carrier groups forming. Consequently, there wasn't sufficient numbers of experienced pilots for Island Air Commands."[35] Japanese forces on the ground were the ones who paid the price. "The American attacks are becoming more furious," a soldier wrote in his diary. "Planes come over day after day. Can we stand up under the strain?"[36]

The stamina of the Japanese defenders was put further to the test as the invasion fleet approached Kwajalein atoll towards the end of January. Setting the scene for the invasion was Task Force 58. It was a formidable manifestation of naval aviation as it had evolved two years into the Pacific War, consisting of 12 carriers and 650 aircraft. Unlike the role that the carriers had played at Tarawa, where they had been mainly tasked with defense against Japanese airplanes, at Kwajalein their purpose was offensive if not aggressive: to annihilate all shipping and aircraft in the Marshalls before the landing began. It was phenomenally successful. At 8am on January 29, two days before D-Day, the last Japanese plane observed in the air over Kwajalein was shot down.[37]

The US commanders were uncertain about the opposition they would meet on Majuro, en route to Kwajalein. Layton, the intelligence officer, offered an estimate of a garrison of just six Japanese at a pre-invasion planning meeting. Marine General Holland "Howling Mad" Smith protested: "You mean six thousand." Layton was adamant. "No, six," he said. Smith offered to bet "a quart of the best bourbon whiskey" that the number of Japanese on Majuro would turn out to be "nearer 600 than 6." When a small force landed on Majuro on January 31, they found it nearly deserted and took the island in a day of bloodless operations. "Howling Mad" Smith conceded he had lost the bet and presented Layton with a bottle of bourbon, wrapped with ribbons of scarlet and gold, the Marine Corps's colors.[38]

Meanwhile, the main invasion fleet was on its way. "We had a big task force," said Marine Richard Sorenson. "You could see ships all around us as far as the eye could see. There were aircraft carriers and planes taking off and air cover all the time." The Marines prepared for the assault by studying detailed mockups of the landing areas, including all known Japanese pillboxes and blockhouses. "We were well schooled as to where we were going to land and what our objectives were. So every man in the squad and every man in the landing teams knew just where we would go," Sorenson said. Watching the accompanying battleships pummel the islands boosted morale even further. On January 31, the Marines landed on a series of small islets at the entrance of the Roi and Namur lagoon, providing a base for guns to be placed in support of the main invasion.[39]

The landings on the main islands took place on February 1. Despite the heavy bombardment, there was still resistance on Roi and Namur, much of it determined, and as the Marines poured out of their landing craft, they felt dangerously exposed. "Roi was all airstrip; all flat; nothing, no humps or bumps or anything on it. You looked around and you wondered, 'Where am I going to hide if somebody is shooting at me?'" recalled Marine Arthur Liberty.[40] He also soon discovered that the enemy in front was not to be written off. "I had always heard, we all had, that the Japanese were little people with big coke bottle glasses; not so. The first thing I saw when I hit the beach was about a 6-foot Japanese marine. That changed my attitude right quick."[41]

Carl Matthews was in the first invasion wave, jumping out of the amphibious tractor that had carried him through the turf and scrambling for cover on the flat beach. "A young Marine lay on the dry sand, rifle pointed in the direction of the enemy, steel helmet held fast by the strap under his chin, his dungarees were spotless and without a wrinkle," he later said. Only then did it dawn on him that the man had already been killed. "That young Marine was dead and I wanted to be sick, but I didn't have time."[42] As more waves piled up in the invasion area, bullets flew in all directions, and most of them were American. "Every wave that hit the island would immediately start firing away," said Marine Baine Kerr. "If you're in one of the earlier waves, you had to get down on the ground flat because these birds were firing madly away. They didn't know what they were shooting at."[43]

In the middle of the first day of fighting, Marines accidentally detonated torpedo warheads stored inside a bunker on Namur. Some Marines thought an unknown volcano had suddenly erupted, and it seemed as if "the whole of Namur Island disappeared from sight in a tremendous brown cloud of dust and sand raised by the explosion," as one of them later recalled.[44] Chunks of concrete landed among the troops on the invasion beach, killing several men and injuring many more, and debris even rained on the vessels anchored in the lagoon. "Trunks of palm trees and chunks of concrete as large as packing crates were flying through the air like match sticks," a Marine officer said about the chaotic scene. "The hole left where the blockhouse stood was as large as a fair-sized swimming pool."[45]

Despite the initial setbacks, the Marines advanced briskly on Roi and Namur, and individual units moved forward at such speed that they lost contact with neighboring outfits. Richard Sorenson's platoon ended the first invasion day well in advance of the frontline, spending the night in a bombed-out building. The morning after, the Marines found themselves surrounded and under furious attack by 250 Japanese. Sorenson was injured by a grenade, which sent 11 pieces of shrapnel into his lower body. Unable to fight, he crawled into a depression. "I thought if they broke through, I would get my throat slit," he later recalled. "They weren't taking any prisoners and we weren't either. As an assault unit, you cannot afford to take prisoners." Eventually, a Marine force fought its way through to the beleaguered outpost, and Sorenson was evacuated. He was put on a Higgins boat and placed next to another wounded

Marine that he knew from his platoon: "We just looked at each other and didn't say anything."[46]

The fighting went on, and the meticulous preparations paid off, as the Marines gradually squeezed out the last Japanese pockets of resistance. The particularly ferocious nature of Pacific combat was in evidence throughout. Lieutenant Colonel Justice Chambers led a battalion on Roi and Namur and was disturbed to come across men under his command in the process of beating the teeth out of a dead Japanese soldier, one of them proudly holding up a gold tooth. Chambers had what he called a "prayer meeting," telling the soldiers, "If I ever see any of you mutilating a body, I will kill you. I am not going to let you people pull yourself down to the level of the men we're fighting."[47]

While the Marines were taking Roi and Namur, the Army's 7th Division was carrying out similar operations to the south on Kwajalein island. Here, too, the invasion force seized several islets the day before the main assault, and Kwajalein was subjected to massive bombardment from sea and air. "The entire island looked as if it had been picked up to 20,000 feet and then dropped," as one observer noted.[48] An American correspondent on board a B-24 Liberator bomber described the scene from above: "The projectiles of the Navy ships geysered in a lagoon and crushed already battered beach areas." An airfield was left deliberately intact by the self-assured attackers. "The Japs built this airfield," an aviator said. "Let's save it for our own use."[49]

Despite the lunar landscape left for the soldiers to invade, there was plenty of fight left in the Japanese. They were waiting in their pillboxes and underground fortifications, and each had to be taken out in the same bloody and merciless fashion. In one battle among many, soldiers of the 184th Regiment overcame a stubborn pillbox. "Quickly taking shelter in a shell hole," the official historian writes, "they started lobbing grenades at the enemy position about fifteen yards ahead. The Japanese merely threw the grenades back and the volley kept up until a flame thrower was brought forward. That, too, proved ineffective; the flames only hit the box and bounced back." At this juncture, a GI crawled within five yards of the pillbox and threw in a white phosphorus smoke grenade, flushing out a group of Japanese who were met by a hail of deadly fire. A sergeant climbed on top of the pillbox: "He emptied his M1 rifle into it, killing the remainder of the Japanese inside. To make doubly certain that the job was done, an amphibian tank was then brought forward to fire both its flame thrower and its 37-mm gun into the aperture."[50]

The fighting after the landing on Kwajalein was a close parallel of Roi and Namur, brutal but brief, and resulting in American victory. Kwajalein was in Army possession after four days, while Roi and Namur belonged to the Marines after a week. A crucial anchorage in the Central Pacific was now in American hands. The planners had aimed to avoid a repeat of bloody Tarawa, and they got precisely what they wanted. Casualties were counted in the hundreds, not thousands. For the Japanese, on the contrary, this was exactly Tarawa all over again, with only a minority surviving and ending up in American captivity. Admiral Raymond Spruance, whose fleet had played a key role in disembarking the troops, wrote to his wife: "Dead Japs were very plentiful, but not so ripe as at [Tarawa], or else I am getting used to the flavor, although I still cannot say that I enjoy it."[51] In the months after the battle, war correspondent Ernie Pyle noted, naval engineers "couldn't dig a trench for a sewer pipe without digging up dead Japanese."[52]

★ ★ ★

After two years of war the Allies, led by the United States, were by early 1944 finding their bearings. It had happened in a costly process of trial and error, much of it paid for dearly in blood, but by now they were learning from past mistakes with astonishing speed. Lessons from Tarawa were applied, within just weeks, on Kwajalein. Most importantly, for a war that to a large extent hinged on control of the vast Pacific, the Americans had mastered the art of amphibious warfare, an area in which the Japanese had been among the pioneers until a few years earlier. This was no mean feat. As Admiral Ernest J. King, the US chief of naval operations, commented: "The outstanding development of this war, in the field of joint undertakings, was the perfection of amphibious operations, the most difficult of all operations in modern warfare."[53]

Infantry tactics had also evolved to account for the special challenges that awaited the men once they had made it beyond the water's edge: a determined enemy entrenched in fortifications that he had sometimes spent years preparing. Marine officer Baine Kerr explained the grim procedure which had proven its efficiency in combat and was now being drilled with thousands of small groups of infantrymen: "What you had to do was to take them under fire—the ones immediately that you were attacking plus ones that could support it with fire—and then send up your demolitions people. They had to crawl up under this bunker, and you had your flamethrowers, and they would toss this satchel charge of explosives inside the bunker; and they would use flamethrowers and shoot them in through the openings into the bunker."[54]

To be sure, the Japanese remained formidable foes, as they showed in both the Kwajalein and Cape Gloucester battles, demonstrating a fanaticism that the United States military encountered on no other battlefield in the world.

The American fighting man could never hope to match his foe's willingness, put on suicidal display at every junction, to struggle on to the last breath of the last man, but he could make up for some of that deficit with a nimbleness of mind that became more pronounced as the war wore on. An example of this, and of the easy routine with which US commanders were now able to move awesome destructive power from one point on the map to another, was Nimitz's ability to seize the momentum and move on to targets lying beyond what had been previously planned, once it was clear that Kwajalein would fall faster than anticipated.

Nimitz had sensed even before the first shot was fired at Kwajalein that he would not have to deploy all the forces at his disposal to seize the islands. He kept his reserves ready for an additional prize, the atoll of Eniwetok consisting of 40 smaller islands at the northwestern edge of the Marshall Islands. Considered an indispensable staging area for future operations into the Marianas to the west, Eniwetok was scheduled for invasion in late spring, but Nimitz saw no reason to wait. "I want you to keep your eye on Eniwetok. I think we will have forces available to go after that place right after Kwajalain but I will clear this with King," he told his staff.[55] The Joint Chiefs of Staff told him "if we wanted to go ahead at once."[56] Nimitz proceeded immediately, but before he could implement the plan to invade Eniwetok, he had to secure his flank and neutralize the threat of aerial attack from the Truk lagoon, Japan's main naval base in the neighboring Caroline islands.

A task force commanded by Spruance set out for Truk in early February. It was a formidable fleet, consisting of nine carriers, seven battleships, ten cruisers and 28 destroyers. Still, Commander Phil Torrey, who headed Air Group Nine, recalled his reaction when it was announced over the loudspeaker on board the aircraft carrier *Essex* that Truk was the target: "My first instinct was to jump overboard."[57] This was partly due to Japanese propaganda, which had spread the idea of Truk as the "Gibraltar of the Pacific," brimming with warships and defended by an iron ring of warplanes. "It was considered impregnable," said Captain Fitzhugh Lee, air officer on board the *Essex*. "At least it had that aura in the minds of most of our sailors out there."[58] Was it to be a suicide mission, as many of the men seemed to think? Only time would tell.

In fact, over the preceding weeks Truk had gradually been emptied of its large warships as the Japanese admirals had come to the realization that they were too exposed given the hasty American advances.[59] The result was that when the attack on Truk went ahead on February 17, it was a hopelessly one-sided affair. In terms of firepower deployed by the Americans, it was a Pearl Harbor in reverse, just many times more powerful. The task force carried out a total of 30 strikes on the Japanese installations in the lagoon, each more devastating than either of the two strikes that the Japanese had launched against the US Pacific Fleet in Hawaii 26 months earlier.[60] "Our planes attacked it successfully, sank a few ships and had very few losses," said Captain Lee. More than 200 Japanese planes were destroyed, while the American pilots found that only moderately sized surface ships were left. Outside the mouth of Truk lagoon, Admiral Spruance personally headed a task group of two battleships, two cruisers and four destroyers with the aim of catching as many Japanese vessels as possible inside the Truk lagoon and sinking them. In the end, he regretted finding only "small fry and merchant ships."[61]

Spruance might not have got the big prey he had hoped for, but the fact that American surface vessels could now move unopposed and unscathed to within just a few miles of the main Japanese base in the South Pacific was evidence that the battle for control of the ocean had shifted decidedly in favor of the Allies.[62] "I doubt," Spruance pondered about the psychological impact on the Japanese enemy, "if their morale was raised any by the operation."[63] The Americans might not have realized it at the time, but in post-war testimony Japanese officers said the assault on Truk, followed by other raids later that spring, was what broke their back in the Pacific. "They could 'endure' Midway. Yes, they'd lost their carriers, they'd lost their carrier pilots, which were more important than the carriers," said Layton, the intelligence officer. "But the Truk raid effectively eliminated any thought of offensive, forward operations of their fleet, thereafter."[64]

While American planes were still reducing Truk to rubble, an invasion fleet off Eniwetok began bombarding Japanese positions. The following day, February 18, Marines and soldiers kicked off landing operations. Despite the level of sophistication that amphibious operations had reached by this time, it was another reminder that this was an activity with many moving parts, and if one of them malfunctioned, everything was at risk. Marine James Day was in a landing craft that was put out of service after hitting underwater coral, and he had to wade the rest of the distance under enemy fire. "We knew that it was going to be tough if we were stopped out in the surf, but you just do not really get a feel for that until you are caught in the middle of all this and see the Marines fall," he said. "It is a pretty lonely feeling having to go across a beach where you are getting fired at. There is no protection that you can possibly have."[65]

Once they had secured a foothold at Eniwetok, the Marines went about fighting an enemy that mostly hid underground, in camouflaged dugouts nicknamed "spider holes." "We got to looking for spots where it didn't look just right, and I remember a couple of them we dug up and killed the Jap that was in those spider holes, because we got smart enough to where we could spot them pretty well," said Al Adkins, a Marine. "It was kind of personal at times."[66] The seizure of Eniwetok island itself took two and a half days, while the combat over two smaller neighboring islands lasted a little longer. The Americans captured the atoll at a cost of over 1,000 casualties, comparable to Kwajalein. The Japanese, as before and after, showed a tolerance of enormous losses, and out of an original garrison of about 3,500 only 66 survived.[67]

The US war machine as it was put on display in places like Eniwetok and Truk was the sharp end of the world's most powerful nation, where all its productive might and entrepreneurial energy was funneled. To take just one statistic, in 1943, Americans plants had churned out 85,898 warplanes against 16,693 in Japan.[68] Still, the aircraft carrier and bomber planes that were winning the war in the Pacific would amount to little if the men that operated them were not of the highest caliber. Every level of command was, with a few exceptions, dominated by officers who were at the top of their game, inspiring confidence in those they led into battle.

This was the result of a process, at work since the start of hostilities, of winnowing out officers in a brutal Darwinian fashion. In what was perhaps the military equivalent of American capitalism, no one from the submarine commander in charge of a few dozen men to the general or admiral overseeing hundreds of thousands of men, could stay in his position if he did not perform. Nimitz, for one, had no compunction about getting rid of officers who did not meet his strict requirements, and he might do so in a brusque fashion. "Young man," he might say to an underperforming junior officer, "you fail to cut the mustard, and I hereby dispense with your services."[69] A system that was this unforgiving placed great responsibility on the people at the top, but both Nimitz and his Army counterpart, Douglas MacArthur, proved, in his own way, capable of shouldering it.

Chester Nimitz's paternal grandfather was born in Germany and, as a sailor on merchant ships, he wielded a profound influence on his grandson's decision to pursue a naval career.[70] While his looks betrayed his North European ancestry, Nimitz was testimony to the speed with which immigrant families made America their home and were formed by the soil where they grew up. "The admiral's eyes were serene and blue, his bushy hair was blond salted with gray, his soft speech still carried a trace of his native Texan drawl," according to two historians of the Pacific War.[71] Captain Henri Smith-Hutton of the US Navy was impressed with the fitness of a man who was, by the time he met his greatest challenge as commander of all Naval forces in the Pacific, approaching retirement. "The Admiral looked to be in wonderful physical condition for a man of his age," he said of Nimitz, who turned 59 in February 1944. "I learned that Admiral Nimitz carried out a schedule of swimming, playing tennis, pitching horseshoes, and other exercises. He looked very bronzed, alert and strong."[72]

Nimitz was not given to mood swings, having learned at an early age to control a hot temper, and once he had risen to the highest rank in the Navy, he never exposed those around him to the temper tantrums that other senior officers might be prone to.[73] Many visitors to his Hawaiian headquarters were struck by the unhurried and calm atmosphere, but the laid-back demeanor disguised an occasionally extreme punctiliousness and a firm determination not to let standards slip. In one memorable episode, Nimitz ordered a sweep of Honolulu, confiscating the liberty passes of all Naval personnel who failed to salute their superiors.[74] He wanted his way, and while he was willing to listen to dissenting opinions, he displayed remarkable willpower when he felt he was right. This was, however, exercised with considerable grace, and he would impose his decisions on his subordinate "in a nice way," said Layton, the intelligence officer: "His eyes would sparkle. He would say it just like he had won a bridge hand by clever finesses. It was just marvelous and he would smile his beatific way."[75]

MacArthur was, in many important ways, Nimitz's polar opposite. Whereas Nimitz's blond looks seemed to reflect an easy-going attitude to life and work, MacArthur's dark eyes and jet-black hair appeared to be testimony to thinly disguised emotions that could explode onto the surface at any time. "Joy and sorrow would set the general off on lusty zooms or steep dives," according to one account. While in times of crisis, Nimitz would relieve tension in his staff by sanctioning a quick break, "the general would, as a rule, sit stonily in his chair, chewing on the stem of a corncob pipe, which usually needed relighting."[76] Like Nimitz, however, MacArthur was the product of a proud family history, being the son of a hero of the Civil War and subsequent Indian Wars, and he shared with Nimitz the ability to hear out his subordinates and listen to reason. "If you felt something should be done in some other way," said an officer who came into frequent contact with him during the war, "or you felt that the timing should be changed on an operation, and you presented your reasons, and if it was reasonable, he would agree to it."[77]

MacArthur had shown great personal courage in World War I, and he put these qualities to use again in the new war, impressing his colleagues with his sang-froid. His close collaborator Robert L. Eichelberger remembered how MacArthur during a staff conference in 1944 studiously ignored repeated Japanese air raids: "Since the Supreme Commander was deaf to the violence around him, the rest of us maintained the elaborate pretense that we couldn't hear any bombs falling either."[78] Captain Charles Adair visited an invasion beach in the South Pacific when Japanese fire suddenly came dangerously close. "Practically all the party had jumped in a ditch or behind a tree, but General MacArthur didn't budge. He refused to duck," Adair said. "He had told people in the past that a bullet hadn't yet been made that was going to get him. And so far as I know, none did!"[79]

MacArthur had an intense interest in public relations, receiving daily newspaper clippings about him and his theater, sent from America by air express.[80] Indeed, at times, he looked more like a candidate running for office than a commander fighting a war, and he had a politician's instinct for appearing forthcoming when necessary. "He was very affable and gave you the impression that he was very glad to see you again (although he had never seen you before)," reminisced an American officer who witnessed him meeting troops at Cape Gloucester.[81]

The Marines tended to dislike him, considering him pompous and referring to him as "Dugout Doug," but those who met him came away with a radically altered impression. Marine Colonel Edwin A. Pollock observed MacArthur visiting Marines on Goodenough island off Papua: "He'd go around and say a few words to the men, pat them on the shoulder or put his arm around them and they thought that was great. And it was his way of mixing with the enlisted men, and it was good."[82] It was more than just words and handshakes. Behind the façade was a master of the art of war, as Bill Filter, a private with the 381st Infantry Regiment, came to realize: "After you fought under him and for him, you found out that he was a military genius, and his plans were carried at a minimum of confusion and bloodshed."[83] Indeed, total casualties suffered under MacArthur's command during the last three years of the war were fewer than those of the Battle of the Bulge.[84]

The outstanding qualities of the commanders could not disguise a deep contradiction inherent in the way the Allies pursued the war in the Pacific. Cape Gloucester on the one hand and Kwajalein on the other were manifestations of two different strategies pursued by the American-led forces in the war against Japan. One was a Southwest Pacific drive led by MacArthur that would allow him to advance along New Guinea and return to the Philippines as he had vowed to do when he was forced to evacuate two years earlier. The other was a Central Pacific route directed by Nimitz, which approached the Japanese isles across the vastness of the ocean. One was largely Army-centered and the other mainly based on the Navy's capabilities, and both would eventually lead to Tokyo, but the question remained whether the twin strategy was an exercise in redundancy, and if victory could be achieved, at a cost of much less Allied blood, by prioritizing either of the strategies.

On the face of it, it would seem the Americans could afford to do both. Towards the end of 1943, and despite an official policy that called for most US military resources to be directed across the Atlantic, the US Army had 13 divisions deployed in the Pacific, the same number as it had sent to the war against Germany.[85] In addition, the Marine Corps was almost exclusively assigned to the task of defeating Japan, meaning that overall, during the first two years of war, the Allied "Germany first" strategy appeared to be in name only. However, by early 1944, this was changing rapidly, and the bulk of Allied supplies went to staging areas preparing for the final assault on Hitler's Fortress Europe, at the expense of bringing down Hirohito's Asian citadel. When US Army Chief of Staff George Marshall paid his only visit to MacArthur's headquarters during the entire war, he was confronted with the paucity of men and materiel. "He said he realized the imbalance and regretted it," MacArthur wrote in his memoirs, "but could do little to alter the low priority accorded to the area."[86]

Faced with a difficult situation and unable to alter the intense focus on Europe consuming planners in Washington, MacArthur did his best to make the case that he should be given the lion's share of supplies arriving in the Pacific. In January 1944 he was visited by Brigadier General Frederick H. Osborn, a staff member of the War Department, and used the opportunity to make his case for a strategy focused squarely on his theater of war and the reconquest of the Philippines. "I do not want command of the Navy, but must control their strategy, be able to call on what little of the Navy is needed for the trek to the Philippines," MacArthur said. "The Navy's turn will come after that. These frontal attacks by the Navy, as at Tarawa, are tragic and unnecessary massacres of American lives."[87] Nimitz did not challenge this view, and for him, too, the bloodbath on Tarawa served as a warning. Worrying that a continued campaign across the Central Pacific would be too costly, he seemed to be quietly resigning himself to a future secondary role as one of MacArthur's lieutenants.[88]

With near-unanimity reigning among commanders in the Pacific, MacArthur looked on the verge of assuming supreme control, causing the

Southwest Pacific rather than the Central Pacific to become the focus of future strikes against Japan, probably supplemented by land operations in China. The Philippines, the scene of MacArthur's first battle in the war and a cause of personal honor, was to be the penultimate prize prior to taking on Japan proper. Everything seemed set, until the proposal was abruptly shot down by Washington. It came in the form of a stern letter from Marshall to Nimitz. In unmistakable prose, the Army chief of staff pointed out that even though the need to recapture the Philippines was beyond debate, the flank of such an operation must be protected through continued massive operations across the Pacific. "The idea of rolling up the New Guinea coast… and up through the Philippines… as our major strategic concept, to the exclusion of clearing our Central Pacific line of communications to the Philippines, is to me absurd," Marshall wrote.[89] Nothing more needed to be said. The two-pronged strategy was to stay and be pursued until the end of hostilities.

Admiral Yamamoto Isoroku, the architect of the Japanese attack on Pearl Harbor, had made only limited promises before committing to the offensive against US and Western possessions in the Asia Pacific in late 1941 and early 1942. He would be able to deliver one victory after the other during the first months of the war while the enemy was still reeling from the initial shock of being attacked, he said, but once that early advantage had been exhausted, the going would become much harder. Now, two years into the war, Yamamoto was dead, shot down by American pilots over the South Pacific, and the US counteroffensive had picked up, pushing back at the fringes of Hirohito's vast empire.

At the dawn of the new year 1944, therefore, many of the emperor's subjects were concerned about the future, and some put their bewildered thoughts on paper. "An important year has come. The days are coming that will decide history," wrote liberal journalist Kiyosawa Kiyoshi in his diary on January 1. There was a pervasive sense that things might not stay the same. In every home in Japan when breakfast was served, he noted, people asked the same question: "Will we really be able to eat in this way next year also?"[90] Yabe Teiji, a political science professor at the Tokyo Imperial University, was more straightforward in his diary entry: "The coming year will be Japan's year of disaster."[91]

The Tokyo Metropolitan Police was keenly interested in the public mood and remarked in a secret report that although some clung on to a vague sense of optimism about the war, a note of caution was clearly discernible. "There are some who are frankly amazed at the quick and mighty strategy of the enemy and fear the threat of invasion of the mainland, some who desire the announcement of the truth, and some who fear for the safety of our fleet," the anonymous author of the report wrote, adding that people who held these views were not few in number. There were other categories of opinion, all reflecting the fact that any early enthusiasm put on display at the start of the war was long gone: "Those who go to the extreme criticize military strategy, exaggerate the announcement of our losses, and consider the war to have already been decided. Also, those who are totally unconcerned with the war situation and show a trend toward defeat and war-weariness, just longing for speedy end of war, have been seen here and there."[92]

By early 1944, even the most optimistic among the 73 million Japanese could no longer fool themselves into believing that life went on as before. In February, the government issued "Outline of Decisive War Emergency Measures," closing high-end entertainment and causing life in the big cities to take on an even drabber appearance overnight.[93] The new rules were expanded to the entire empire with immediate effect, as Admiral Ugaki Matome found out when he stayed over in Japanese-occupied Shanghai and was entertained one evening by Japan's governor general. "Banquets, restaurants, and geishas have been banned, as in Japan proper, but the governor general still seemed as full of life as before," Ugaki wrote in his diary.[94] The kimono, the colorful traditional Japanese dress, was also largely gone from the streets of Japan. As one observer noted, "to be a woman, basically, is not patriotic."[95]

As the war economy gradually caused an increasing share of available resources to be allocated to the military, getting enough to eat was suddenly a daily struggle for average Japanese families. There were lines of usually about a hundred people outside Tokyo food shops, and on any given day thousands of residents would leave the capital to buy supplies directly from farmers.[96] The hard times were felt particularly keenly by the Westerners who had been caught inside the borders of the Japanese Empire when war broke out. In January, Red Cross delegate H. C. Angst visited a camp for civilian internees set up inside a Catholic monastery near Yokohama and subsequently described the poor conditions that the inmates lived under: "Space is insufficient and overcrowded. Some sleeping on tables. Light sufficient. No heating."[97] The anti-foreign mood showed up in other ways as well. Baseball, a favorite sport for the Japanese in the prewar years, was allowed to continue but was being cleansed of English-sounding vocabulary. *Sutoraiki*, an attempt to reproduce the word "strike" in Japanese, was replaced with the much more indigenous-sounding *honkyū*.[98]

At the senior political level, a somber mood also prevailed. Kido Kōichi, Hirohito's closest advisor, sensed that the options available for the empire were closing rapidly, given the pitiful state of its Axis partners, with Italy defeated and Germany pressured on all fronts. "I am wondering about the course of the war for the coming year," he wrote in his diary on January 6. "First, we must consider whether we should take measures to end the war in the event that Germany is beaten or surrenders unconditionally... Second, in such a situation, I believe that the only terms of peace on our part that would be acceptable to our enemies would be those which involved considerable concessions."[99] In his diary, he outlined a peace plan that he thought would appeal to the Allies as it involved a Japanese withdrawal to the areas under its control prior to the invasion of China in 1937, leaving it with the puppet state of Manchukuo in the northeast. Such a proposal was "conciliatory and weak-kneed," he admitted but there was no other choice, given "the terrible attrition of our national power."[100]

Few in Kido's elite circle of political and military heavyweights were prepared to go as far as he, at least not openly. The overall strategy dictating all decisions in early 1944 called for the establishment of an "Absolute National Defense Zone" delineated by a line stretching from Kuriles, via the Bonin Islands, the Marianas, the Carolines, Western New Guinea, and the Dutch East Indies to Burma. This defensive perimeter was to be held at all costs while the imperial forces built up the necessary strength to hand a devastating blow to the Americans by the middle of the year.[101] Or at least that was the theory, but not even a month into the new year, the plan began to unravel as the invasion of Kwajalein in the middle of the Marshall Islands moved the American vanguard dangerously close to the defensive line. Hirohito, who had shown growing unease at the changing fortunes throughout 1943, took to chiding his own generals for their shortcomings. "The Marshalls are part of Japan's territory," he said scornfully. "Why can't you do anything when it is being taken by the enemy?"[102]

Belying the speculation in the American camp that the Central Pacific approach might be a costly waste of time and resources, the capture of Kwajalein, followed by the seizure of Eniwetok and the strikes against Truk, forced the Japanese commanders to completely revise their plans for the coming year. While they had initially scheduled a large buildup in New Guinea in preparation for the mid-year offensive, most available reserves were now diverted to the Central Pacific instead.[103] Far from all supplies reached their destination. The devastating efficiency of the US submarine force, combined with American airpower, caused a large proportion to end up on the bottom of the ocean. In February 1944 alone, 500,000 tons of Japanese shipping was sunk, more than half pre-war estimates of losses of 800,000 tons not per month, but per year.[104]

Compounding the ills besetting the Japanese war effort, the Army and the Navy were hampered by mutual hostility that made inter-service rivalries on the American side seem downright mild by comparison. One point of particular controversy was the Navy's difficulty in securing the absolute defensive line while the Army accumulated reserves, and after one particularly heated argument between the services, Hirohito burst out with exasperation, "What has been the meaning of the meetings we have held up to this point? Why have we taken the trouble to do all that?"[105] One attempt to achieve unity was made in February 1944, when Premier Tōjō Hideki, who was concurrently minister of war, consolidated his power by taking over as chief of the Army General Staff. Unsurprisingly, the Navy protested at the prospect of an Army man hoarding this much power, but Hirohito made a desperate plea to the admirals: "The arrangement is an exceptional measure at this time of emergency and requires caution. But do offer your cooperation to make it work."[106]

Perhaps morale remained highest where it mattered the most: at the frontline among the junior ranks who did most of the fighting and the dying for the Emperor and had little knowledge of the grand strategic picture. In 1944 the common Japanese soldier still considered an Allied victory a remote possibility. The British officer Frederick Spencer Chapman was briefly kept prisoner by a Japanese patrol in the Malay jungle in 1944 before being able to escape. He told one of his captors that he was looking forward to when the British returned to Malaya, which the Japanese soldier considered highly unlikely: "At this he gave a scornful snort, and thought the story so good that he passed it on to the others, who shouted with laughter."[107]

CHAPTER TWO

Ichigō

March–May 1944

For months, US Army Staff Sergeant Frank Ficklin toiled away in the humid Burmese jungle with thousands of other Allied prisoners, building what was later to be called the Death Railway. It was back-breaking work, lasting up to 16 hours a day. Although the area was inimical to any kind of human activity, everything had to be done by hand, and there were no mechanical tools available, although occasionally the Japanese would muster an elephant to lift heavy logs. Ficklin, who was six feet tall and had weighed in at 185 pounds before the war, now had a body weight of just 112 pounds, for food was scarce and consisted mostly of soup. "We used to call it Air Raid soup because it was all clear," he said later. "Our clothing wore out, would be mildewed. Your shoes fell apart. For the remainder of our time in prison camp, we wore something that was indigenous to the native American Indians, a little loin cloth."[1]

Abuse was omnipresent, and guards recruited from the Japanese colony Korea, who ranked lowest in the military hierarchy, were notorious for letting their frustration out on their prisoners. However, disease was the biggest killer. "The Nips there refused to recognize malaria as an illness," a British medical officer wrote. "They forced men out to work with fever on them, and many collapsed on the railway trace. They had nothing like enough quinine."[2] The prisoners got used to the telltale signs of comrades who had lost the will to live. Their hygiene would drop, and they would develop dysentery and begin to dehydrate, and eventually lose interest in food. "Then they'd get to where they were unconscious, and for a time they'd lie there with no stir in their body," a former POW remembered. "Their mouth would open, and sometimes their eyes wouldn't close. When this happened, it indicated that death was not far away."[3]

A total of 61,000 prisoners took part in the construction of the railway, and of these, more than 12,000 died, including 6,318 British, 2,646 Americans and 2,490 Dutch.[4] There was, in the words of Japanese engineer Futamatsu Yoshihiko, who took part in the project, "a death for every ten meters of the entire length of the railway."[5] This did not even take into account the 270,000 laborers from Burma itself as well as those from Malaya and Thailand who were either forced or cajoled into work on the railroad. Postwar estimates are that between 70,000 and 90,000 of them lost their lives during the inhuman regime imposed by the Japanese as they pushed relentlessly towards the completion of the railway.[6]

By early 1944, the prisoners were pulled out of the jungle. Their job was done, and the railroad was ready, linking Burma with Thailand and Singapore for the first time ever. The Japanese needed this transportation link badly. They were preparing a powerful thrust northward, across the border into British-held India. It was to be carried out by three divisions of the Fifteenth Army assisted by a smaller force of former Indian prisoners, recruited to fight against the British and organized into the Indian National Army. The troops, commanded by General Mutaguchi Renya, were to head for the city of Imphal and, further up north, the town of Kohima. Once they had been taken, the Japanese aimed to march on further to the strategically located city of Dimapur, thus cutting off transportation links between India and China. If successful, it was an operation that could decisively affect the course of the war in mainland Southeast Asia.

Japanese soldier Fujiwara Yuwaichi was in high spirits ahead of the operation. This could be the attack that would end years of stalemate. There were reports of a strong anti-British movement in India, triggering hopes that a successful offensive could bring about an actual rebellion against colonial rule. Most of all, however, Fujiwara based his optimism on the track record of the Japanese Army in the Burmese jungle in the years that had passed since the war started. "We had been successful because the British always fought on roads and in motor cars. The Japanese crossed jungle and attacked the British rear. The British were not tough. The Japanese were tough," he said.[7]

It was an appraisal on which Japan's foes agreed, however reluctantly. The Japanese Army retained its reputation of near-invincibility, not because of the capabilities of its officers, nor due to any natural skill in jungle warfare, since Japan had as little tropical rain forest as England. The secret was elsewhere, according to Field Marshall William Slim, the commander of the Fourteenth Army, which defended Burma. Japan's real strength was its individual soldier. "He fought and marched till he died. If five hundred Japanese were ordered to hold a position, we had to kill four hundred and ninety-five before it was ours—and then the last five had killed themselves. It was this combination of obedience and ferocity that made the Japanese Army, whatever its condition, so formidable, and which would make any army formidable. It would make a European army invincible."[8]

Against this fierce enemy, Slim's Fourteenth Army, a multinational force consisting of British, Indian, and African soldiers, had initially seemed inadequate, but it had gradually learned to stand its ground, as it showed in early 1944. As Japan amassed troops for the attack north, it also launched a separate but smaller offensive in February against the region of Arakan on the Burmese west coast in a bid to divert British attention from the area around Imphal. The 7th Indian Division faced the brunt of the Japanese onslaught, and it held its positions to the angered surprise of the attackers, who let out their ire on the prisoners they took, including personnel and patients at a main dressing station. "The helpless men on their stretchers were slaughtered in cold blood," Slim wrote, "the doctors lined up and shot, the Indian orderlies made to carry the Japanese wounded back, and then murdered, too."[9]

The determined defense carried out by the 7th Indian Division was supported by supplies being airlifted in from India, while on the ground it

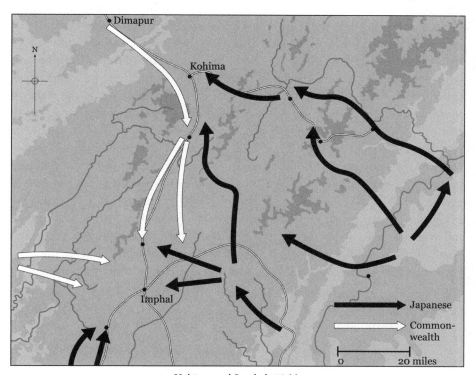

Kohima and Imphal, 1944.

was bolstered by reinforcements moved up to frontline, most importantly British forces in American-built tanks. Among them was Norman Bowdler, a soldier with the 25th Dragoons. Moving only at night and with their noise deliberately drowned out by aircraft flying overhead, the tanks drove through a treacherous pass, along roads with a drop of 600 feet on one side. "It was a bit dodgy, getting a thirty-ton tank around these S-bends. Some of the bends were so severe that you had to go backwards and forwards, backwards and forwards to negotiate them," he said.[10]

The defeat of the Japanese at Arakan contributed to demolishing the myth of their superiority in jungle warfare, but it came at a high price. As elsewhere in the Asia Pacific, the terrain was often as deadly as the actual enemy. An unpublished Indian divisional history describes the green hell in telling detail: "The average soldier who saw it through... will remember patrols long and short out in the rain; leeches in the jungle... socks that shrank because they were never dry; the whiskers that grew overnight on his boots and the fungus that dimmed his binoculars. He will remember dragging mud-clogged feet up the slippery hillsides which were shrouded with mist for days on end, and landslides that threatened to carry away . . . engulf him in their downfall."[11]

The successful defense at Arakan was to a great extent a reflection of the increased vigor on the British side following the establishment of South East Asia Command in late 1943. It was headed by Admiral Louis Mountbatten, who was related to the British royal family and brought with him an offensive spirit and a determination to end the habit of withdrawing at the sight of the Japanese. This he combined with a new doctrine for fighting the war in Burma, calling for his troops not to fall back on their supply lines when the Japanese attacked, but instead to dig in and wait to be supplied from the air.[12]

More than anything, Mountbatten had a genius for inspiring new confidence in his subordinates. He traveled around the region, inspecting his troops and giving versions of the same pep talk everywhere: "I hear you call this the Forgotten Front. I hear you call yourselves the Forgotten Army. Well, let me tell you that this is *not* the Forgotten Front, and you are *not* the Forgotten Army."[13] Foot soldiers said Slim, affectionately known as "Uncle Bill" and conversant in Urdu and Gurkhali, was an even bigger source of inspiration with both British and Indian infantrymen. "I was impressed by [Mountbatten's] handsome appearance and charm, plus the attendant aura of royalty, but it was Slim who left the more lasting impression," recalled a former British soldier.[14]

Regardless of where exactly the credit belonged, Mountbatten was happy with how his troops performed. In his diary, he proudly related the instance of the commanding officer of one Indian mule company, which was alerted to the presence of Japanese: "Instead of turning tail he formed his mules into a circle and put half his muleteers around them, to protect them. The remaining half he formed into battle patrols and went forward to engage the Japanese!"[15] It was a far cry from the early days of war in Burma where the mere suspicion that the Japanese were approaching would strike fear into their enemies.

If the new, more energetic, doctrine was put to the test for the first time at Arakan, it had its real trial by fire when the Japanese Army unleashed its main offensive in mid-March. The city of Imphal, meant by the Japanese to be only the first in a series of lightning victories, instead became the scene of weeks of bloody fighting. For the infantrymen in their trenches, it was a dirty war where the Japanese were rumored to even booby-trap their wounded. Sharpened bamboo sticking out of the ground, known as *pangyis*, were used as primitive anti-personnel weapons on both sides. "They would smear excrement on the *pangyis*," said Private Peter Hazelhurst of the Border Regiment. "So we did that too, and put them in front of our positions."[16]

Despite the brutal nature of the fighting, the defenders did not budge, but forced the attackers to stop, aided by a steady supply of reinforcements and materiel from the air. Mountbatten was only able to do so because of assistance from US airpower. In the end, he had 61,000 American air and ground crew under his command, out of a total of 176,000 airmen in the theater. "I just don't know what we would have done without them," Mountbatten said after the war. "At Imphal, air reinforcement, air evacuation, air supply and air support steadily counteracted all the Japanese advantages. Instead of our army dwindling under attack, we were able to build up its strength."[17]

Further up north, the Japanese 31st Division was racing to capture Kohima. Satō Kōtoku, the divisional commander, summoned his officers for a toast in rice wine on the eve of the battle, informing them that their chances of getting out alive were minuscule. "I'll take the opportunity, gentlemen, of making something quite clear to you," he said. "Miracles apart, every one of you is likely to lose his life in this operation. It isn't simply a question of the enemy's bullets. You must be prepared for death by starvation in these mountain fastnesses."[18]

The battle turned out as desperate as Satō had predicted. For ten terrible days in April, the small, beleaguered garrison at Kohima held out against the Japanese forces, with the two sides often separated by just a few yards of no man's land. Bert Harwood, a sergeant major at the Royal West Kent Regiment, described how the injured were carried behind the frontline and placed in hastily dug trenches with no cover from the elements, giving them only a minimum of protection from enemy fire, or from supplies flown in and dropped at random. "On occasions the parachute wouldn't open and one of these… hit a couple of casualties in the trenches and killed them. That sort of thing happened," said Harwood. "The shelling killed people that were in the trenches, waiting."[19]

★ ★ ★

General Tanaka Shin'ichi, commander of the Japanese Army's 18th Division, was on a mission in northern Burma in early 1944 directly linked to the attempt at Imphal and Kohima to cut through the British lines and reach the Indian border. With his battle-hardened men, he was to cover the right flank of the Japanese forces engaged in the main offensive and tie down as many Allied forces as possible. At the same time, he was to pursue a separate and arguably more important objective, penetrating as deeply into enemy territory as possible. For him, too, the ultimate objective was to disrupt the supply lines between India and China.

Like the Japanese further south, Tanaka was up against a multinational enemy, but of a different kind. Facing him in the north Burmese hills and jungles were the products of one of the most precarious and unwieldy alliances of the entire war—that between China and America. He was an experienced officer who had taken part in most of Japan's conflicts since the early 1930s, but he had never before confronted the Chinese in battle. When he finally had the opportunity in the spring of 1944 near the village of Yupang Ga, he was surprised. "The unexpected stubbornness of the Chinese troops in the fighting around Yupang Ga," he wrote in post-war comments, "led the Japanese to believe the troops that faced them were far superior in both the quality of their fighting and in their equipment to the Chinese troops they had been fighting in China for years."[20]

The Chinese troops fighting at Yupang Ga were from the New 38th Division, the result of long months of Sino-American cooperation following the US entry into the war. The most visible sign of this cooperation was the trademark M1 helmet worn by the Chinese soldiers, as well as the many examples of state-of-the-art equipment and weaponry they were carrying into battle. More importantly, the soldiers had been through months of US-led training at camps in India and had been instructed in the methods of modern warfare. The hard work was not wasted and the Chinese pushed the Japanese back at Yupang Ga. To the young Chinese soldiers, it was an immense morale boost, and likewise to their officers, who still remembered the first humiliating battles with the technologically superior Japanese during the preceding decade. "The

Chinese soldiers talked of it over and over again," according to the official history. "The first victory is never forgotten."[21]

The Japanese, under pressure from the Chinese divisions, retreated back south. In this situation, General Joseph Stilwell, the senior US officer on the Asian mainland, decided to bring to bear what American forces were available to him, in the shape of the newly formed 5307th Composite Unit (Provisional). Dubbed "Merrill's Marauders" after its commander, Brigadier General Frank Merrill, it was the first major US Army unit to go into combat in Stilwell's area of responsibility. The Marauders represented an attempt to beat the Japanese at their own game, as its members were trained to infiltrate through enemy lines and roam deep inside hostile territory.

The British had pioneered this effort on the Allied side with their Long-Range Penetration Groups, known unofficially as the Chindits, under the command of the unorthodox Major General Orde Charles Wingate.[22] The Chindits had first been placed into battle in 1943, and by 1944 they had built up enough skill and experience to arguably have an impact on the overall conduct of the war. Elements of two Japanese divisions were engaged in

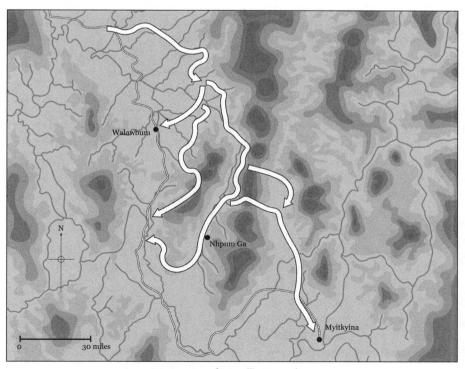

Movements of Merrill's Marauders.

fighting the Chindits, and Japanese General Mutaguchi, who led the offensives against Imphal and Kohima, argued that if either division had been able to release just one regiment from these operations, it "would have turned the scales at Kohima."[23]

Given the experience in the Chindits, it was perhaps not surprising that the Marauders had originally been meant to fight under British command, but Stilwell had vetoed the idea. It was a question of American honor. The United States ought, in his view, to make its unique contribution in this theater, and he had high hopes for their performance. "Tough-looking lot of babies," Stilwell thought as he saw the Marauders off before they disappeared into the Burmese jungle, on their mission to cut off the retreating Japanese.[24]

The fact was, however, that even though they had trained hard, the Marauders were not all elite material. They were from a variety of units, and many had signed up simply in the hope of escaping back stateside. "We were told that if you volunteer, you make one mission and… if you live, we'll send you home," one of them said. It was tempting: "I had been there long enough that it just seemed that what I had lived in the United States was a dream. It wasn't real anymore."[25] Even before going on their first mission, many suffered from malaria and other disabling maladies. "We found many chronically ill men," commented Captain James E.T. Hopkins, a field surgeon with the Marauders. "Many brave men came but also numerous psychiatric problems as well as men with chronic disturbances who believed that they might get treatment if they could get away from their outfits."[26]

The Marauders began a grueling trek through dense forest, with the aim of intercepting the 18th Japanese Division and preventing its withdrawal to the south. The first roadblock was set up in early March near a village called Walawbum. Tanaka, the Japanese division commander, knew the Americans were waiting and attempted to annihilate them in a series of mass attacks, but suffered heavy losses for no gain. "We had several banzai attacks and we killed over four hundred Japanese," said Hopkins.[27] Confusion spread when the Chinese, who had been pursuing the Japanese, unexpectedly caught up and were involved in the fighting. "We wounded two or three Chinese before we found out who in the hell they were. They looked like Japanese, as they had the same color uniforms."[28]

What followed was a series of battles as the Japanese continued their retreat south, pursued by both the Chinese and the Americans. Thomas Phillips was an expert marksman and killed several Japanese snipers during the campaign. "It's a good feeling to take on a sniper," he said, remarking how civilians would often not understand the emotions soldiers had towards killing the enemy. "That's what you are in the army for, you don't go in there to serve tea."[29] A particularly unnerving factor was the Japanese habit of taunting their adversaries in a form of primitive psychological warfare. In one instance, they tried to lure the Marauders to bayonet fights, shouting at them in perfect English, "General Merrill eats K rations."[30]

The Japanese 18th Division eventually escaped, but at great cost. At another blocking position at the village of Nhpum Ga in April, military journalist David Richardson observed the carnage as the Japanese attempted frontal assaults at prepared positions: "They came in waves, banzai attack with flags and everything. Out of the bush, one wave then another," he said. "Well, it was like sitting ducks. We had high ground, we were protected. We just mowed 'em down, wave after wave... We were good marksmen, so we killed eight hundred of them in one day. Bodies strewn all over like the Civil War was at Gettysburg."[31]

As the effort to halt the retreating Japanese was ending, the Marauders' mission was over, or so they thought. They had been promised to be relieved, but soon the rumor was spreading that they had one last job to do. The strategic city of Myitkyina and the adjacent airfield remained in Japanese hands. "Incredible as the rumor was, it persisted, like a mosquito whining about your head," one account read. "You wanted to bat it away from your ears. 'For Christ's sake, will you lay off that story,' someone would explode. 'Are you *asking* for it?'"[32]

It was more than just a rumor. Stilwell needed Myitkyina, and the Marauders were the only ones available for the task. The exhausted Marauders now set out on a last, arduous march across the Kuman Mountains, 6,000 feet high and covered in vegetation. For Captain Fred Lyons every step on the trek was like "beating an open wound." He had reached a stage where he no longer cared if he was overrun by the Japanese: "All I wanted was unconsciousness."[33]

Immediately upon arrival, accompanied by Chinese and Burmese troops, they moved in on the airfield, guarded by a few hundred surprised Japanese. They seized it with little difficulty even though the Japanese threw everything and everyone they had into the battle, including patients from the 18th Divisional Field Hospital.[34] Once the airfield was secure, the Marauders confirmed by radio that Allied planes could fly in supplies and reinforcements, using a pre-arranged code signal: MERCHANT OF VENICE.[35]

The Marauders had by now been on a 1,000-mile trek through dense jungle and inhospitable terrain, intermingled with brutal fighting. The hardship had incapacitated more than half the force, according to Richardson, the combat journalist who shared the hardship with the infantrymen: "Our casualties were not so much from Japanese bullets, they were from disease, sixty percent, seventy percent were diseased and they were just beat up," he said, describing how the soldiers were falling apart, quite literally, due to malnutrition. "We were losing teeth… We looked like skeletons. It was very rough, and yet we were supposed to fight this battle."[36]

The fighting in northern Burma in the spring of 1944 saw the closest cooperation thus far between American and Chinese forces in a coordinated effort to trap the Japanese soldiers under Tanaka's command. While Merrill's Marauders received most of the attention in the American press, Chinese units, trained and equipped by the US Army in India and known as X-Force, took part in the operation from the outset. Meng Huaxin, a captain in the Chinese New 38th Division, described the shock he and his soldiers inflicted when attacking Japanese positions at the town of Mogaung, scene of one of the major battles during the pursuit of the 18th Japanese Division. "They believed we were airborne troops," he said.[37]

In some instances, the Chinese, haunted by the superiority of the Japanese for years, managed to score quick victories. One Chinese company surprised a group of Japanese officers in the middle of a meeting. "Our sudden strike and encirclement scared them and sent everyone running around in chaos," a member of the company said.[38] However, it was not a walkover. Shi Linxian, a regimental chief of staff in the New 22nd Division, also part of X-Force, recalled moving into Japanese-held territory where there were booby-traps at every step, and the constant risk of ambushes from hidden positions. "The enemy's 18th Division had built semi-permanent fortifications along the river for more than a year," he wrote. "Plus the stubbornly resistant and unyielding character of the Japanese, it made this battle the toughest yet."[39]

A separate Chinese army, appropriately named Y-Force, had been trained and equipped in southwest China, and in the spring it was sent towards the Chinese frontier with eastern Burma, with the ultimate objective of linking up with X-Force. Unknown to the commanders of Y-Force at the time, the Japanese had captured a codebook and a cipher table, enabling them to read the Chinese messages and anticipate several major actions.[40] Still, the Chinese forces succeeded in reaching their initial objectives, prompted by the words with which their leader, Generalissimo Chiang Kai-shek, had sent them into the battle: "The prestige of the Nationalist army is at stake, as is the outcome of the war."[41]

In spite of this message there was, in fact, little appreciation at home for the hardship suffered by Chinese forces. Chiang, holed up in the wartime capital of Chongqing, would have preferred it if they had not been fighting the Japanese in the Burma area in the first place. He had supplied troops to the campaign only with great reluctance, displaying a recalcitrant attitude which in turn gave rise to considerable frustration among his Western Allies. Sometimes the frustration surfaced, as in Mountbatten's quip when China's First Lady Madame Chiang Kai-shek sent him a large basket of Jaffa oranges: "Oranges? They should have been lemons."[42]

Fundamentally, Chiang believed his resources were better spent closer to home, where the Japanese Army posed a much more imminent danger. After nearly seven years of war, the frontline had frozen in many places, but battles still continued to erupt. Furthermore, his unwillingness to send troops to Burma only intensified in early spring when his attention was directed towards the region of Xinjiang along China's northwestern frontier, where Soviet-backed Mongolian troops suddenly made an incursion. While the Mongolian operation was primarily probing in nature and did not constitute a full-scale invasion, it was enough to deepen Chiang's sense of insecurity and dissuade him further from military adventures in far-off locations.[43]

It did not ingratiate Chiang with the Americans, whose views on the China theater had changed markedly in the roughly two years that had passed since the beginning of their war with Japan. Back then, Admiral Ernest King, the US chief of naval operations, had spoken for many when he had argued that "just as Russia warranted support to drain off German strength, China had to be kept in the war so as to occupy on the mainland of Asia heavy Japanese land forces and some Japanese air forces" and that "the key to a successful attack upon the Japanese homeland was the geographical position and the manpower of China."[44]

By 1944, it was still feasible that the Chinese mainland would play a role in the eventual Allied offensive against the Japanese home islands, but the possibility of this ever happening was becoming more remote as the rapid advances in the Pacific opened alternative and ultimately more promising roads to Tokyo. The decreasing likelihood that China was to become a major battleground also meant that it was not the first priority when assigning senior American personnel to service overseas. Rather, it had become "the dumping ground for men whom Eisenhower and MacArthur did not ask for," in the words of an American advisor.[45]

Even so, the United States maintained its steady stream of supplies flown from India across the Himalayas to areas controlled by Chiang's forces in western China. The air route, known as the "Hump," was as risky as it was epic and claimed numerous American lives, more due to extreme weather condition than to enemy action. Alan "Buck" Saunders experienced the physical hardship of flying over some of the world's most inhospitable terrain. With no winter equipment, he was forced to fly in khaki pants, and often ended up with a coat of ice over both legs. "When you take off, you're in the monsoons," he said. "As you climb up the rain comes in, the water comes in, blows in. Then you get into snow, then snow pellets, then you get to where it's too cold for any moisture, but that water that blows in freezes because it may be 45 below zero outside."[46]

Randy Watson, another "Hump" pilot, was surprised by the variety of different cargoes he was required to take into China. On one occasion it consisted of sanitary napkins. "What in the Sam Hill," he asked. "We don't have any women over in China. Why are we carrying this?!" A member of the ground crew replied, "The Chinese use it as battle dressings." Another time, he was required to risk his life to take large bails of Chinese money across the Himalayas, for use in the war economy. Before departure, a man came up to Watson with a can of kerosene and a box of matches. "If you crash, burn the money." Watson shot back, "If I crash, I'm not going to worry about that money!"[47]

The need to fly in cash to prop up Chiang's regime, at the risk of inflation spiraling out of control, was testimony to his weakening command of his people's loyalty. His chief domestic challenge was the Communist Party, which controlled huge swathes of territory in the north and proved highly capable of securing the backing of the rural population. Evans Carlson, an American Marine officer, had visited Mao Zedong's partisans and believed they held the real answer to the Japanese invasion: "They are making it impossible to control China politically (and Japan cannot possibly produce an army big enough to do it)," he wrote in a dispatch. "They are making it difficult for the Japanese to move supplies over their lines of communication, or to obtain them from the people. They are making it impossible for Japan to exploit the natural resources of the country."[48]

Carlson's description was necessarily general in nature, and in a country as vast as China, there was room for countless local peculiarities. The country never formed a united whole in the struggle against Japan but encompassed a variety of responses to the foreign threat, from active armed resistance to downright collaboration, and murky arrangements in between. A report prepared by the US War Department described a complex, almost surreal situation in between war and peace in the eastern province of Jiangsu, where a tacit agreement existed between the Chinese Communists and the Japanese: "In return for the communists not attacking the trains and railroads, the Japanese will not construct walls and dikes along the railroad as they have done elsewhere, and which would make crossing by the communists next to impossible."[49]

The complex interplay among Chiang's Nationalists, Mao's Communists, and the Japanese was taking place against the vast, gray backdrop of the enormous Chinese population, predominantly rural and overwhelmingly poor. To many of them, it mattered little who held sway, either in their province or in the national at large, since to many it had never even occurred that they were part of a larger Chinese nation. "Away from the towns and the roads," wrote the American Graham Peck, most people "knew nothing of what threatened them. Many would probably not know until they heard the guns on the horizon." He described the instance of a semi-educated church worker who lived a mere 18 miles from a major city about to be engulfed by a Japanese offensive: "The Japanese would arrive within two weeks if they kept up their present momentum, but until he reached the city that morning, he had heard nothing of the new invasion."[50]

Despite all this, China remained the Russia of Asia, as Admiral King had stated. "China had a vast territory and a dense population," argued Chinese general Li Zongren. "The Japanese army sent one division at a time to China, which was like sprinkling sauce into a body of water until a bottle of sauce was finished and disappeared into the water. In this manner Japan dropped sixty or seventy divisions into China, to become bogged down in the mire until the nation faced inevitable death."[51] In addition, China was important as a potential base for strategic bombing against Japan. This worried the Japanese, too, and it was a major rationale for their decision to launch their biggest offensive operation of the year 1944. The operation, known as Ichigō, was to come as a shock to the Chinese and the Americans, even though there had been plenty of warnings.

In late 1943, the American diplomat Everett Drumright, on a tour of central China's Henan province to inspect conditions near the frontline, sent an alarming telegram to the US ambassador in the Chinese capital of Chongqing. "The Jap garrison on [the] south bank [of the] Yellow River... has been increased and the old railway bridge is being repaired."[52] Clearly, the Japanese were preparing something big. Other warnings followed, and some months later, they reached all the way to the White House. In a report to Roosevelt,

Claire Chennault, argued there was a strong probability the Japanese would unleash a major offensive drive down the middle of China. "Preparations for these offensives have recently been going forward apace. Movements of troops and equipment up the Yangtze River, for example, have never been so heavy," he wrote. "I wish I could tell you I had no fear of the outcome."[53]

In fact, by the time Chennault's letter was being telegraphed to Washington, the Japanese offensive was already getting underway. In the early hours of April 18, an army of some 140,000 soldiers began crossing the Yellow River and moved into Henan province.[54] This was the beginning of Operation Ichi-Go, in which the Japanese would eventually deploy half a million solders, 100,000 horses, 1,500 pieces of artillery, 800 tanks, 1,500 mechanical vehicles and a large number of airplanes.[55] It was the largest operation in the history of the Japanese Army, dwarfing anything it had carried out so far in Burma or the Pacific, or indeed in any other war it had ever taken part in.

Lieutenant General Liu Changyi, the commander of the Chinese Fifteenth Army, which was located in the path of oncoming Japanese forces, was awakened in the middle of the night when report of the attack started coming in, and he rushed to the frontline with his staff. On the way, he encountered signs of emerging chaos, including a column of more than 30 trucks with the families of senior officers who were fleeing the battlefield along with their belongings. Dismayed by this sign of defeatism, but unable to do anything about it, Liu simply ordered the fugitives to keep good order and avoid panicking. "Don't upset the people in the hinterland," he shouted, and added, for emphasis, "Or you will be shot!"[56]

The offensive, which had taken the Chinese defenders by almost complete surprise despite intelligence that a buildup was underway, served several purposes, including the capture of air bases that US forces had established in southeast China.[57] This was the aim cited when Emperor Hirohito approved the plan in January, reflecting growing concern about the role that a potent American air force in China could play.[58] According to a Japanese account, the attacks of US aircraft were hindering the supply of key forces in central China, and there was no choice "but to plan to destroy Chennault's bases of operation from the ground."[59] Aside from his tactical consideration, and more worrying for the longer term, there was also the prospect that China could increasingly become the base of long-term strategic bombing of the Japanese home islands.[60]

A secondary motive was to create a direct transportation link to Japanese-controlled territories in the south of China. This was the result of a Japanese reevaluation of its strategic options following the series of Allied wins in the

Pacific. The growing American dominance on the ocean made the sea routes to Japan's resource-rich possessions in Southeast Asia insecure, and the Japanese high command hoped a land corridor down the middle of China, relying on trains rather than ships, would provide an answer for the future.[61] Third, the Japanese planners believed that a successful campaign in China could result in the toppling of Chiang Kai-shek's regime.[62] This reflected a belief that the enemy camp only had a fragile hold on the public's loyalty, similar to the expectation that the simultaneous offensive in Burma would trigger rebellions in India.

While the three overall goals were basically sound, the entire operation nevertheless reflected an emerging departure from reality and a belief in miracles, not unlike the fantasies about wonder weapons that sustained the Nazi leadership as Germany marched towards the precipice. Lieutenant Colonel Imoto Kumao, an officer active in the Japanese Army's Operations Section, described how the section's chief carried out wargames prior to the Ichigō offensive, arriving at unrealistic results that spoke volumes about the wishful thinking dominating minds in Tokyo. "The plan had as its final goal the launching of a major offensive in the Pacific from northern Australia or the southern Philippines in about 1946 to bring the war to an end. Yet there were no concrete prospects of this happening, and the sole objective seemed to be to keep hopes alive for the future."[63]

The optimism was far-fetched, even allowing for the limited perspective available to Japanese planners at the time but the initial momentum of the Ichigō offensive in Henan province nevertheless showed that the Japanese Army retained much of its fighting potential from the early years of the war, especially when pitted against a foe of uneven quality such as the Chinese. Chinese defenses along the Yellow River consisted of 21 nominal divisions, but of these only 11 were combatworthy.[64] Further aggravating the problems on the Chinese side, the senior command initially did not see the danger they were in, perhaps because they did not wish to see. Chiang Kai-shek only paid attention to the Japanese operations in his diary two days later, and even on April 22, he seemed not to appreciate the severity of the situation: "In Henan, the enemy has moved around foolishly," he wrote in his diary.[65]

In fact, there was nothing foolish about the Japanese advance. Chen Zhengfeng, a staff officer with the Fifteenth Army, described the unequal fight between Chinese troops with obsolete equipment and little training, fighting an army boosted by tanks and airplanes. "The officers and the men had entered into battle, with no provisions whatsoever. They had been fighting fiercely and were exhausted, and they received no supplies or reinforcements.

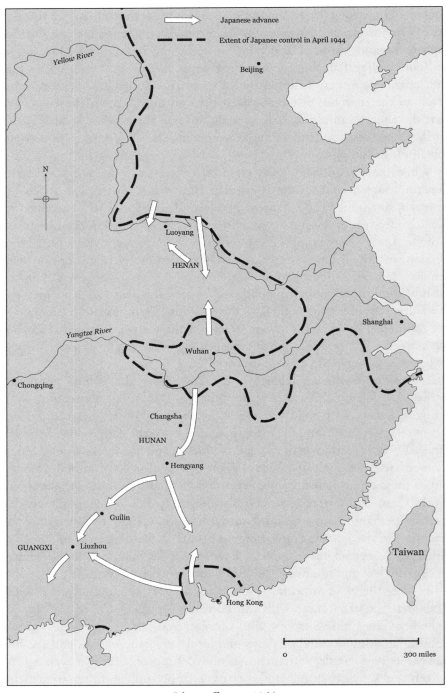

Ichigō offensive, 1944.

They had no choice but to gradually retreat." The flat, featureless terrain was perfect for tanks, and put infantry at a severe disadvantage. "The battlefield we were fighting in consisted of sandy ground, and it was hard to find materials to build fortifications… We tried to set up roadblocks, covering behind ruins and toppled walls, crouching in ditches and hiding in forests."[66]

At a time when Axis forces were retreating everywhere else in the world, the Japanese troops were making rapid advances. After seven years in China, the Japanese Army also appeared to have learned a thing or two about hearts and minds. The Japanese soldiers taking part in the invasion had learned a new marching song, which included lines suggesting a new approach to the civilian Chinese:

Taking loving care of trees and grass,
The Japanese troops march through Hunan province.
How kind their hearts are!

The song ended with a line aimed at the common enemy, the "Anglo-Americans, the white-faced demons."[67] Any sympathy the Japanese might have attained by this approach evaporated from day one, as they behaved no differently from previous campaigns, looting and burning villages as they went.[68] At the same time, airplanes attacked refugee streams on the roads, as Lutheran missionary John Benson saw repeatedly: "As it got light planes appeared and strafed the traffic. We hid twice in the wet wheat. The roads were crowded with refugees streaming out of the city, carrying their precious belongings or a baby or an aged, crippled mother—always forced to be on the lookout for planes who were mercilessly strafing traffic on the roads."[69]

Japanese aircraft were not the only danger. Chiang Kai-shek recorded in his diary how US Army Air Force bombers cost the lives of numerous Chinese due to tragic mistakes: "The American bombers were expected to bomb the railway bridge over the Yellow River three times, but yesterday they did it only once, and there was no effect. They were supposed to continue until they had reached the objective, but in today's mission, they decided to turn around halfway towards the target and fly back to [the southwestern city of] Kunming. They decided to drop their bomb load en route, killing and injuring Chinese civilians on the ground. It breaks my heart."[70]

It was hard for ordinary farmers in the war zone to really distinguish friend from foe, and in many parts of central China, the Chinese Army had made itself extremely unpopular due to its behavior over the preceding years, while a relative lull had dominated the frontline. The Chinese soldiers, who often came from completely different parts of the country and spoke an unintelligible dialect, frequently behaved like an army of occupation, extracting grain from farmers who were already under severe stress. So, when the Chinese Army retreated, it received little support from the civilian population, and sometimes direct opposition. "People in the hills of west Henan attacked our units, taking our guns and ammunition, and even mortars and telephone poles. They surrounded and killed our troops," Jiang Dingwen, a senior Chinese commander, wrote after the war. "They sacked our barracks and cleared the fields so some units went without food for days."[71]

Anarchy reigned in areas vacated by the Chinese Army, and in the lawless conditions, bandits roamed the countryside, looting anyone unable to defend themselves. The common people were the big losers in this situation. Greta Clark, a Canadian missionary fleeing the fighting, was hiding inside a small cave with her assistant Miss Wang and other refugees when eight men armed with revolvers and swords entered, demanding money. "They took all Miss Wang's belongings and many of my things, including my reading glasses," Clark later explained.[72]

In this maelstrom of people, the two armies continued their battles, and by May, the fighting concentrated in and around the ancient city of Luoyang. Liu Yaxian, a logistics officer with the Fifteenth Army, described the ferocity of the battles inside the city's narrow streets: "Soldiers of the 64th Chinese Division were in hand-to-hand combat with Japanese infantrymen over control of one of the buildings. The Japanese attacked with bayonets fixed to their Type 38 rifles. One of the Chinese soldiers tried to grab the bayonet of one of the attackers and wanted to push it downwards. The Japanese soldier hastily pulled back his rifle, causing the man to lose his fingers."[73]

By May 24, the situation in the city had become untenable for the Chinese defenders. While the Japanese sent in aircraft and had their artillery shell the Chinese-held districts mercilessly, their tanks rolled in from several directions, followed by infantry. Chinese soldiers placed on rooftops along the route of advance tried desperately to hold back the attack with rifle fire and, when they had exhausted their ammunition, with bricks. It did not change the fact that the battle was lost. Members of Luoyang's fifth column set fires throughout the city, adding to the overall chaos. An officer who had inspected the frontline stumbled into the field headquarters of the Fifteenth Army, sat down with a dejected look on his face, and muttered, "It's over."[74]

★ ★ ★

While Japan was pushing away everything in its path in the last successful major offensive of any Axis power, thousands of miles to the south, it was placed irreversibly on the defensive and lost the initiative, never to seize it again. By early spring, the harbor of Rabaul, its South Pacific fortress, had been almost completely surrounded, in accordance with the US strategy of circumventing major obstacles if at all possible, rather than expending men and materiel to capture them for little long-term gain. To the east, American forces had moved up the Solomon Islands chain, and to the southwest, they had taken major positions along New Guinea's coastline. The most important missing piece was the Admiralty Islands, straddling sea routes northwest of Rabaul leading to Japanese possessions in the East Indies and Philippines.

The Admiralties, including Los Negros with its strategically placed Monote airstrip immediately east of the main island Manus, were scheduled for invasion by a US Army division in late March, but aerial reconnaissance of the islands had revealed almost no Japanese activity, leading key members of MacArthur's staff to the conclusion that it could be taken one month early with little or no opposition. "Los Negros is ripe for the plucking," said George Kenney, the Army air force commander in the region. Intelligence officers disagreed, citing Japanese radio communication suggesting a large presence of troops. The final decision rested with MacArthur. Listening to Kenney, he paced back and forth, nodding occasionally, and then suddenly stopped, exclaiming with reference to the geographic location of the islands which virtually blocked Japanese access to Rabaul: "That will put the cork in the bottle."[75]

The move against the Admiralties ahead of schedule was similar to Nimitz's bold grasp for Eniwetok a few weeks earlier and revealed the same nimbleness of mind and preparedness, at extremely short notice, to seize an opportunity when it emerged amid better-than-expected fortunes on the battlefield. Indeed, MacArthur was in all likelihood prompted in part by the rapid advances made by Nimitz, leading him to fear that the Philippines might not be liberated by his Army moving up along New Guinea, but instead by Navy and Marine forces approaching from the sea. That would make a mockery of his pledge to "return" which MacArthur had made when hastily departing in early 1942. Now was the time to act and avoid being left entirely behind in the race to Manila.[76]

The invasion of Los Negros was scheduled for February 29, just four days after MacArthur had given the green light. Not only was the period left for preparation extremely brief, but the troops assigned to the operation had also been significantly reduced from those originally earmarked for the seizure of the islands. The invasion force now consisted of reinforced elements of the 1st Cavalry Division's 5th Regiment, which were to make a probing attack,

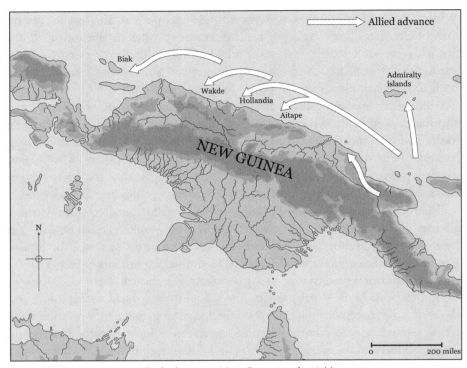

Allied advance in New Guinea, early 1944.

and only if Japanese resistance was as limited as expected were reinforcements to be sent in.

MacArthur was accompanying the invasion fleet, leaning against the rail of the cruiser *Phoenix* on the eve of the landing, when an aide expressed concern about deploying the 5th Cavalry, still untested in this war, in an operation this risky. MacArthur was completely at ease, describing how as a boy of four, when his father was stationed at Fort Selden in New Mexico, he had seen the very same regiment, then a true cavalry outfit, ride to the rescue during battles against the Apache chief Geronimo. "I can still remember how I felt when I watched them clatter into the fort, their tired horses gray with the desert dust. They'd fight then and they'll fight now. Don't worry about them."[77]

Only hours later, the men in the first wave of landing craft approached the invasion zone through a narrow channel formed by two promontories on the eastern end of the island. As the Japanese defenders still kept low after the preparatory bombardment, they were able to storm the beach without suffering casualties, and stumbled ashore, almost unable to believe their own good luck. The following waves were not so lucky, as the Japanese had now returned to their positions, and some of the boats were subjected to intense fire, cutting many of the men to pieces in their craft.[78]

A correspondent for *Yank* magazine described the scene inside one of the landing craft immediately after it had been hit: "Up front a hole gaped in the middle of the landing ramp and there were no men where there had been four. Our barge headed back toward the destroyer that had carried us to the Admiralties. White splashes of water were plunging through the 6-inch gap in the wooden gate." At this point, a sergeant ducked from his position at the starboard gun and slammed his hip against the hole to plug it. "He was firing a tommy gun at the shore as fast as wounded soldiers could pass him loaded clips. The water sloshed around him, running down his legs and washing the blood of the wounded into a pink frappe."[79]

Despite the Japanese fire, the 5th Cavalry was able to maintain a steady stream of men and equipment onto the invasion beach, and by afternoon on the same day, they had not only secured a foothold but had reached the airfield that was the main objective. MacArthur now went ashore and was pleased with what he saw. "Hold what you have taken, no matter against what odds. You have your teeth in him now. Don't let up," he said.[80] Getting back onto the *Phoenix*, he ordered reinforcements sent to Los Negros in preparation of taking the rest of the Admiralties. He had been vindicated, he felt. In fact, he was just lucky. There was indeed a large Japanese force on Los Negros, but their commander had placed them on the opposite end of the island, facing a more likely invasion beach.

The ensuing days and weeks saw protracted fighting as the remaining Japanese sought to regain control of the airfield. Fred Faiz, a machine gunner with the 1st Cavalry Division, recalled Los Negros as one great swamp with no trails where all movement had to take place by foot. "It was just jungle. We had a machete that we cut our way through with," he said, recalling close encounters with the island's wildlife: "You'd be sleeping at night there and there'd be a snake crawling all over you."[81]

There were, of course, much greater dangers. The regiment's soldiers had been warned beforehand by battle-hardened Marines not to sleep in their hammocks, because the Japanese would crawl up in the middle of the night and butcher them while asleep. Instead, they set a trap, filling the hammocks with their ponchos rolled up to resemble sleeping soldiers and their helmets placed at the end. After dark, the Japanese appeared, armed only with knives and grenades. Faiz and the other men were waiting for them in trenches outside the area and opened fire when they could not miss. The battle was over almost immediately. "We had the guns and they didn't have any," Faiz said. It was a ruthless, brutal kind of war, played out as a dirty game with no rules but with huge stakes, because it was a question of life and death for those involved. "There is no fair play in soldiering," according to an American officer who served in the South Pacific. "You shoot the enemy in the back without warning. You allow them no protection. What is cowardly in kid games is good tactics to a soldier."[82]

Deadly firefights could erupt at any moment. Martin Gonzales, the assistant in a two-man team operating a Browning Automatic Rifle, or BAR, was on a small patrol and had moved on more than a hundred yards into the jungle when his squad ran into a group of Japanese. Both sides began firing, including the man with the BAR. "I was the assistant so I had to feed the clips to him. Big old, 30-caliber, 20 rounds a clip. So I was feeding the clips and then he got shot." As the injured man collapsed to the ground, Gonzales picked up the BAR and began firing: "You're shooting away and you lose track of time."[83]

By early March, Los Negros was largely in American hands, and the invading force turned its attention to neighboring Manus island. Given overwhelming US superiority, the Japanese garrison was forced to withdraw inland, and over the subsequent weeks its soldiers became prey not only to American patrols but also the harsh elements. The diary found after the battle on a dead Japanese soldier described the hardship that accompanied the last defenders during their final days. "We have been wandering around and around the mountain roads because of the enemy," read one entry toward the end of the month. "Our bodies are becoming weaker and weaker, and this hunger is getting unbearable."[84]

Manus and Los Negros were both secured by April 1. It was a triumph for MacArthur's penchant for bold strategic moves, and from the newly won harbor facilities in the Admiralties he was about, in the second half of the same month, to launch an even more daring operation, which would push the frontline 500 miles to the west, and closer to the Philippines, virtually overnight. The ultimate target was the jungle-covered region of Hollandia, which was well inside the former Netherlands New Guinea and boasted three strategically positioned airstrips.

The capture of the airfields was to take place in an operation codenamed Reckless and led by General Robert L. Eichelberger, one of MacArthur's trusted lieutenants. It required landing in three different locations. The US Army's 24th Infantry Division was to disembark on the west side of Hollandia, while the 41st Infantry Division landed on the east side. The two divisions were to make their way inland and meet at the airfields in the heart of Hollandia. Further to the east, at the town of Aitape, another force was to disembark in order to establish a stepping stone towards Hollandia. The invasion forces would hit the Japanese where they did not suspect it and therefore maintained a limited number of troops. Much denser concentrations of troops along the north coast of New Guinea were simply bypassed.

All three landings took place nearly simultaneously on April 22 and achieved maximum surprise. The few Japanese defenders were stunned, and casualties were light. It was a logistical feat as much as a military one. Eichelberger later pondered the challenges associated with carrying out a sophisticated military campaign in a part of the globe where great powers had never before waged war: "The white man's influence had penetrated only a few miles inland from the seacoast. Planning a military campaign on the basis of word-of-mouth information and air reconnaissance has its hazards, but a campaign must be planned. Then it must be fought."[85]

Operation Reckless was a prime example of exactly this. The airfields in the center of Hollandia had seemed to be tempting targets in the aerial reconnaissance carried out before the invasion, and they had been primary objectives of the landings, but once the Americans reached them, they proved of questionable value. The ground was too soft for use by heavy American bombers, and extensive engineering work was required.[86] We have captured a "lemon," an Army Air Force officer said. Even the roads leading to the airfields were in a deplorable state, and Eichelberger had to spend four miserable hours to get there, employing a variety of transport means, including "jeep, buffalo and on foot."[87]

While in terms of air power the results of the operation would have to await the efforts of the army engineers, in other ways it yielded immediate results. At Aitape, the US troops achieved an intelligence bonanza. A diver salvaged a steel box containing key Japanese codebooks from a Japanese barge that had been sunk during the fighting. The Japanese had set fire to the codebooks inside the box and believed they had all been consumed by the flames but had forgotten that books must be burned page by page to really disintegrate. The books were flown to Brisbane where Australian scientists employed various chemicals and were able to restore 85 percent of the codes listed in the original books.[88]

Overall, MacArthur sounded a note of triumph, if not retribution, in his official communique announcing the operation at Hollandia, describing it as the mirror image of the situation he himself had experienced two years earlier when forced to leave his beleaguered forces on the Philippine peninsula of Bataan: "[The Japanese enemy's] invested garrisons can be expected to strike desperately to free themselves and combat will be required to accomplish the annihilation, but their ultimate fate is now certain. Their situation reverses Bataan."[89]

CHAPTER THREE

"Turn on the Lights!"

June 1944

By early summer, the Japanese Army had reason to be satisfied with Operation Ichigō. It had brushed aside most Chinese resistance, and it was now ready for the second stage of the offensive. The objective was the populous Hunan province. This was key in any attempt to secure control of the railroad south to the large city of Guangzhou, and at the same time it was an important area which the Japanese needed to control if they were to neutralize the threat of American bombers based in China. To achieve this aim, three massive Japanese columns moved south out of the Yangtze city of Wuhan, marching along a 100-mile-broad front towards Hunan's capital of Changsha.[1]

The decision to proceed along three different routes, cutting a broad belt down through Hunan, was a very deliberate one. This was the Japanese Army's fourth attempt at seizing Changsha, and each of the three earlier offensives had failed for roughly the same reason. Each time, it had sent a narrow column of soldiers south towards the city, allowing the Chinese to carry out flanking maneuvers and cut off the Japanese supply lines in the rear. This had threatened the Japanese with envelopment and had forced them to withdraw prematurely. To prevent a repeat of these previous debacles, the Japanese not only dispatched three columns but made sure this time to place their strongest forces in the two outer columns, deterring Chinese attacks on the wings.[2]

The Chinese side was divided on how to react to the Japanese advance. A majority of commanders wished to abandon the railroad to Guangzhou, which also implied giving up Changsha, and instead move their defenses further inland. "My anger silenced others at the meeting," remarked Xu Yongchang, a Chinese general who was in favor of defending the railroad, writing in his diary.[3] Eventually, Chiang Kai-shek overruled the proponents of a withdrawal, determining that Changsha was to be defended after all. Zhang Deneng, a general with two decades of battle experience, was ordered to hold the city as the commander of the Fourth Army, and planning for the defense went ahead.[4]

The Chinese commanders expected that the formula which had saved Changsha three times already would be effective once again, and they only gradually realized they were wrong. Any attempts to slow down the advancing invasion force foundered on the powerful flanks, especially the Japanese left wing, which occupied mountainous areas and prevented Chinese reinforcements being sent in from the neighboring war zone. As a result, the Japanese reached Changsha less than three weeks after the opening of the offensive, leaving the fate of the city in the hands of Zhang Deneng and his Fourth Army, known as the "Iron Army" because of its record during China's civil wars nearly two decades earlier.[5]

Zhang Deneng's forces held two main positions. One was Changsha proper, while the other, across the Xiang river, was Yuelu Mountain. The Chinese command had positioned a large amount of modern artillery on the mountain, meaning for it to play a decisive role in the upcoming battle by shelling the advancing Japanese. The senior officers watching the battle from the hinterland also tended to think that the main effort should be placed on the mountain in order to defend the precious equipment and prevent it from being seized by the Japanese, thus displaying an old penchant for valuing materiel more highly than people. Zhang was not convinced. "Our mission is to defend Changsha to the death. If we don't hold onto Changsha, it will be impossible to evacuate the positions on Yuelu Mountain anyway."[6]

Once the Japanese arrived, Zhang was eventually convinced to send reinforcements from Changsha across the Xiang River to Yuelu Mountain. The maneuver was complicated by the fact that it was taking place while the battle was already on, and it was further hampered by a lack of vessels to transport the troops safely across the river. From early on, the losses began piling up on the Chinese side. Zhang was caught in a situation where he decided that a pullout would save lives and enable him to fight another day. Ignoring instructions to battle on to the last man, on June 18 he ordered the full-scale withdrawal out of the burning city, leaving behind most of the artillery on Yuelu Mountain.[7]

Chiang Kai-shek was furious, especially since a large number of modern artillery pieces and mountain guns as well as over 50,000 shells had fallen into Japanese hands when they conquered Yuelu Mountain, with no apparent attempt to try and disarm them before withdrawing. "The Fourth Army's reputation appears to have been completely without merit, an empty shell," Chiang wrote in his diary, and added ominously: "There is no way around punishing the commanding general severely." A few days later Zhang Deneng was sentenced to death and executed.[8]

Even though the Japanese offensive had only met with success up until that moment, the senior commanders in Tokyo were concerned that Ichigō could still end up a failure due to the excessive ambitions of the officers in the field. Since the planning phase, Tōjō's focus had been on eliminating the American airbases, whereas he saw other objectives such as the destruction of Chiang Kai-shek's regime as risky diversions. In early June, he sent General Hata Hikozaburō, the vice chief of the General Staff, to China to make sure that the priorities stayed in place. "There seems to be an emphasis on the extermination of enemy forces. But... the prime objective of the operation is to destroy enemy airfields," said Hata upon arrival.[9]

In spite of this criticism coming straight from Tokyo, the Japanese field army maintained an emphasis on seeking to engage and wipe out as many Chinese troops as possible. In order to lure a greater portion of the enemy army into battle, the Japanese moved on from Changsha to the city of Hengyang, further south along the railway to Guangzhou. Hengyang was an important transportation center, where the main north-south railroad was linked to a secondary line further into Chinese territory, while also offering avenues into several key provinces not yet under Japanese control. In addition, a major American air base was located nearby.[10]

A young American civilian, Graham Peck, visited Hengyang just as the Japanese were moving in on the city, describing a population confused by wild rumors and torn between fear and hope. Given the Japanese record of barbarity towards the people they conquered, the only rational solution was to leave as soon as possible, but as had been the case with other major cities threatened by Japanese occupation over the past seven years of war, only the wealthy had the means to do so. "A missionary who called on one official reported he had been received in an empty house and his host contentedly told him that he had just sent all his possessions, two boxcars full, down the railway," Peck wrote. "But few ordinary people were leaving. It was too difficult and expensive. They could not make up their minds to go until they were sure there was no choice but to run."[11]

Even though the Chinese tactics of luring the enemy in deep and attacking the flanks and the rear had failed in the battle of Changsha, the exact same approach was picked in the defense of Hengyang. The Japanese moved swiftly despite Chinese attempts at delaying their offensive, and on June 23, a mere five days after the fall of Changsha, they were at the gates of Hengyang. Once again, the Chinese command was divided on the proper approach, and only at the last moment did Chiang Kai-shek decide in favor of defending the city. The stage seemed set for another quick Japanese victory in the manner of Changsha, but it would turn out differently this time around.

It evolved into one of the bloodiest and most protracted urban battles of the entire eight-year Sino-Japanese War. This happened as world public opinion was increasingly directing its attention towards China, in a negative way. At a time when the Allies were advancing everywhere else—in the Pacific, in France after the Normandy invasion, and on the Eastern Front following a massive Soviet summer offensive—China was the only exception, and the only place in the world where Axis powers were not retreating but in fact advancing by hundreds of miles. The opinion spread among several of China's senior commanders that it was necessary to make a stand at Hengyang, even if it did not necessarily make sense militarily speaking. Emotions ran high. At one meeting, Chiang Kai-shek was said to be "shaken to the core and pounding the table again and again."[12]

Hengyang became a city under siege. Everything was in short supply on the Chinese side: ammunition, food, medicine, even water, and efforts to airdrop supplies often failed and ended up inside Japanese-held territory.[13] A hellish atmosphere descended over the streets, compounded by the almost unbearable summer heat and the ubiquitous insects. Japanese snipers outside the Chinese perimeters hit their targets with uncanny precision.[14] Even so, the Chinese persevered, and their determination to hold on to Hengyang resulted in desperate seesaw battles over key positions. By early August, after one and a half months of fierce fighting, the Chinese forces had no choice but to withdraw out of the city. Although the Chinese launched several counterattacks against Japanese forces around Hengyang over the next weeks, it did nothing to change the final outcome. Hengyang was securely in Japanese hands.[15]

A common complaint among Chinese commanders was the emergence of fifth-column elements at key moments during major battles, starting fires and causing confusion in the hinterland. This reflected the fact that Chinese armies were often fighting far away from home, in provinces where language and customs were different from their own, like in a foreign country. Likewise, the civilians often had no particular loyalties and saw both the Chinese and the Japanese as foreign armies fighting for control of their soil. Chiang Kai-shek saw this as a major shortcoming during the Ichigō operation: "Our biggest humiliations in the battles of Henan and of Hunan was that the Japanese used Chinese people as plain-clothes personnel, while we were not able to do so. With the exception of one general, no Nationalist army unit was able to mobilize our own people in our service."[16]

Overall, the relationship between the Chinese soldiers and the population they were supposed to be defending was often shockingly bad. The main issue was a corrupt mentality at the core of many Chinese units, as Chiang Kai-shek argued while expressing his dismay in a speech to officers at his summer retreat at Huangshan near Chongqing towards the end of the Hengyang battle: "This time during the battle for Henan, some American and Soviet officers retreated along with our troops. According to their testimony, the local population surrounded our troops during their withdrawal and seized their weapons. Of course, that kind of army can only lose."

Chiang went on to describe the conditions in a straightforward manner which only the man at the top could afford: "The horses and wagons in our army did not carry weapons or ammunition, but smuggled goods. Once the situation turned critical, if the goods were not stolen by civilians, they were simply left by the roadside, and the horses and wagons were used to transport family members instead. Once the soldiers and the horses were exhausted, they could move no longer and were killed by the people." Worse yet had happened, Chiang said: "The army had lost all morale and was rotten to the core. While they were retreating, some soldiers and officers went about raiding every place they passed, looting people's homes and raping the women, taking away the very means that people relied on to survive. How can such an army exist in today's China?"[17]

In the summer of 1944, the region of Indramayu on the East Indies island of Java exploded in violence. A student at an Islamic boarding school who was known only by the name of Mi'an began distributing holy water among the peasants in the area, telling them it would make them invulnerable to attacks from non-Muslims. They needed it, for they were preparing an uprising against their Japanese-supported rulers over grain levies that made life almost unbearable. A couple of low-ranking Javanese officials in the village of Bugis were the first to feel the wrath of the peasants. Angry mobs attacked them in their homes, beating them up and destroying everything inside. The Japanese military police rushed to the scene and confronted the protesting crowd. After attempting to threaten the peasants to disperse, the soldiers opened fire, mowing down the men and boys, who were carrying only sticks and machetes. About 200 people died on that blood-soaked day.[18]

Many had expected a clash sooner or later. Tensions had been building up in this part of the former Dutch East Indies since the spring, as village after village had protested at the rising grain acquisitions, and some had openly rebelled. "We would rather die in battle than die of hunger," they shouted when officials tried to convince them to go home. Instead, the desperate villagers went on rampages, hunting down tax collectors and others who acted as the face of the regime at the grassroots level. One was stabbed to death by a crowd wielding sharpened bamboo sticks, another was killed along with his son.

Anger was directed as much at local officials as at the Japanese, but it was the Japanese who had the power to enforce the unpopular decisions on the poverty-stricken people of Java. Few protesters were killed on the spot. Most individuals deemed to be the ringleaders of the riots were simply driven away, never to be heard from again. Still, even the Japanese did not have the power to rein in the escalating chaos following the riots during the summer months, and as roving bandits moved through the unpoliced countryside, attacking ordinary people and looting their homes, everyone suffered.[19]

The unrest in Java reflected larger problems afflicting the Japanese throughout their vast empire by the middle of 1944. In the Dutch East Indies, the Japanese had ostensibly been attempting a policy of unifying the various ethnicities. On Java, this philosophy of a "fraternal order," bringing together Japanese, Indonesian, Chinese, Arabs, and Eurasians, was propagated, in direct opposition to the "divide and rule" tactics that the former Dutch colonial masters had carried out, with significant success. In most Asian areas, Japan made the pretense of supporting indigenous government of some form, in conformity with its stated objective of ridding the region of western imperialism. The one exception until the end of the war was Indochina, where the French colonial administration remained in place.[20]

In some cases, regular friendships had evolved between Japanese and representatives of the local population. An Indonesian journalist later explained his relationship with one of the Japanese officials, who had a genuine concern for the fate of the East Indies. "He was a frank and sympathetic friend, almost like a brother to us. His Indonesian was excellent... and we had many discussions with him about politics, Japan's objectives and Indonesian independence. He helped us in a lot of ways; for instance, sometimes if articles we had written did not pass the censor, he would somehow try to get them in print."[21]

The reality, however, was often the reverse of the rosy images of inter-racial harmony described in the Japanese illustrated magazines. Since the early days of the occupation in 1942, the requirements of the local population had to yield to the demands of the Japanese military. After all, access to the rich natural resources of the East Indies had formed the entire basic rationale for Tokyo's decision to unleash the Pacific War. "I had only to know how much exploitation the native population could endure," said Major Miyamoto Shizuo, an officer in charge of logistics planning.[22]

It was highly ironic that by 1944 Japan was reaping extraordinarily little actual gain from its possessions in Southeast Asia. Prior to Pearl Harbor, Japanese planners had calculated with Indonesian oil meeting most of their 7.9-million-ton oil requirement per year, but Allied sinking of Japanese transport shipping had caused the amount actually shipped to other parts of the Japanese empire to gradually dwindle, and for the fiscal year beginning April 1, 1944, no oil at all was transported from the East Indies. The output of other strategic materials such as rubber and coal also dropped to a fraction of their prewar levels, meaning essentially that the entire war had been in vain, insofar as it had started out as a grab for vital resources.[23]

Only one resource was plentiful and could be exploited directly on the spot: labor. Young men known as *romusha* or "work soldiers" were recruited, often forcibly, and set to work at various large-scale projects under the supervision of Japanese engineers. They were often promised good treatment before their departure, but many never returned. Of 300,000 from Java who were sent off to islands elsewhere in the huge Indonesian archipelago, only 77,000 made it home again.[24] What happened to the others is clear from an eyewitness account of the scene at a remote mountainside, where hundreds of workers hacked out a tunnel with adzes and hammers. "Their bodies were thin and parched—bone wrapped in skin," the testimony reads. "Corpses were just like rubbish—walking skeletons no longer shocked people."[25] Another account detailed the abuse they were subject to: "Because of their weakened condition, they almost did not have enough strength to walk, so that they staggered on their feet like drunkards. To rest for a moment meant running the risk of getting abuse and blows."[26]

Resistance movements emerged throughout Asia and the Pacific and, as in Europe, they differed widely in terms their means and aims, and the circumstances that gave rise to them. Some operated in close cooperation with the Allies forces, while others were anti-colonialist organizations with a socialist agenda. In addition, there were movements arising at the local level emerging because of economic grievances, as the one on Java in the summer of 1944.[27]

The situation could become extraordinarily complicated if several resistance groups vied for control of the same area. An example of this was the province of Ilocos Norte in the northern Philippines, where civil war-style conditions ruled, and one group of partisans, led by an American officer who had escaped capture during the Japanese invasion, introduced a reign of terror in a campaign against suspected collaborators. Mariano Marcos, the chief of propaganda in the region and also the father of the future dictator Ferdinand Marcos, was executed by the guerrillas and hung from a tree as a warning to others.[28]

Despite the vast differences among various localities, Japanese brutality was the big constant throughout the Asia Pacific, alienating vast numbers who had initially extended a cautious welcome to rule from Tokyo, believing it could be no worse than the colonial regimes it replaced. Even at the official level, among members of the collaborationist governments, patience was wearing thin. It was dawning on some of them that even though the previous colonial administrations of the British, the Americans, and the Dutch might have been flawed, what they had got instead was, on balance, many times worse.

In a remarkably candid letter sent in June 1944 to Japan's embassy in Manila, the Philippine Foreign Minister Claro M. Recto criticized the behavior of the Japanese occupation forces, giving as an example an incident in his hometown of Tiaong, where one hundred people had been summarily executed. This was far from an isolated event, he explained: "Thousands of cases have been reported of people being either burned alive, killed at the point of the bayonet, beheaded, beaten without mercy, or otherwise subjected to various methods of physical torture, without mercy, without distinction as to age or sex. Women and children below fifteen years are known to have been among those who were victims of such punishment."[29]

Lord Mountbatten was in high spirits on the first day of June. He was visited at his headquarters in Ceylon by the world-famous playwright Noel Coward and enjoyed his clever conversation immensely. "We never had a dull moment," Mountbatten wrote in his diary.[30] Half a world away, in London, the Southeast Asian commander's relaxed attitude could be mistaken for happy indifference at a time when the Japanese Army was pushing ahead with its most ambitious offensive in Burma since the beginning of the war, and Field Marshal Alan Brooke, the chief of the Imperial General Staff, was intensely worried. The situation in Burma was "heart-breaking," he wrote in his diary. He elaborated: "I see disaster staring us in the face, with Mountbatten incapable of realizing it."[31]

In fact, Brooke's pessimism was misplaced, because of events which by then were just a few hours old. The day before, Satō Kōtoku, the commander of the Japanese Army's 31st Division, which had been laying siege to Kohima since early in the offensive, had decided to defy his superiors and beat a retreat. Although he had been ordered to hold out for ten more days, he felt he had no choice. "It seems the Army cannot grasp the real situation: no supplies and men wounded and sick," he reported back in a message. "I wish to inform you that, according to the situation, the divisional commander will act on his own initiative."[32]

Satō's action, which earned him a court martial, betrayed an alertness that had not characterized his conduct so far in the campaign. To his main adversary, Slim, Satō was the "most unenterprising" of all Japanese generals he encountered during the war. He could have left a small force to keep the Allied garrison at Kohima busy and moved the majority of his force forward to more important objectives, but instead he had followed his orders slavishly. "He had been ordered to take Kohima and dig in," Slim wrote in his memoirs. "His bullet head was filled with one idea only—to take Kohima. It never struck him that he could inflict terrible damage on us without taking Kohima at all."[33]

A similar stubbornness reigned throughout the Japanese military hierarchy. Key officers in the Fifteenth Army, which had overall responsibility for the operation, displayed remarkable unwillingness to see the situation for what it was, and even to the extent that they understood the gravity of the situation, they were determined to prevent that knowledge from reaching Tokyo. "No staff officers were sent to the front if they were likely to report that the Imphal operation was going to fail," said an officer touring the region in early June.[34] What is more, in the few cases where the facts actually reached Tokyo, the implications were ignored. When confronted with reports suggesting a withdrawal, Prime Minister Tōjō Hideki was adamant: "The battle must be fought to the end."[35]

Only at the sharp end was it impossible to deny the rapidly deteriorating situation. "By the end of May the monsoon had started, and our campaign had already failed," Japanese private Fujiwara Yuwaichi said.[36] An Allied counteroffensive was already getting underway, albeit slowly. For the Japanese soldiers in the frontline, it was no longer a question of whether they would succeed with their operation, but whether they would get out alive. Still, a withdrawal was not ordered until July. "Almost all Japanese soldiers were suffering from malaria and starvation. Many soldiers died," said Fujiwara, adding that the route back got the sinister nickname "death road."[37]

At Myitkyina, where Merrill's Marauders had captured an airfield in May, the battle continued to take the city proper. It was a coordinated Sino-American enterprise, with all the difficulties that entailed. Casualty figures spoke their distinct language about the different challenges Chinese and US soldiers faced, and how they coped with them. During the three months of battle in and around Myitkyina, US forces counted 1,227 killed and injured, whereas Chinese lost 4,156 soldiers, testimony to the continued Chinese propensity for mass frontal assaults. By contrast, a massive 980 American soldiers were rendered unfit for combat by disease, as opposed to 180 Chinese. This was put down to natural Chinese immunity, as well as habits the Chinese soldiers has brought from home to always boil their water and cook their food.[38]

Even though the Western soldiers in Burma continued to battle with disease, gone were the days when the Japanese were facing an adversary unaccustomed to the jungle, or even scared of it. Layer by layer, civilization was peeled off, and life before became a faint, distant memory. Michael, a British special operations officer, noticed an odd change in the men who had spent a long time in the Burmese theater. "Strangely enough, although all units which first started to fight in Burma disliked the jungle and complained about the poor visibility, having been in the jungle for a while they were now subject to agoraphobia, dislike of open spaces."[39]

At the same time as the Allied soldiers gained the skill and experience needed to beat the Japanese, they were assisted by superior materiel, which could be brought to bear even in intensely difficult jungle terrain 5,000 feet or more above sea level. General George J. Giffard, in command of the 11th Army Group, pointed out the crucial role of armor: "Hazardous and difficult as the nature of the country made every movement or operation, tanks often proved the decisive factor in the fighting up and down these mountainous ranges, where they climbed almost precipitous slopes to blast Japanese bunkers at a range of 10 yards."[40]

Superior technology, and the ability to apply it on a sufficient scale, was paramount. Nothing did more to turn the tables in Burma than air power, which put every part of the theater within easy reach for the Allies. This provided invaluable support for the ground forces, according to Keith Park, the commander of Allied air forces in the region: "Continually outflanked by Allied forces, to whom the manna of air supply gave an unprecedented degree of mobility, and continually harried by our close support aircraft, the enemy was never allowed to consolidate the new positions that he occupied along the line of his retreat."[41]

The Japanese air force was now the underdog and unable to counter this growing threat, with attrition playing a big part. "The pilots got worse, but the planes got better," aviator Kawaguchi Susumu said in a post-war interrogation.[42] Morale was high despite heavy losses, sustained by a mixture of pep talks and better living conditions than in the army, which included an ample supply of rice wine, sake. "Like the Luftwaffe," a former pilot later reminisced, "they continued flying until they were killed, or were so severely wounded or struck down by tropical diseases that they were unfit for further service."[43]

In the South Pacific, too, the Allies were keeping up the pressure on the Japanese. Men of the US Army's 41st Division, elements of which had taken part in the landing at Hollandia, were involved in early summer in a new amphibious operation, which eventually moved the frontline a further 300 miles to the west. When one of the division's regiments landed on the island of Wakde off the north coast of New Guinea to seize a Japanese airfield, it met a total of 800 enemy soldiers dug in and prepared to defend their position with the same tenacity as everywhere else. "One prisoner, a Hawaiian-born Jap marine, who spoke excellent English, walked into a supply dump and surrendered. He was the only captive taken at Wakde," wrote General Eichelberger in his post-war memoirs.[44]

Meanwhile, on the New Guinea mainland, American soldiers were moving up the coastline, capturing some positions of strategic value while bypassing others. When they encountered concentrations of Japanese soldiers, as they did around the town of Sarmi, where they landed in mid-June, the resistance was ferocious. Ramon Arcuna, a soldier with the 158th Regimental Combat Team, experienced the ultimate horror of taking the brunt of a nightly Japanese suicide attack: "They hit us, I don't know how many times. That night was so dark, you couldn't see anything. They just kept coming in and leaving their dead, or dragging their dead back, and coming in again. They were completely just bombed out on sake. They were all drunk, screaming."[45]

A primary, hotly contested feature in the Sarmi area was known as Lone Tree Hill. The official US Army history describes one instance in which a Japanese unit wearing American helmets and carrying American weaponry approached the US lines: "The battalion initially held its fire, thinking that the enemy force might be a friendly patrol, and the Japanese were able to advance to within fifteen yards of the battalion lines before being recognized. It was an hour before the results of this error could be corrected—an hour during which both the 2nd Battalion and the Japanese suffered heavy losses. The hour ended with an enemy retreat."[46]

The Wakde and Sarmi areas were needed mainly as stepping stones towards the island of Biak, off the northwestern coast of Netherlands New Guinea and of key importance in any further advance by MacArthur's forces. This was because of its airfield, placed near the village of Mokmer, which was the only one in the area capable of supporting heavy bombers. The Japanese

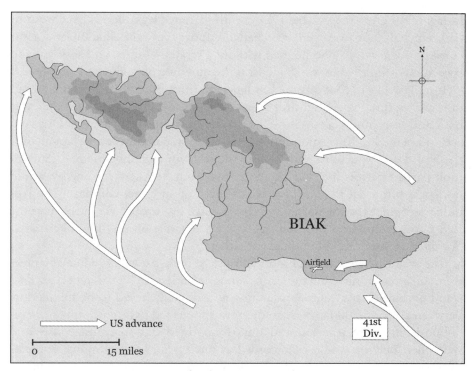

Invasion of Biak, May to September 1944.

knew the value of Biak and introduced a new form of tactics to make the expected American invasion as costly as possible. Rather than seeking to stop them on the beaches, they allowed them to move inland before striking from prepared positions. The result was a far more savage experience than anything the soldiers of the 41st had been though up till then.

Disembarkation, a few miles to the east of the airfield, was deceptively easy, and hopes grew among the soldiers that this could be one of the rare bloodless invasions. They were disappointed. On the second day of the operation, one of the division's battalions moved down a coastal road towards the airfield when it was surprised by Japanese lying in hiding with machine guns, knee mortars, and heavy coast artillery. "They're plastering the hell out of us," the battalion commander reported back to his regiment: "One of my three tanks was knocked out by a lucky hit. The other two are out of gas. Send me ammunition, blood plasma, morphine and water. It's urgent!"[47]

At night, the Japanese emerged suddenly from nowhere and assaulted the American positions, taunting their enemy in broken English, "Wassamatta, Yank, fraid to fight?" The US field hospitals were filling up with casualties, maimed and dying soldiers as well as those who had given in to the intense horror of the green tropical hell. "Boys with shattered legs, bloody head wounds and faces half shot away were stretched out under every available shelter," a war correspondent wrote. "Some men without a scratch—dazed and shocked and speechless—huddled in the shade with the quietude of frightened children."[48]

It took weeks to root out the last Japanese from Biak. "We were in and out of it all the time, you'd fight for a few days or a week or two and then come back and rest," said Calvin Stowell a private from the 41st Infantry Division, acting as a medic. "It was a mopping up operation with pockets of Japs all over the island and you went and hunted them down and shot them."[49] Stowell took part in patrols into the jungle at Biak, but he knew the enemy would not spare him even though he was not involved in direct combat. "The Japs didn't recognize the medic or anything else like in Europe. We didn't have the Red Cross painted on our helmets in a white circle or anything like that… We didn't respect anything on them either."[50]

The aviation hero Charles Lindbergh visited Biak in late July, while US forces were still attempting to kill the last Japanese defenders. In his dairy, he described standing outside his quarters watching as a ridge, believed to be manned by between 250 and 700 Japanese soldiers, was subjected to heavy bombardment: "If positions were reversed and our troops held out so courageously and well, their defense would be recorded as one of the most glorious examples of tenacity, bravery, and sacrifice in the history of our nation. But, sitting in the security and relative luxury of our quarters, I listen to American Army officers refer to these Japanese soldiers as 'yellow sons of bitches.' Their desire is to exterminate the Jap ruthlessly, even cruelly. I have not heard a word of respect or compassion spoken of our enemy since I came here."[51]

While noting that "Oriental atrocities are often worse than ours," Lindbergh also wrote about American soldiers shooting Japanese soldiers on sight even if they had raised their hands in a sign of surrender, and described the casual manner in which enemy dead were treated: "I would have more respect for the character of our people if we could give them a decent burial instead of kicking in the teeth of their corpses."[52] This latter practice was noticed by others. A US Army engineer noticed a particular feature of Japanese corpses he saw in the South Pacific: "All the skulls are minus their teeth because souvenir hunters use them for bracelets."[53]

Japanese soldiers were making themselves culpable of even worse handling of dead bodies. Cannibalism was widespread, and the view of the enemy as a protein source even crept into some of the soldiers' language. They referred to Western soldiers as "white pigs," while indigenous people were called "black pigs."[54] More than anything else, the consumption of human flesh was forced by circumstances. Virtually no transports made it through to New Guinea, and indeed the Japanese soldiers stranded on the huge landmass were abandoned to their own devices. In these circumstances, they devoured not only their foes, but also those among their own ranks who had succumbed to wounds, disease, or starvation. Even so, out of a total of 157,646 Japanese soldiers serving in New Guinea, only 10,072 survived to the end of the war.[55]

But for a very specific circumstance, the invasion of Biak could have ended in abject failure for the Americans. A powerful Japanese fleet was poised to pounce on the US invasion force off the island and could have wreaked havoc. "The Japanese battleship force could have been to Biak, sunk our ships, destroyed the landing, and left," said Captain Charles Adair, US Navy, who played a key role in the planning of amphibious operations. Instead, the Japanese fleet was called off to a separate American offensive in the Central Pacific. "The attacks that were made in the central Pacific in those various islands helped us very much in keeping the strength of the Japanese Navy pointed in that direction rather than in our direction. We had nothing to fight it off with, so we would have been sitting ducks, as far as that goes," said Adair.[56]

The focus of the American offensive in the Central Pacific, taking place nearly simultaneously with the Biak operation, was the island of Saipan, a Japanese possession since 1914. Three American divisions two Marine and one Army, stormed onto its beaches on June 15, nine days after D-Day in Europe. It was the start of a battle as ferocious as the struggle for northern France. The invasion force that carried the men to the battle consisted of 535 combatant ships and auxiliary vessels, not by any means comparable to the fleet that crossed the British Channel, but the logistical challenge was far more complex. While the armies landing in Normandy that same month had to travel less than 100 miles from southern England, Saipan was 3,500 miles from Pearl Harbor, and 1,017 miles from the atoll of Eniwetok, the closest advance base. "No operation on so vast a scale, with a final thousand-mile 'hop,' had ever before been planned," in the words of the US Navy's official historian.[57]

A central part of the Marianas archipelago, the 13 miles of rock and limestone known as Saipan was a vital station on the road towards Tokyo, not least because it would enable American bombers to begin long-distance missions against the Japanese home islands. In this respect the neighboring island of Tinian, separated from Saipan by three-mile-wide channel, was

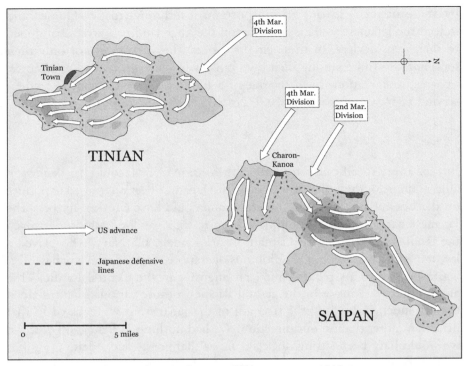

Landings on Saipan and Tinian, summer 1944.

even more important. Being nearly flat, Tinian offered excellent geographic conditions for air bases, and it was also targeted in the operation.

Apart from their use as a base for the coming bomber offensive, the twin islands formed a vital node in Japan's overall defensive network in the Pacific, alongside Guam, the biggest island in the Marianas. "Saipan was Japan's administrative Pearl Harbor," remarked Marine General Holland M. Smith, in charge of ground troops during the operation. "It was the naval and military heart and brain of Japanese defense strategy."[58] Saipan was also home to a sizable population of civilian Japanese, which was to give the battle an even more cruel character.

The pre-invasion bombardment, carried out while men of the 2nd and 4th Marine Divisions were getting ready in their amphibious craft, was as devastating as anything the US Navy had organized so far in the war, and highly targeted. The battleship USS *California* got within 3,000 yards of Saipan. "We were almost patting them on the head," said Robert Ellinger, in an antiaircraft division aboard the ship, remembering how suddenly the Japanese guns opened up. "We had shells coming around our ship. They hit and killed a man and injured an officer and four or five other men. Then we knew we were at war."[59]

Meanwhile, the Marines approaching the beach were also subjected to deadly Japanese fire, standing densely packed in their landing craft. "They were all crowded and standing up, so there really was no room to get down," said Baine Kerr, a young Marine officer. A captain was hit: "A 20-millimeter shell hit him just square in the head, splattered his brains all over everybody else on the boat."[60] Marine Captain Carl W. Hoffman, the commander of George Company, had the radio call sign George 6. On his way towards the beach, he was taken aback, to suddenly receive communication from a voice speaking with a clear Japanese accent: "Georgie, Georgie 6 come in." The voice tried to give him confusing instructions about where to land and stayed on his frequency throughout. "The accent was unmistakably Oriental, and his pronunciation of words tipped us off, but it was interesting that the Japanese were attempting that."[61]

Hoffman's company was required to make a turn after landing on the beach, and to avoid firing into the flank of neighboring Marine units, it had been equipped with short-range shotguns. This was fortuitous, since Hoffman's unit found itself in a maze of World War I-type open trenches full of Japanese who had survived the naval bombardment and were ready to fight, armed with bayonets and sabers. "We had a lot of hand-to-hand fighting, and there's nothing more effective in hand-to-hand fighting than shotguns," he said. "The Japanese would dart in and out of various little coves in the trench line and do battle with the courage that characterized everything they did."[62]

Marine Lieutenant Colonel Raymond Murray had just landed when a mortar shell hit right behind him. He passed out for a moment, and when he came to, his trousers had been blown completely off, and when he looked down, all he saw were some tatters and blood everywhere. "Well, this is it," he said. "This is what it means to get killed in the war." His orderly was trying to inject morphine into his arm but was shaking so violently he had to give up. Murray began feeling better, muttering, "Oh, God, I'm not going to die after all." He was right and although seriously wounded, he survived. His orderly was not so lucky. Murray saw him a few minutes later. "He had been just decapitated," he said in an interview after the war. "Another mortar shell had landed and caught him."[63]

The Marines started moving warily inland, firing at any object that might be hiding an enemy. "We directed round after round of small arms fire into the tops of palm trees just in case a sniper was positioned there," said Marine Carl Matthews. "Sometimes the rounds found their mark and we could see the sniper fall from the tree or dangle from a rope tied to the sniper and to the top of the tree."[64] Arthur Liberty, another Marine moving inland at the same time, was startled by a Japanese soldier charging at his unit out of nowhere. One man standing next to Liberty fired all 15 rounds of his carbine into the Japanese, but he still kept coming. Another man with a shotgun took aim and fired. "He hit him twice before he dropped him. They must have been hopped up on something."[65]

The defenders, a force of 32,000 soldiers mostly from the 43rd Japanese Infantry Division under the Thirty-First Army, were waiting in pillboxes and foxholes, in caves and tunnels, ready to unleash a hail of deadly fire, and in some instances, they were hiding where the Marines least expected it. At the village of Charon-Kanoa, the Marines took several casualties from uncannily precise enemy mortar fire. It was only after several deadly rounds that they realized they were being watched by a Japanese observer hiding near the top of a three-story-high smokestack at a bombed-out sugar factory. A barrage of artillery fire put an end to his activity.[66]

According to a senior Marine officer, the "most critical stage of the battle for Saipan was the fight for the beachhead," and by nightfall, this had been accomplished, with two Marine divisions put ashore.[67] Unsurprisingly, however, the dark hours brought no rest for the invaders. During the first night, the Japanese attacked again and again with wild cries of "Banzai, banzai." An American BAR man shouted back at the oncoming wave of Japanese, "Banzai yourself, you sons of bitches," as he fired his weapon.[68]

Some Japanese abandoned blunt force and used a merciless kind of stealth. In front of one of the Marine battalions, a line of approaching civilians emerged out of the dark, apparently seeking to give themselves up to the invaders. Only at the last moment did the Marines realize that the refugees were being used as a shield, and that groups of infantrymen were following close behind. They called in artillery support, and the attempted attack was crushed in a blanket of 105-mm shells. It was one of the first signs that Saipan's civilians were being actively mobilized by the Japanese military to take part.[69]

After a busy night of fighting, the chief of staff of Japan's Thirty-First Army acknowledged that the defenders had been unable to dislodge the Americans, mainly due to their advantage in tanks and firepower. "We are reorganizing," he vowed, "and will attack again." In Tokyo, the news about the American landing, while expected, was received with great concern and determination to push the Americans back into the ocean. "Our soldiers on the front line are putting up a good fight, but aren't our forces inadequate compared with the enemy forces?" Hirohito asked Prime Minister Tōjō. "If we lose Saipan, there will be more and more air raids in Tokyo. We must hold [Saipan] at all costs."[70]

★ ★ ★

The Japanese Navy wasted no time once the American operation in the Marianas was underway. At 8:55am on June 15, a mere 11 minutes after the first Marines set foot on Saipan, Admiral Toyoda Soemu, the commander-in-chief of the Combined Fleet, sent a message to Admiral Ozawa Jisaburō and his First Mobile Fleet anchored off Borneo in the Dutch East Indies: "On the morning of the 15th a strong enemy force began landing operations in the Saipan-Tinian area. The Combined Fleet will attack the enemy in the Marianas area and annihilate the invasion force. Activate A-Go operation for decisive battle."[71]

The A-Go operation was the most recent version of the long-held plan to engage the Americans in a decisive battle that would force them to accept a negotiated peace. The target was the US Fifth Fleet led by Admiral Raymond Spruance, and in particular its fast carrier force under the command of Admiral Marc Mitscher. Ideally, the Japanese admirals would have preferred to fight it further south, closer to the refined oil of Southeast Asia, but they had no choice. The attack on the Marianas posed an existential threat to the Japanese Empire.[72] "[American forces] had approached and penetrated what we had decided was our last stand line, and we were forced to commit our ships," Nakajima Chikataka, a senior officer with the Combined Fleet, said in post-war interrogations.[73]

Admiral Ozawa was forced to fuel his fleet partly with substandard oil from the Borneo fields, and he went into battle with only about 500 aircraft, or half the planes that the Americans could field from their carriers, although he was led to believe that he would be assisted by an equal number of land-based Japanese planes in the Marianas. In addition, he had a key advantage. His aircraft had a longer range than the US Navy's planes, enabling him to strike the Americans from a distance where they would not be able to hit back. His intention was for his planes to fly to the American task force, carry out their attacks, and then land on the Marianas. After refueling and rearming they were to make another attack on the American fleet and then return to the Japanese carriers.[74]

There were high hopes with senior Japanese commanders that the plan would work. "We had expectations that Ozawa's fleet would crush [the] carrier groups," said Nomura Minoru, an officer with the Naval General Staff in Tokyo. "We hoped that [the] battleships would rout the US vessels that crowded around Saipan and relieve the Japanese soldiers fighting desperately on the island."[75] The Americans, proud sailors and soldiers of the Fifth Fleet, were equally confident of victory for their side, from the admiral down to the lowliest sailor. Quartermaster Michael Bak, on board the destroyer USS *Franks*, described the feeling of invincibility sailing with a powerful fleet: "You looked out on the horizon and you saw these aircraft carriers, saw all those battleships, and you saw 30 destroyers in a circle. With all this firepower, you felt pretty safe and confident that you could take on anybody."[76]

The historical significance of the battle was lost on neither side. On the eve of the clash, Admiral Toyoda, the commander of the Combined Fleet, sent the same message to his men that Yamamoto had done two and a half years earlier, before the attack on Pearl Harbor. It was a message that echoed a signal that legendary Japanese Admiral Tōgō Heihachirō had composed prior to Tsushima, the most decisive battle of the war with Russia in 1905, and it even referenced back to the British Admiral Horatio Nelson at Trafalgar: "The fate of the Empire rests upon this single battle. Every man is expected to do his utmost."[77] At Trafalgar, Tsushima, and Pearl Harbor, empires had been made and unmade. This would be no different. The stakes could hardly be higher.

By June 18, two Japanese fleets were approaching the American task force in the Philippine Sea west of the Saipan invasion beach. The main body under Ozawa moved carefully through the Philippine archipelago towards what he hoped would become the long-awaited decisive encounter with the US foe, while another fleet under Admiral Ugaki Matome was heading in the same direction from the south. By nightfall, both Japanese forces were positioning themselves to strike the following day. A tense atmosphere settled as the hour of decision neared. Even Ugaki allowed a note of doubt to slip into his diary on the eve of battle. "Can it be that we'll fail to win with this mighty force?" he wrote late in the day, but then dispelled the uneasy thought completely: "No! It can't be!"[78]

Positioned in waters near Saipan known as the Philippine Sea, the US fleet was alerted to the presence of the Japanese and the imminence of the attack, and many were similarly concerned about the battle that lay ahead. "Word is that we're going out after the Jap fleet," naval aviator Joseph E. Kane wrote in his diary in the evening of June 18. "Gives you plenty to think about, particularly about getting to the States—not by Christmas—but getting back period."[79]

Admiral Raymond Spruance, the commander of the Fifth Fleet, prepared to go to sleep on board his flagship, the heavy cruiser USS *Indianapolis*, after spending the past two days pondering one simple but crucial question, "Now what would I do if I were a Japanese with these capabilities in this position?" The answer he settled on in the end was that, if he were a Japanese admiral, he would go for the transports that had brought the invasion army to Saipan, not the aircraft carriers protecting them. Therefore, Spruance would not send his carriers west on a wild chase after the Japanese foe, leaving the transport vessels defenseless. When he turned in at 9:30pm, he had decided that he and his forces would remain near the invasion area.[80]

As dawn broke over the Western Pacific on June 19, Spruance stuck to his plan, waiting for the Japanese to strike, and limiting his offensive actions to bombing a Japanese airfield on Guam further south. "We Airedales down in ready rooms were a little unhappy," US pilot James Ramage recalled, using the canine slang expression for naval aviator. "We said 'Let's go get them, they are out there'."[81] The tactic, while telling on the nerves of the airmen, made sense from Spruance's point of view. "Planes from the carriers would attack him, then rearm and refuel at the Marianas bases, and bomb his forces while returning to their carriers. A true shuttle bombing," said Navy intelligence officer Edwin Layton. "He was smart enough to realize these options open to the enemy, and to stay close to the invasion area, which he had been instructed to defend, while he clobbered the enemy airfields in that area so they can't be used for such shuttle bombing."[82]

Ozawa could not know that the Americans had seen through his plans, and in the morning of June 19 he dispatched aircraft to locate the enemy carriers. When the Japanese reported that they had observed American vessels, Ozawa sent off his first attack wave. Shortly before 10am the Japanese planes appeared on the American radars, and now the relative inactivity on the US side ended. All available American planes, including those engaged in bombing Guam—were called back with the radio message "Hey, Rube!" which was a traditional slang phrase used by the workers in traveling circuses calling for help. All the might of the American fighters was to be made ready for the Japanese.[83]

Alex Vraciu, in his Grumman F6F Hellcat, was among the fighter pilots sent to meet the oncoming Japanese. Seeing the swarm of enemies, he thought to himself this was a "fighter pilot's dream." In quick succession, and within a span of just eight minutes, he downed six aircraft. He remembered seeing the rear gunner in one of these doomed aircraft peppering away at him as he disappeared in an increasingly sharp arc downward: "For a split-second, I almost felt sorry for the little bastard." When it was all over, he glanced back in his cockpit to where it had begun. "In a pattern thirty-five miles long, there were flaming oil slicks in the water and smoke still hanging in the air. It didn't seem like just eight minutes—it seemed longer. But that's all it was—an eight-minute opportunity for the flight of a lifetime."[84]

The Japanese were the underdogs, and not just because their technology could not keep up. Their most experienced fighter pilots had mostly been killed, and they sent newbies into battle. "The big problem was that they just didn't have the talent, and our fighters made mincemeat of them on the 19th," said James Ramage, the impatient pilot.[85] As if this were not enough, the numerical inferiority of the Japanese was even more pronounced than they realized. The hundreds of planes that Ozawa had been promised from airbases in the Marianas failed to materialize, despite promises to the contrary. The officer who made the pledge apparently never intended to fulfill it, and only wanted to "save face."[86]

Abe Zenji, one of the few Japanese pilots who had been at war since Pearl Harbor, remembered being pursued by a group of aggressive Hellcats, or what he referred to as a game of "Hellcat-hide-and-seek," which lasted for the better part of an hour. "These Hellcat pilots were really tenacious," he wrote, describing how he was unable to shake them off, despite his years of experience in the cockpit. "With daylight beginning to fail, I had no idea when our engine might stop and prompt me to dive into the sea crying 'Long reign the Emperor!'" In the end he managed to land his aircraft on a small island in the Marianas still fully in Japanese hands.[87]

Many of Abe's comrades were not that lucky. Wave after wave of Japanese aircraft assaulted the ships of the Fifth Fleet, running into dense swarms of enemy fighters and the deadly barrage from the surface vessels. Out of a total of 373 Japanese aircraft committed to the attack on June 19, only 130 returned. In addition, about 50 Japanese planes were destroyed in the bombing of Guam.[88] In the middle of the day's combat, a pilot, Lieutenant Junior Grade "Ziggy" Neff, yelled in adrenaline-filled excitement, "Hell, this is like an old-time turkey shoot." The remark was overheard by Lieutenant Commander Paul Buie, who used it in his after-action report and gave rise to the expression "the Great Marianas Turkey Shoot."[89]

The full Japanese losses were even more extensive than that, as the carriers *Shokaku* and *Taiho*, Ozawa's flagship, were sunk by US submarines in separate actions.[90] Therefore, the day after, on June 20, Spruance finally felt confident that he could go searching for the Japanese foe without putting the transports at undue risk. "We knew that those ships would have to be sunk sometime as the Japanese were determined fighters and they'd continue to fight as long as they had ships left to fight," said Arleigh Burke, chief of staff to Admiral Marc Mitscher, commander of the Fifth Fleet's fast carrier task force. "The more ships we sank now, the less we would have to sink sometime in the future. But before we could sink those ships we had to know where they were."[91]

At the Naval General Staff in Tokyo, a similar sense of uncertainty was prevalent on the same day. A large number of planes had not returned to their carriers the day before, but the extent of the disaster was still unknown. "We could only pray that these planes had achieved as yet unreported victories," recalled Nomura Minoru, an officer on the staff. "But the fact that enemy carrier groups had steamed halfway to the Philippines, when earlier they had stayed close to the Marianas, indicated to us that Spruance had confidence in victory. The gloom in the Operations Room was at its deepest."[92]

The American fast carrier force spent most of the day in a futile attempt to locate the Japanese fleet, and only late in the afternoon did one of its planes spot it, just on the edge of the range of the US aircraft. Admiral Mitscher now faced one of those difficult command decisions that make or break careers, and might potentially cost innumerable lives: should he send off his planes in the direction of the Japanese ships, in the knowledge that many might not make it back to their carriers due to the lack of fuel?

He decided to run the risk and sent off his aircraft. With just hours before sunset, the planes of the fast carrier force took off, one after the other. James Ramage in his SBD Dauntless dive bomber was among them. On the way he sighted a group of Japanese oilers but decided to give them a miss. "There was no question about what the priority was. It was carriers, and carriers, and carriers." Eventually, they were sighted, and oblivious to the Japanese fighters flying patrols around the ships, the American pilots went in for the kill. "We peeled off and went into the dive," Ramage said. "I put my pepper as they called it just ahead of the bow, headed into the wind and released it at about 2,000 feet, and pulled out."[93]

The attacks were only moderately successful. Aircraft carrier *Hiyu* was sent to the bottom of the sea, but three other Japanese carriers escaped to fight another day. And now the American pilots were in for the long flight back. Some did not have enough fuel and were forced to land in the ocean, and the ones who made it back to the carriers were struggling with the dark. "There were planes landing all over the place," said Cecil King, chief yeoman on USS *Hornet*. "It didn't matter what carrier they were from. The minute anybody flashed ready deck, somebody landed on it. Almost every landing was some kind of deck crash. They were running on fumes. There were planes going in the water everywhere."[94]

At this point, Mitscher issued the command, disregarding for a moment the threat from enemy submarines and planes: "Turn on the lights." As the vessels turned on glow lights, running lights and signal lights, and each group flagship pointed a searchlight vertically in the air, the pitch-black night became "a Hollywood premiere, Chinese New Year's and Fourth of July rolled into one," in the words of an aviator watching the scene from above.[95] Ramage also had just enough fuel in his Dauntless to reach the fleet. He landed on the first available carrier. Stumbling out of the cockpit, he asked the deck crew rushing to his assistance, "What ship?" "*Yorktown*," they answered. It was not his carrier, but he did not care. He was home, and he was alive.[96]

On Saipan, it was clear by now that the Americans had secured a foothold, and that with their superiority in every material category, dislodging them was close to impossible for the Japanese. On the second day, the two Marine divisions were reinforced by units of the Army's 27th Infantry Division. The defenders were coming under ever greater pressure, facing the near-certainty of violent death. "There is nothing to do but be trampled under by the enemy tanks," naval officer Nagata Kazumi wrote in his diary.[97]

To be sure, the 27th Infantry Division, manned mainly by National Guardsmen considerably older on average than their Marine counterparts, initially made meager progress. Holland Smith, the Marine general in overall command of ground forces, sent a message to 27th Division, stating that he was "highly displeased." The division's commander, General Ralph Smith, agreed himself that the division was not carrying its fair share of the burden, stating to a visitor that "if he didn't take his division forward tomorrow he should be relieved." This proved prophetic. Soon afterwards, he was dismissed and replaced.[98]

The battle for Saipan now formed an endless series of small encounters, each of which merited perhaps no mention in any official history book but was nevertheless fraught with drama and tragedy. A Marine, who was still only in his late teens, was shot by a Japanese sniper. His injuries were lethal, and while he was conscious and his comrades told him he was going to be all right, he instinctively knew that he had no chance. "I don't want to die," he said. "I'm too young to die." He was dead two or three minutes later.[99]

The ferocity increased over time as the soldiers on both sides saw their buddies die next to them. A Marine company attacked a Japanese position after seeing several from its ranks mowed down by enemy fire. They vowed to make the defenders pay dearly. Every bush that moved, and any warm body that exposed itself was showered with bullets fired by angry Marines. "One older man, emerging from a hole in the ground, was shoved back in the hole by the force of bullets hitting his body. Concussion grenades were tossed into the hole," a Marine said later. "It was all over in a few minutes, but we'd all aged a lifetime."[100]

Soon after landing, the Marines began using flamethrowers as a matter of routine wherever they had a suspicion there might be Japanese. "I always felt bad when the Japanese would run out of their holes almost naked but with fuel and fire from the flamethrowers covering their body, screaming and dying," said Marine Carl Matthews. "But if we gave them half a chance we would have been the ones dying."[101] One night, a wounded Japanese was lying in front of the American line, screaming and moaning. This disturbed the GIs who were trying to sleep, and one of them yelled out, "Will someone please shoot that son of a bitch so I can get some sleep." Before dawn, the screaming and moaning gradually ceased. "We assumed that the poor soul had died," one of the Marines later commented.[102]

The fact that Saipan had been under Japanese rule for decades gave rise to one of the special horrors of the battle. The island had a sizeable civilian population, who were ordered to take their lives in one last meaningless act of defiance once defeat was certain. Lieutenant Colonel Wood B. Kyle was involved in a vain effort at getting the civilians to give themselves up rather than to sacrifice themselves pointlessly for a lost cause. "The disheartening thing was that you really couldn't stop these people," he said. "You couldn't get them to surrender."[103]

War correspondent Robert Sherrod described a group of about 50 Japanese, including small children, standing in a circle while gaily tossing hand grenades to each other, "like baseball players warming up before a game," he said. "Some seemed to make a little game out of their dying—perhaps out of indecision, perhaps out of ignorance, or even some kind of lightheaded disrespect of the high seriousness of Japanese suicide." Suddenly six Japanese soldiers darted out of a cave, lined up in front of the civilians, and blew themselves up with hand grenades. The civilians immediately did the same.[104]

Mopping up was a dangerous operation as the remaining Japanese would often not be armed, except everyone seemed to have a hand grenade. "They always saved a hand grenade," said Wood Kyle. "This was the thing that you had to be very careful about, because if you closed in on one of them and you got close to him he'd throw a grenade at you. It was a pretty ticklish proposition to try to capture the soldiers."[105]

Even militia-style Japanese units proved hard or impossible to induce into surrender. During an advance, a Marine unit ran into a group of Japanese armed only with pitchforks. They tried for 10 to 15 minutes to persuade them to give themselves up, but to no avail. Then the battalion commander came up to the spot and was furious at the delay. It was the kind of incident that could get Marines killed. "Shoot the bastards!" he yelled, which they did.[106]

Nagata Kazumi, the Japanese navy officer, was still alive but not for much longer. "The decision to make a final stand has at last been announced," he wrote in one of the last entries in his diary. "This is fate; it had to end this way."[107] By now, some parts of Saipan which had seen particularly vicious battles were covered in Japanese bodies, which were often allowed to stay in the sun and rot. Lieutenant Colonel Justice Chambers remembered driving through a field and suddenly running over a large number of dead Japanese. "We rolled across so many that burst, and we were all vomiting," he said later.[108]

CHAPTER FOUR

"Hell is on Us"

July–September 1944

The sun was shining from a bright Pacific sky, but Admiral Ugaki Matome's mood was much more accurately reflected in the dreary seasonal showers that he knew were now hitting the Japanese home islands. As commander of one of the fleets that had been beaten so profoundly off Saipan, he was fully aware of the implications. "It will be extremely difficult to recover from this disaster and rise again," he wrote in his diary. "When I think the prospect of a victory is fading out gradually, it's only natural that my heart becomes as gloomy as the sky of the rainy season."[1]

Back in Tokyo, the humiliation was felt equally intensely. Retired Admiral Yonai Mitsumasa was in despair. "Although I do not know [the] exact details, Japan has lost the war," he told a colleague. "We have been defeated beyond doubt. Whoever leads the war, there is nothing to be done."[2] Hirohito was in a daze and spent his time gazing at fireflies in the Fugiake Garden of the Imperial Palace. "Under the circumstances, there is nothing better for him than to divert himself and to recuperate," his second cousin Irie Sukemasa wrote in his diary.[3]

Vice Admiral Miwa Shigeyoshi spoke for many when he commented: "Our war was lost with the loss of Saipan. I feel it was a decisive battle. The loss of Saipan meant [the Allies] could cut off our shipping and attack our homeland."[4] Rear Admiral Takata Toshitane, the deputy chief of Military Affairs at the Navy Ministry added, "We knew that from then on the war was going to be pretty tough. We realized that with the destruction of our industrial capacity, our production would naturally drop to practically zero."[5] Nagano Osami, the emperor's supreme naval advisor, put it succinctly: "Hell is on us."[6]

The few foreigners left in Japan felt the different atmosphere. The Vice Admiral Paul Werner Wenneker, German Naval attaché to Tokyo, noted a clear change in the mood of the Japanese governing elite after the debacle at

Saipan, an actual piece of Japan, and not recently conquered territory. "Saipan was really understood to be a matter of life and death," he said. "About that time they began telling people the truth about the war. They began preparing them for whatever must happen. Before that, they had been doing nothing but fooling the people."[7] A few days after the loss of Saipan, Tōjō did indeed tell the public that "Imperial Japan has come to face an unprecedentedly great national crisis."[8]

In Europe, Germany was facing a possibly even more desperate situation, being pressured by huge offensives on both the Western and the Eastern Front, forcing a rethink in Japan of the entire strategic situation. Officers in charge of long-term planning at the Imperial General Headquarters produced a top-secret report which was astonishingly frank in its advice: "Since Japan will face a gradual decline from now on, we all came to the conclusion that Japan should make plans to end the war... Therefore, although it is very difficult, the empire must seek to conclude the war through political maneuvers and offensives. In such a case, the only condition for peace should be the preservation of the national polity."[9]

Prime Minister Tōjō came under pressure over the loss of Saipan. His wife received phone calls from people who did not give their names and simply asked, "Hasn't Tōjō committed hara-kiri yet?"[10] In an indication that after years of war Japan was nowhere near becoming a hard dictatorship like Germany, Tōjō faced criticism that he was amassing too much power in his own hands. Some even compared him with Adolf Hitler, arguing that it was the German dictator's insistence on making all the big decisions himself that had led to the disaster at Stalingrad in early 1943. Tōjō was unperturbed: "Chancellor Hitler was a corporal. I am a general."[11]

In what could have been an almost perfect parallel to the attempted assassination of Hitler in July 1944, two Japanese officers in the same month planned to throw a bomb at Tōjō's car as it passed through the grounds of the Imperial Palace in Tokyo, but their plan was thwarted, and they were sentenced to death—and later granted a stay of execution.[12] Instead, political pressure built on Tōjō to resign from his post. An alliance of court officials and senior naval officers had been seeking to oust him for months but had been prevented from achieving their aim by Emperor Hirohito's strong support of Tōjō.[13]

They had been waiting for the right moment to strike, and now with the fall of Saipan, the opportunity was there. They acted by the middle of July, preparing a resolution to Hirohito stating that "the minds and hearts of the people must be infused with new life if the empire is to survive... a powerful new cabinet must be formed that will surge forward unswervingly."[14] With the loss of the emperor's backing, Tōjō was doomed. On July 18, a deeply disappointed Tōjō was forced to tender his resignation. He was replaced by General Koiso Kuniyaki, who was not Hirohito's first choice as head of the Cabinet, being seen as too easy to sway and with a dangerous penchant for mystical nationalism, probably the last thing Japan needed at this particular time.[15]

While the Tōjō administration was in its death throes, American forces were preparing yet another assault on Japan's crumbling Pacific empire. The objective was Guam, the largest island in the Marianas. Unlike Saipan and Tinian, it had been an American possession since the US war with Spain at the turn of the century. Even so, the US forces had to start from scratch when preparing the landing. "We had owned the island of Guam since 1898," said Edwin Layton, a Navy intelligence officer stationed in Pearl Harbor. "Yet—you won't believe it—we didn't have good maps of our own island. The Japanese had better maps of Guam than we had, and they had occupied it only in 1941."[16]

The naval shelling and aerial bombing of the Japanese positions were of a length and intensity that, in the words of a Japanese report completed after the war, approached "the limit bearable by humans." Some soldiers receded into a stupor, while others, "like lunatics" seemed to gather more strength after being under days of continuous fire.[17] An example of the latter was a young enlisted man, who wrote in his diary, "I will not lose my courage, but now is the time to prepare to die! If one desires to live, hope for death. Be prepared to die! With this conviction one can never lose... Look upon us! We have shortened our expectancy of 70 years of life to 25 in order to fight. What an honor it is to be born in this day and age."[18]

The men who were to face this type of fanaticism—the 3rd Marine Division scheduled to land north of the Orote peninsula, and the 77th Infantry Division reinforced by the 1st Provisional Marine Brigade landing south of it—were awakened at 4am on the day of the invasion, July 21, and rushed to place their equipment on the topside of the ship. "They had a church service if anybody wanted to attend, and everybody was there," said Ralph Ketcham, a Marine.[19] They got their first inkling of what was awaiting them as, moments later, from their Higgins landing vessels they were watching the pre-invasion bombardment of Orote, where an important airfield was located. "The cliffs on the peninsula gradually fell into the sea, opening up underground tunnels that looked like large apartment houses without the front wall," one of them recalled. "The Japanese soldiers were living like ants underground."[20]

The Higgins boats were circling until 8 am, when the Navy raised the shelling. "Then we started in for the beach," Ketcham recalled. "About two-hundred of them Higgins boats in a straight line. When we got there, there was a big coral reef, and that's as far as they'd go." The Marines had to walk the last 600 yards to the beach, amid Japanese shelling which struck with cruel randomness. Some units made it onto dry land without a single casualty. Others were heavily decimated by just one shell exploding in their midst. A group of ammunition handlers crouched in fear on the beach, refusing to move. A sergeant yelled, "If you don't move you're going to get killed." They still would not move Ketcham recalled. "So, one of them Japs dropped a shell about fifty feet from them in the water and they moved quick as they could."[21]

The Marines and soldiers set up positions around their respective beachheads and set about expanding them little by little. As in other island battles, the Japanese on Guam used stealth as part of their tactics. One evening, Marines guarding a road watched a group of three men coming towards them, singing Yankee Doodle. The Marine sergeant said, "Kill 'em, they're Japs, Kill 'em." The Marines hesitated, and he repeated his order, "I said kill them, damn

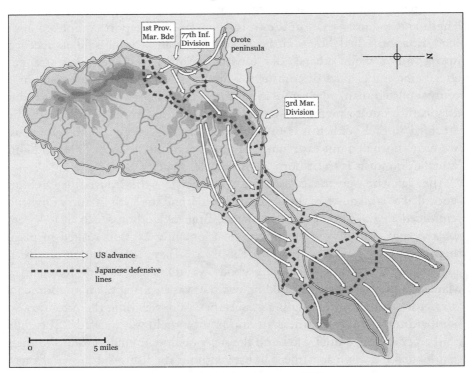

Guam invasion, July and August 1944.

it." They opened fire and searching the three dead bodies, they realized they were indeed Japanese.[22] Episodes such as this caused the men to be extra alert, and in some cases it led to tragic misunderstandings, a Marine said: "Another group had come down and the machine gun opened up on them too. Only the second group wasn't soldiers, they were just Guam natives."[23]

On the fifth day of the invasion, the Japanese commanders decided to stake everything on massive counterattacks against both invasion beaches, north and south of the Orote peninsula. Most Japanese soldiers knew they were probably going to die, and they prepared in ways suggesting that not all were imbued with the suicidal displayed by the young diary writer. "Some took out photographs of their parents, wife, or children and bid farewell to them; some prayed to God or Buddha, some composed a death poem and some exchanged cups of water at final parting with intimate comrades," according to a post-war Japanese account. "Few were able to be ready to rush out through the enemy line courageously. However, all of the officers and men were generally prepared for their fate, because of their honour, sense of responsibility and hate for the enemy."[24]

When the Japanese unleashed their attacks, it became clear to the Americans that their enemies were sustained by more than just high morale. "We had a few banzai attacks—both individual and otherwise—in which we were able to prove that they were loaded," a Marine recalled.[25] The attackers formed a grotesque spectacle. Led by sword-wielding officers, soldiers armed with normal infantry weapons mixed with others clutching pitchforks, sticks, ball bats, and pieces of broken bottles.[26] The Americans fired their weapons into this wall of stumbling, drunken humanity, and the results was terrifying, according to a nearly contemporary account: "Arms and legs flew like snowflakes. Japs ran amuck. They screamed in terror until they died."[27]

The Japanese lost most of their strength, carefully husbanded and honed over years of waiting and training for the invasion, on that day. Now that the back of the Japanese resistance had been broken, the Americans advanced out of their beachheads. While the 3rd Marine Division and the 77th Infantry Division headed towards the north of the island, the 1st Provisional Marine Brigade moved down the Orote peninsula for the airfield. Marine raider Raymond Strohmeyer recalled how that attack ended: "Further down there was a cliff down on the end of the airfield. A bunch of them pulled back on it and just dived off that cliff and committed suicide. They were great on committing suicide."[28]

The advance towards the north of Guam changed the nature of the battle and exposed the men to the harsh jungle terrain. "The distance across the island is not far, as the crow flies, but unluckily we can't fly," as one soldier said.[29] James L. Day, a Marine who had trained at Guadalcanal, was surprised: "I thought that nothing could be worse than Guadalcanal and nothing was as far as the thickness of the foliage, but Guam had its share," he said. "So it was a slow and tedious process moving in that type of an area."[30] The dense vegetation occasionally caused the opposing forces to get within just yards before becoming aware of each other's presence. One Marine suddenly saw himself face to face with a Japanese, his hand raised, clutching a grenade. Both men froze. "You know seven seconds is like hours, it seemed like an eternity we stood there and stared at each other before his hand grenade went off and his head disappeared."[31]

In the early hours of August 6, two Japanese tanks, trailed by a group of Japanese infantrymen, caused havoc in the bivouac area of A Company, 305th Infantry. The company's soldiers immediately opened fire, and a Japanese soldier on top of one of the tanks yelled, "American tank—okay, American tank—okay." This did not fool the defenders, who kept up the fire, but still the tanks managed to break into the defense perimeter. Panic erupted in the American ranks, as some soldiers had been prevented by the hard coral from digging trenches. The Japanese had an eerie understanding of the bivouac area, having probably reconnoitered beforehand, and the two tanks roamed around with blazing machine guns, while the crew threw hand grenades from the turret. One wounded American soldier tried to stagger to safety but was crushed by one of the tanks. Small-arms fire against their steel hulls had no effect, and the bullets ricocheted off, hitting yet more Americans. When the tanks disappeared into the darkness, they left behind 16 killed and 32 injured.[32]

It was one of the last major actions on Guam. Within days it had fallen to the Americans, adding to the rapidly expanding area of the Pacific securely in Allied hands. Still, the Japanese put up a fight till the very end. "The enemy met the assault operations with pointless bravery, inhuman tenacity, infiltration, cave fighting and the will to lose hard," Nimitz wrote in a report.

Tinian was the last part in the three-piece puzzle that the Americans were laying in the Marianas, and the 4th Marine Division landed on July 24. The battle for Saipan, within sighting distance, was still not over, and the struggle for Guam was only just getting started. To take the island, the Marines opted for a feint. The obvious invasion area was a stretch of even, broad sandy beach just below the island's main city, Tinian Town. This was where the Americans concentrated the vast majority of their preparatory fire prior to the invasion.

However, the Marines carried out the actual landing at two tiny sand spits at the part of Tinian closest to Saipan. "With the enemy focusing nearly all of his attention in the wrong place—the smoke and confusion at Tinian Town was tremendous—our Marines funneled ashore over those two tiny beaches," said Marine Captain Carl Hoffman. "By the time the Japanese commander figured out what was happening, we had a secure lodgement on that portion of Tinian."[33]

Most of the Japanese artillery as well as many of their heavy machine guns were pointing at the wrong beach, and they could not be moved around easily to fire at the Marines in the corner of the island where they went ashore. "The enemy commander had about 9,000 troops at Tinian. I must say that he didn't make very effective use of them because he was so badly outmaneuvered," said Hoffman. "It was a brilliant scheme of maneuver and it worked beautifully. It made the Tinian campaign almost a perfect campaign."[34]

The Japanese gradually understood that the US landing had taken place in a different section than they had expected, and they decided on a massive, suicidal night attack. "They conveniently charged right into our fire. They came in with our infantry all set up and alerted," an eyewitness said. "Some of the enemy troops rode on the tanks, officers waving their sabers, as they approached our lines."[35]

Again, American material preponderance was a decisive factor. The landing on Tinian was facilitated by the proximity to Saipan and the fact that artillery batteries that gradually became idle as the battle died down there could not be put in use for the new invasion. On Tinian, the air force played a major role both in the pre-invasion raids and as tactical support during combat. Marine Arthur Liberty described the effect of strafing by American warplanes: "All you could see were pieces of Japs. They just chopped them up into hamburger."[36]

The last Japanese defenders became increasingly desperate, and similar to the situation on Saipan and Guam, their tactics in the end amounted to little more than running straight into deadly American machine-gun fire. Carl Hoffman described the defense of a Marine position that began as a banzai attack but soon evolved into full-scale slaughter: "The strange thing the Japanese did here was that they executed one wave of attack after another against a 37-mm position firing cannister ammunition... That gun just stacked up dead Japanese. The enemy kept attacking the same position and the 37-mm gun kept whacking them down... Soon we were nearly shoulder high with dead Japanese in front of that weapon. Still the Japanese assaulted that one weapon. They never were able to overrun it."[37]

A large part of Tinian was covered in sugarcane fields. One risk when navigating this terrain was losing men to heat exhaustion in the hot and humid weather. Another risk was that the sugarcane might catch fire and trap the soldiers in a rapidly expanding inferno, but sometimes the Americans used it to their advantage. "When we had the enemy cornered in areas like that, we actually set the cane fields afire in order to flush them out or to trap them in there," said Hoffman. Tinian was another example of Pacific island fighting at its most grueling, and a few days exposed to the constant danger was enough to wear down most men. The assistant commander of the 2nd Marine Division, Merritt A. Edson, asked one of the men under his command at Tinian, "Son, how do you like this kind of war?" The private's answer was telling in all its candid brevity, "General, I don't like any kind of war!"[38]

Great care was taken to ensure US President Franklin D. Roosevelt's personal safety as he made it across the Pacific from the US west coast to the Hawaiian Islands in late July. There had been reports of Japanese naval vessels 200 miles north of the archipelago, and to minimize the risk of a hostile encounter, the president's cruiser USS *Alabama* zigzagged its way to its destination. Once in Honolulu, Roosevelt's staff warned against placing him too close to American soldiers of Japanese descent for fears that a secret admirer of Hirohito might attempt an assassination. Hearing about the concerns, Roosevelt dismissed them as overblown and overruled any restrictions on GIs being allowed near him on ethnic grounds.[39]

Roosevelt was in Hawaii, where the war with Japan had started 33 months earlier, to meet with his two principal commanders in the Pacific, MacArthur and Nimitz. The conference was taking place against the backdrop of the newly gained advantageous positions in western New Guinea and the Marianas, and the aim was to determine how to proceed from here against the Japanese empire. The issue basically boiled down to one alternative: should the main stepping stone before the final assault on Japan be Taiwan or the Philippines?

Taiwan, known at the time as Formosa to Westerners and a Japanese colony since 1895, was pushed by senior planners such as Admiral Ernest B. King, the chief of naval operations, who continued to see China as a vital part of the overall plan to defeat Japan. It was an unsinkable aircraft carrier which could be used, in conjunction with pieces of territory seized on the east coast of China, as a staging area for troops preparing to deal the final blow to Hirohito's empire. Seizing Taiwan would be a vital step in severing Japan's links to its

Southeast Asian possessions, King argued, while also providing the bases for "the speedy and effective further advance of our forces to the complete defeat of the Japanese war machine." Indeed, time was of the essence, King warned. Since they would probably fortify Taiwan in reaction to their setbacks in the Pacific, it was important to "beat the Japanese to the punch in this area."[40]

It was tempting, in this view, to simply bypass much of the Philippines in the way that the majority of the Dutch East Indies was being left aside as the American forces picked a more direct route north towards the Japanese home islands. At this point, however, politics and even honor became a factor. MacArthur had made a pledge to the Philippine people to return and liberate them, and he felt duty-bound to make good on the promise. "Practically all of the 17,000,000 Filipinos remain loyal to the United States and are undergoing the greatest privation and suffering because we have not been able to support or succor them," MacArthur had argued in a letter to Washington the previous month. "We have a great national obligation to discharge."[41]

In addition, there were valid strategic reasons for picking the Philippines over Taiwan, and MacArthur made sure to emphasize these, too. An American foothold on the Philippines would also cut Japan's links to the south, and it entailed fewer of the risks entailed in assaulting Taiwan, with a large garrison, and the possibility of easy reinforcements from Japan. "The hazards of failure would be unjustifiable when a conservative and certain line of action is open," MacArthur argued in talks with Roosevelt, referring to the Philippine option.[42] At one point during their talks, the general provided what might have been the decisive argument, convincing Roosevelt, who was running for a fourth term in November: "I dare say that the American people would be so aroused that they would register most complete resentment against you at the polls this fall."[43]

Nevertheless, at the meeting in Hawaii, MacArthur and Roosevelt, who had not met for seven years, found unexpectedly good personal chemistry, and the general was allowed to make the argument forcefully in favor of landing on the Philippines, rather than in Taiwan. Once he was done, he believed himself to have won over Roosevelt, and he was right. Although the formal decision was only made at a later date, at the end of September,[44] plans were now in motion for seizing the Philippine island of Leyte, followed by a larger invasion of Luzon. After the meeting, Roosevelt told reporters, "We are going to get the Philippines back, and without question General MacArthur will take a part in it."[45]

For Admiral King, the chief proponent of the Taiwan option, more bad news was in the offing. Since Pearl Harbor, he had considered the Pacific an exclusively American enterprise, and while he appreciated China's contribution in keeping large Japanese land forces tied down, at sea he "did not want anyone else to intervene in his own pet war."[46] However, at a US-British summit held in Quebec a few weeks later, in the first half of September, Roosevelt accepted an offer by British Prime Minister Winston Churchill to place under US command sizable Royal Navy forces once the war in Europe was over. "The British delegation heaved a sigh of relief, and the story went the rounds that Admiral King went into a swoon and had to be carried out," wrote Lord Ismay, Churchill's chief military assistant.[47]

At a follow-up meeting between Roosevelt and Churchill held at the American president's home in Hyde Park in upstate New York, an issue of world-changing importance emerged. Both leaders were intimately familiar with the top-secret Manhattan Project aimed at producing an explosive device of unimaginable power. While the bomb was meant for use against the Nazi threat, in line with the Germany-first strategy adopted early in the war, the Allies now were moving towards a consensus that Japan could also be targeted. An aide memoire initialed by both Roosevelt and Churchill at Hyde Park made this clear: "When a 'bomb' is finally available, it might perhaps, after mature consideration, be used against the Japanese, who should be warned that this bombardment will be repeated until they surrender."[48]

While the American and British decision makers were meeting, important information arrived from the western Pacific. Admiral William Halsey, leading a group of fast carriers near Philippine waters, reported that there was "no shipping left to sink," that the Japanese enemy displayed a "non-aggressive attitude" and that essentially, "the area is wide open." A downed carrier pilot had even been told, erroneously, by his Filipino rescuers that there were no Japanese soldiers left on Leyte. The report caused both Nimitz and MacArthur's staff to reconsider the time schedule for returning to the Philippines and advise a more direct approach.[49]

The proposal reached Marshall and King in the evening of September 15, while they were having a formal dinner with Canadian officers in Quebec. The senior US commanders withdrew from the table and within 90 minutes drafted a new masterplan for the downfall of Japan. The invasion of Leyte was to take place not on December 20, as previously planned, but on October 20. The liberation of the Philippines was to be moved up by two months. In fact, during the very hours when Marshall and King were working on the plan, what could be seen as the first step in the Philippine campaign was already underway: the seizure of the island of Peleliu.

★ ★ ★

Peleliu was to go down in history as the unnecessary battle. With the benefit of hindsight, it was clear that it could have been bypassed like so many other Japanese-held islands scattered across the Pacific and left to "wither on the vine." Instead, Admiral Nimitz insisted that the island, part of the Palaus, had to be seized as a necessary staging ground ahead of the reconquest of the Philippines. "It is questionable whether the advantages gained offset the terrible cost," wrote Nimitz's otherwise sympathetic biographer.[50]

General William H. Rupertus, the commander of the 1st Marine Division, was sanguine about Peleliu. "He felt that it was going to be a two-or-three-day operation and as a matter of fact, said as much to the newspaper correspondents with the effect that there wasn't too much coverage of the operation," recalled Benis M. Frank, a Marine of the same division.[51] Major Jonas M. Platt participated in an officers' briefing and was struck by the breezily optimistic mood. "Something was said about getting the Japanese commander's sword on the first day," he said. "It was generally the feeling that it was not going to be a real tough operation and, of course, it was."[52]

The cheerful attitude was passed down the ranks to the Marines, who were left with the impression that they were in for a cakewalk. As a result, when they ran into stiff opposition, they were in for a rude shock, said Platt, who saw it as a personal lesson: "If you are going into an operation and the Marines involved believe that it's going to be very tough and it turns out just to be tough, they think they have gotten a bargain. If they go into it and think it is going to be easy, and it turns out to be tough, the shock involved is quite a price to pay."[53]

The Marines were alerted to the strength of the Japanese defenses even as they were making their way towards the beaches on D-Day, September 15, and shells began falling in rapid succession and with uncanny precision among their landing craft. "When we were goin' in, they was shellin' the hell out of us and we got caught up on a reef and got stuck just for a few seconds," said Romus Burgin, a mortarman. "Just as we pulled out from that reef a shell landed directly in front of us. And I believe till this day if we hadn't got stuck on that reef that artillery shell woulda dropped right in the boat."[54]

Worse was still to come. In the words of one of the Marines getting off the landing craft, "it became a new ballgame immediately after we got ashore."[55] The Marines, stumbling over the sides of their landing craft, were met by hails of small-arms ammunition, fired by an unseen enemy. It was a "very, very hot beach," according to Platt, who recalled the first minutes on dry land: "When we got ashore, there was a lot of incoming mortar, artillery, direct small arms fire… We had rounds ahead of us and rounds behind us."[56]

Tom Lea, a war artist assigned to cover the invasion even though it had been expected to become a non-event, described the horrific sight of a wounded Marine staggering towards the landing craft: "His face was half bloody pulp and the mangled shreds of what was left of an arm hung down like a stick, as he bent over in his stumbling, shock-crazy walk. The half of his face that was still human had the most terrifying look of abject patience I have ever seen. He fell behind me, in a red puddle on the white sand."[57]

By the end of the first day, the Marines had secured a beachhead, and at about 5pm, they dug in for the night. "Long experience with the Japanese in rugged and overgrown country had taught us to eschew night attacks and be prepared for night counterattacks and infiltration efforts," Oliver P. Smith, the assistant commander of the Marine division, wrote later.[58] In fact, the Japanese did more than infiltrate, and even attempted an armored assault. On the first night, a Japanese tank drove down the beach from one side, practically with one tread in the water, until a Marine stopped it with a bazooka.[59] The Japanese commander, in his official report, praised the tank unit for its "cat-like spring," expressing his overall satisfaction with the day.[60] His upbeat mood was not unwarranted. Even though the Marines had made it ashore, their losses had been high: 1,111 casualties, including more than 200 dead.[61]

What the Marines encountered on Peleliu was a novel and even deadlier Japanese tactic that prioritized a defensive posture over an offensive one, turning the battle into a series of costly struggles for fixed positions. The approach, inspired by the lengthy defense of Biak which Lindbergh had witnessed during his brief visit, abandoned costly and ultimately doomed attempts to halt the enemy at the beachline.[62] "The new doctrine discouraged the traditional grandiose suicidal attacks in favor of limited but stinging counterattacks," a Marine officer wrote later. "The objective was to play for time, bleed the enemy and fight a protracted battle of attrition. The deadly significance of these revised tactics would become evident during the Marine's last three great battles of the war: Peleliu, Iwo Jima and Okinawa."[63]

Peleliu was perfect for this new kind of tactic, not least because of a ridgeline in the north of the island, soon nicknamed "Bloody Nose Ridge," which was eminently suited for defense. According to Marine Robert Leckie, it formed "a monster Swiss cheese of hard coral limestone pocked beyond imagining with caves and crevices. They were to be found at every level, in every size—crevices small enough for a lonely sniper, eerie caverns big enough to station a battalion among its stalactites and stalagmites."[64] Here the Japanese had spent months preparing their defenses to the extent that they had adapted themselves to a subterranean existence. "They weren't *on* the island, they were *in* the island," said Romus Burgin, a mortarman.[65]

The Japanese had developed a complicated cave system that allowed them to pop out and back in within seconds. "They could kill guys before you could get to them," said Lieutenant Colonel Lewis J. Fields.[66] "If you got your head around a rock, the chances were at this time that you'd get plugged between the eyes. Marines were getting killed daily like that."[67] Burgin had the same experience, and got to the point where he could never rest: "They'd come out and shoot you from one of those caves and then they'd go back in. And then at night they'd come out and infiltrate your lines so actually you were in real danger 24 hours a day."[68]

Sergeant Martin Clayton was one among thousands of Marines who spent weeks on the inhospitable island, fighting an invisible enemy hiding underground in cave systems three or four stories deep, while enduring hellish natural conditions: "At one time it was over 110 degrees and you can imagine that heat coming down on this white coral reflecting back on you. Oh, it was a mess!"[69] The Marines employed everything they had, from flame throwers to 155 mm Long Tom guns, but it was like throwing "sand up against a wall," he said. "You had to dig them out of these caves one at a time out of each cave. Sometimes we were able to blow the caves shut. That didn't do any good. They had paths all down in there and they even had their mess halls. They had their barracks in there, their communications in there, their officers' quarters, they had everything in these caves."[70]

Eventually, Peleliu became a more than two-month-long battle for attrition, as the last stubborn Japanese defenders continued their resistance long after the island was lost to them. Again, it became a display of overwhelming American might. Once the main airfield was in US possession, it was used by airplanes providing close tactical support to the infantry on the ground in a mechanical manner, like trucks lining up to dump waste into a landfill. "All I can remember was just looking up watching 'em drop napalm on top of that doggone Bloody Nose Ridge," a Marine said. "Planes... wouldn't even raise their wheels up; they'd just take off, drop it, next turn, come back and land."[71]

If one were to point to one vital factor that tilted the balance against the Axis across the globe, it was, in addition to the Soviet willingness to shed blood, the juggernaut of American industrial might. To be of any use it had to be taken from the assembly lines in the United States to where it was needed, and by

1944, it was reaching the farthest corners of the Pacific. It was a miracle of transportation, but it did not come easy or cheap: for every combat division that was deployed in the war against Japan, twice the number of service troops was needed to ship it to the region and keep it supplied.[72] This was a feat that probably no other power could accomplish but the United States, skilled in the operation of a modern continent-sized economy, with maritime commercial ties spanning across the globe to match. The war in the Pacific was a logistical contest as much as a military conflict, and America was uniquely prepared for it.

The peculiar nature of the war changed the face of the Pacific, and it brought the 20th century, with all its technological prowess and organized violence, to areas that sometimes were just emerging from the Stone Age. At Nadzab in New Guinea, originally a mission station with a tiny airfield for small planes, one of the world's largest airports and transportation hubs had emerged from practically nothing. It was the western terminus of the Air Transport Command's trans-Pacific flights,[73] and by 1944, it was a beehive of frantic activity, as Navy airman Charles Furey later recalled: "During the daylight hours, the sky is filled with hovering airplanes, and airplanes taking off and landing. Hardly a day goes by when there isn't a fiery crash on one of the runways. We hear a deep rumble, and then an obelisk of black smoke appears in the sky, a brief monument to some unlucky flight crew."[74]

Later in the year, Ulithi atoll in the Carolines became for a period the world's largest fleet base. It was seized against no opposition on September 23, and within weeks, it was home to not only harbor facilities, but also an airstrip and a hospital, and shortly afterwards "Radio Ulithi" began broadcasting. The base even boasted modest facilities for rest and recreation for weary soldiers and sailors, on the small island of Mogmog, ruled by the Micronesian King Ueg, who agreed to move his people to the neighboring island of Fassarai for the duration of the war.[75] At one point when the lagoon was particularly crowded, Mogmog was "so full of bluejackets in shoregoing whites that from a distance it looked like one of those Maine islands where seagulls breed," according to the official US Navy historian.[76] Still, there was little entertainment: "You would sit around and drink beer and that was about it, and maybe try to go for a swim. But the coral was so sharp that it would cut your legs up and you couldn't even get in the water," a serviceman recalled.[77]

Michael Bak, quartermaster on board the destroyer USS *Franks*, remembered the immense size of Ulithi, which seemed large enough to hold the entire US Navy: "One of the interesting things about Ulithi was that there were so many ships in the fleet coming in that everybody aboard ship had a buddy on another ship. They would come up to the bridge, where the signal gang had a record of the ships in the lagoon. The signalmen always knew, because we had to watch our division commander's mast for signal messages which were given off on the yardarms. And one of the fellows from our crew would come to the bridge and ask if we could call different ships to see if so-and-so was aboard, and maybe get him to talk," he said.

"Many times I would give them a light and let people know what ships were in the fleet. Then I would be calling the different ships and asking if Sam Jones was aboard; so-and-so from his hometown was there. He would say, 'Yes, we'll get him for you,' and then there would be a five- or ten-minute delay, and a flashing light would come back at us. And somebody would say, 'This is Sam Jones,' and 'This is Charlie'. They would talk back and forth—'How are you?' They would never see each other, but they would just talk by signal light. It was a highlight of their experience."[78]

Logistics was one of the many areas where the Japanese material inferiority was being exposed in 1944. While the United States transported its hardware across vast distances, Japan was gradually proving incapable of moving freely even within the shrinking perimeters of its battered empire. At the beginning of the war, the Japanese military had commanded 2,150,000 tons of shipping, but three years later, that number had shrunk to 250,000 tons.[79] To make up for this huge material deficit, coming at a time when the logistical needs had multiplied rather than declined, planners in Tokyo made it a priority to build new transport vessels in 1944, and during the year they earmarked up to 40 percent of all funds allocated to civilian enterprises in its Southeast Asian possessions for that particular purpose.[80]

The ambitions came to nearly naught. Most new ships were simple wooden structures, and because of the severe lack of modern engines, most were equipped only with sails. At a time when their adversaries were employing all their innovative powers to keep a modern army and navy supplied in the Pacific, the Japanese were banking increasingly on 19th-century technologies, and even by those outdated standards, they often fell short. At one shipyard in Singapore, seasoned shipwrights brought in from occupied south China were astonished by the absence of professionalism. "Bolt holes were bored larger than the bolts," according to a postwar account. The same account stated that no vessel built in the shipyard made more than one trip.[81]

★ ★ ★

In the second half of 1944, China remained the one bright spot in a universe of gloom for the Japanese. The Ichigō offensive continued with undiminished vigor, bringing yet more territory under Japanese control. With a vigor and speed more impressive than the American and British advances in France at the same time, the Japanese were driving a deep and broad wedge down the middle of China, threatening the complete collapse of the nation and its elimination as a major Allied power. The Japanese success left Chiang Kai-shek severely dejected. "1944 is the worst year for China in its protracted war against Japan," he wrote. "I'm fifty-eight years old this year. Of all the humiliations I have suffered in my life, this is the greatest."[82]

As the Japanese advanced, with their reputation for unbridled ferocity preceding them, the civilian population of the big cities often embarked on a mass, panicked exodus which ended up killing huge numbers. Graham Peck, the young American, described how in a major southern city several hundred refugees packed on a railway track were killed when a train crew, anxious to escape the Japanese, drove their locomotive through the mass of people. In another incident that Peck was told about, a train traveler explained how seven passengers in his car were killed in one day. "It was a freight car with two makeshift floors inside, to hold extra layers of crouching refugees, while hundreds rode on its roof and rods," Peck wrote. "In that single day, three people were scraped off the roof in tunnels and two fell off the rods, under the wheels. In the mass of bodies inside, an old man was killed by a heart attack and a woman died in childbirth."[83]

The mass flights reflected a view of the Japanese Army as a force of nature that could only be evaded but not resisted let alone stopped. This again revealed a fundamental absence of trust among the Chinese in their own army's ability to perform. This poor impression was only exacerbated by the behavior of some particularly undisciplined Chinese units. In an especially notorious incident, an entire Chinese army, led by General Chen Munong, disintegrated and started looting the local population in a south Chinese province. Chiang Kai-shek had to send in troops led by a more competent general to disarm the delinquent soldiers.[84]

After seven years of war, even China's enormous population was proving insufficient, and the available resources of manpower fit for military service were dwindling. There were still some first-rate troops, many of them manning the units trained and equipped by the Americans, which were now deployed in Burma. Even so, the vast majority of new recruits came from poor backgrounds, with little or no education, and often with stunted growth due to long periods of failed harvests and imploding rural economies. Ray Huang, a future historian, then a platoon commander, had little regard for the standard of the Chinese army: "The approach was to train those who had basic skills with a cram course. The rest received little training. Officers only wanted these soldiers to show up during a battle to show the Japanese that we have a lot of people."[85]

The main problem with the Chinese army, however, was its senior officers. In a continent-sized country where a feeling of nationhood was still only taking hold sporadically, personal loyalties came at a premium, and Chiang Kai-shek was forced by circumstances to promote his closest allies. Li Zongren, a leading Chinese general and not a part of Chiang's inner circle, described great difficulties cooperating with other senior officers who were closer to the generalissimo. They were referred to, often sarcastically, as the "disciples of the son of heaven." "They took orders only from Chiang himself and even went so far as to evade orders from the commanding officer of the war zone, who controlled their operations directly," he said in a post-war interview. "They seldom reported situations to the commanding officer, and their pride and arrogance were beyond description."[86]

Chiang's wife, Chinese First Lady Song Meiling, once asked him why he used a general by the name of Liu Zhi, an officer whose skills were in low regard everywhere. Chiang replied, "It is true that Liu Zhi is a bad commander in war. But where can you find a man who is so obedient?"[87] It was a deliberate trade-off between skill and loyalty, but in the end, Chiang may have received neither from the generals he picked for key commands. "Among themselves there was considerable friction," said Li Zongren, "but all had a common desire to deceive the generalissimo, so that the supreme commander knew nothing of actual conditions in the army. It is easy to see that such an army could not fight."[88]

There was growing discontent within Chinese ranks with Chiang's leadership and resentment about the power he had been able to monopolize in his own hands, combined with emerging concern about what the post-war future would bring. Many members of rival factions were beginning to consider if they would be better served by throwing in their lot with the Communists. "Will there be a possibility that I can safely negotiate an alliance with the Communists?" Li Wenhui, a warlord in southwestern Sichuan province, asked the American advisor Owen Lattimore. "They are anti-Chiang Kai-shek and I am anti-Chiang too. Maybe I shall be able to recover my lost influence in the province."[89]

Chiang's most important enmity was with his chief American advisor, Joseph Stilwell. The relationship had been strained since the beginning of Stilwell's mission two years earlier, but by the second half of 1944, the confrontation was coming to a head. Stilwell, who referred to Chiang as "Peanut," had been frustrated since his arrival, pointing out that while his mission had been to train dozens of new divisions, Chinese foot-dragging had bogged him down. "To get this mission accomplished I have never had any means of exerting pressure," he wrote in a letter to Marshall in Washington.[90]

Stilwell had a valuable point, but the general, known as "Vinegar Joe" due to his penetrating, acerbic wit, was his own worst enemy, capable of making mortal foes within friendly ranks. A member of Merrill's Marauders, angered at the way the unit was pushed to the utmost at Myitkyina, with little in return in terms of thanks and recognition, put it bluntly: "If I'd had him in my sights at Myitkyina, I'd have shot him."[91] Still, the British commander in Burma, General Slim, was capable of seeing the qualities hiding within the complexities of Stilwell's personality: "To my mind he had strange ideas of loyalty to his superiors, whether they were American, British, or Chinese, and he fought too many people who were not enemies; but I liked him. There was no one whom I would rather have had commanding the Chinese army that was to advance with mine. Under Stilwell it *would* advance."[92]

The position Stilwell was placed in was one where diplomacy was called for, but it brought the worst out in him. "He was a masculine type who could have been a great general in battle but was ill-suited to staff work behind the lines," a Chinese general said.[93] David Richardson, a journalist for *Yank* magazine, got to experience Stilwell up close, and saw an individual in constant battle with his surroundings, and perhaps with far too high an opinion of himself. "He hated everybody. He hated Chiang Kai-shek and he hated the British. Stilwell was not a very balanced individual, to put it mildly," he said. "It was almost as though he wanted to be Emperor of China to show Chiang Kai-shek that he could take Chinese troops and make his own Army and go back into China and get the Japanese out. He would need no help. Now this was crazy."[94]

Stilwell had Roosevelt's backing almost until the end. In September, the American president sent a stern letter to Chiang, accusing him of inaction: "I have urged time and again in recent months that you take drastic action to resist the disaster which has been moving closer to China and to you." Roosevelt made a suggestion that was anathema to Chiang, proposing that Stilwell be put in charge of all forces in China as soon as possible. "It appears plainly evident to all of us here that all your and our efforts to save China are to be lost by further delays."[95] Stilwell insisted on handing the letter to Chiang personally. "The harpoon hit the little bugger right in the solar plexus," "Vinegar Joe" wrote in his diary.[96]

Stilwell's triumph was brief. Chiang's reply was yes to putting an American general in command of all forces in China, and no to Stilwell being that general. "The officer chosen... must be one in whom I can repose confidence, and must be capable of frank and sincere cooperation... General Stilwell has shown himself conspicuously lacking in these all-essential qualifications."[97] At this point, Roosevelt completely reversed his position. He was fighting a tough electoral battle, and the last thing he needed was an American general presiding over a military fiasco in China. Stilwell had to go. He was replaced by the less openly undiplomatic Lieutenant General Albert Wedemeyer, who assumed the post of Chiang's chief of staff, not overall commander in the China area.[98]

Stilwell's dismissal was a surprise to the American public, which now for the first time was alerted in more detail to the problems existing on the China front. Prior to his departure, Stilwell complained that Chiang Kai-shek "will squeeze out of us everything he can get to make us pay for the privilege of getting at Japan through China. He will do nothing to help unless forced into it."[99] The fact was that this advantage was being diminished by the seemingly unstoppable Japanese offensive down through China, placing in doubt the entire idea of the vast nation as a feasible staging ground for the final offensive against Japan. Especially since the Americans were advancing rapidly in the Pacific, China might not even be needed any longer.

Even so, the United States could not contemplate the idea of relinquishing China in its entirety to the Japanese. One scenario that this could produce, US strategic planners feared, was for Japan to surrender its home islands but continue the fight indefinitely from the Chinese mainland. By the fall of 1944, while Stilwell was being sent home, this appeared a very real possibility. Ichigō had reached into the southern province of Guangxi and the picturesque town of Guilin was now under threat. As the Japanese approached, chaos reigned in Guilin, and mutual suspicions thrived. Four spies within the Chinese ranks were put on a brief trial and immediately executed.[100]

By early November, Guilin had fallen. "The so-called three-month-long 'fight to the death' ended up lasting less than one night," wrote Tan Geming, deputy chief of staff of the Guilin defense.[101] The day after, Liuzhou, the other strategically important city in Guangxi, was also evacuated. From here, the Japanese advanced at a rate of more than 13 miles a day. American Colonel John Hart Caughey, part of the US mission to Chiang's capital in Chongqing, was oiling his heavy shoes and placing chocolate bars in his knapsack, preparing to have to evacuate and start walking to India. "It looked as if China was on her last legs. That we were too," he wrote in a letter to his wife. "Yes, those were bleak days."[102]

In fact, the Ichigō offensive, which had lasted for most of 1944, was coming to an end. The Japanese general in overall command of the operation would have preferred to continue on to Chongqing and capture the city that had been the symbol of Chiang's regime for the past more than six years, but his request was denied by Tokyo.[103] The Imperial General Headquarters had no intention of creating a "continental fortress" in China, despite American fears, but prioritized the preservation of forces to prevent US bombing of Japan from Chinese bases. To a large extent, this has been achieved. Ichigō ended not because of Chinese or American resistance, but because it had essentially succeeded.[104]

CHAPTER FIVE

Decisive Battles

October–December 1944

By October, the soldiers and sailors at the vast Ulithi atoll sensed that a major operation was being prepared, and rumors were rife about where they were headed next. "We knew something big was coming up, because there were more and more ships coming out, more and more people," said Michael Bak, quartermaster on board the destroyer USS *Franks*. The men understood instinctively that they were watching the beginning of the end, and that they were now approaching Japan proper, where the enemy would be at his most dangerous. "We had already secured a lot of islands," said Bak, "and we were getting closer toward the enemy homelands."[1]

In fact, they were going to the Philippines. This was the logical next step in view of the likelihood that an invasion of Japan proper would be necessary in order to bring the empire to its knees, explained Robert Eichelberger, the commander of the US Eighth Army in the Southwest Pacific. "We needed the deep-water harbors, the great bases, and the excellent training areas available in those islands, which, in the main, had a friendly and loyal population," he said. "We had no knowledge of the atomic bomb; indeed, it was not until almost a year later that the first atomic bomb was exploded experimentally in New Mexico."[2]

The Philippine archipelago, which was also required in order to cut Japan off from its possessions in Southeast Asia, had now definitively been picked over Taiwan, but it had to be taken one piece at a time. Geographically speaking, it would seem sensible to invade the large southern island of Mindanao first, since it was the part of the Philippines closest to American-held territory in New Guinea, except Mindanao's Japanese garrison numbered more than 60,000 troops. The smaller island of Leyte further north had only 25,000 defenders, explained Captain Charles Adair, US Navy, who played a key role in planning of amphibious operations. "It was much better to go to Leyte and follow the same policy we had of 'going where they weren't' as far as we could," he said, paraphrasing MacArthur's much-cited phrase of "Hit 'Em Where They Ain't."[3]

In the days prior to the planned invasion of Leyte, the Third Fleet under Admiral Bill Halsey sortied out into waters northeast of the Philippines, launching air raids against Japanese-held islands off the Chinese mainland. Okinawa was hit, but Taiwan was the main target, since its importance as an unsinkable aircraft carrier had been multiplied following the loss of many of Japan's real aircraft carriers in the battle off Saipan. The task for Halsey's pilots, therefore, was to lure the planes based on Taiwan into a fight that would knock them out and eliminate them as a serious threat to the impending Leyte operation.[4]

The air war over Taiwan culminated on October 12, when a total of 1,378 sorties were carried out by Japanese planes from airfields and ships in the area. Fukudome Shigeru, the commander of army air forces on the island, had high hopes for the outcome, believing that his planes were numerically superior to the Americans and at an advantage because this was their home turf. Intense dog fights broke out in the air over Taiwan, some of them even above the base where Fukudome himself was standing. "Well done! Well done! A tremendous success!" he exclaimed, clapping his hands, as he saw the first planes falling down, enveloped in flames. "Alas!" he wrote in his memoirs, "to my sudden disappointment, a closer look revealed that all those shot down were our fighters, and all those proudly circling above our heads were enemy planes!"[5]

It was a devastating defeat for the Japanese air force in Taiwan. In one day, it lost over 300 planes to more experienced American pilots flying better armed and better protected aircraft.[6] Still, the Japanese aviators, many of them green and easily excited, wildly overstated their victories. Once their overblown reports reached Tokyo, commanders in the Japanese capital came under the impression that the air battle over Taiwan had, in fact, been a major triumph. "The exaggerated report caused Imperial General Headquarters to commit, though temporarily, a mistake in its estimate of the war situation," remarked Fukudome. "It made the nation indulge in a false celebration and created the illusion that the empire could turn the tide of the war."[7] The result was a disastrous decision to adopt a more aggressive stance in the battle of the Philippines.

That battle began on October 20, when an American invasion fleet of 738 vessels emerged off the east coast of Leyte. Supported by Halsey's Third Fleet, consisting of 18 carriers, six battleships, 17 cruisers and 64 destroyers, it was, in the words of the US Navy's official historian, "the most powerful naval force ever assembled."[8] On board the transports were four divisions,

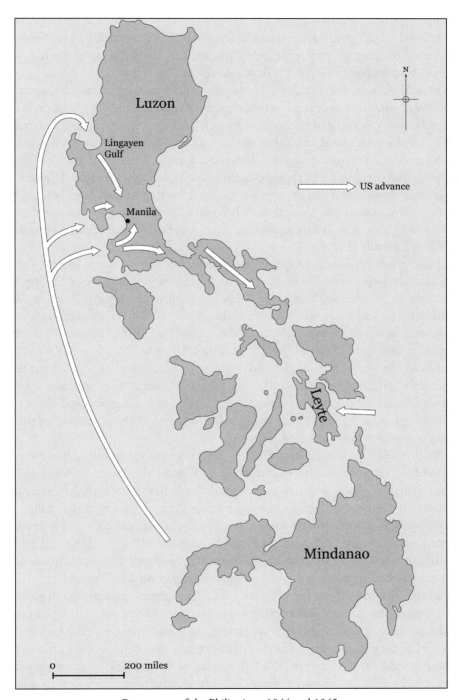

Reconquest of the Philippines, 1944 and 1945.

including the now battle-hardened men of the 1st Cavalry. They had proved worthy of MacArthur's trust when carrying the heaviest load in Los Negros, and now once again they were being put in front as the general made good on his vow to return to the Philippines.

In addition to the usual naval shelling and bombing from the air, the invaders brought rocket ships, firing dozens of missiles onto the landing area. "The boats went right in behind the rockets and we kept moving the barrage right up the beach and behind it to the rear area as the troops landed," said Adair, the amphibious specialist. The rockets proved highly effective: "They cleared out every bit of Japanese resistance, and they even killed Japanese that were in the area that were not touched by fragments. The concussion knocked them out, and cleared the whole area, our troops got ashore at Leyte and were walking, standing up, a mile from the beach. Now that, I consider, is a good assault landing."[9]

MacArthur set foot on Leyte a few hours after the invasion, eager to pull off as early as possible the great symbolic move of stepping onto Philippine territory in person. Soldiers of the 24th Division were fighting Japanese 300 yards inland, and there was a distinct atmosphere of danger all over the beach area, according to George Kenney, MacArthur's air force commander, who accompanied him. "Four of the big landing craft, beached where we went in, had been hit by Jap mortar fire and one was burning nicely when we landed. One light landing craft had just been sunk," he wrote in his memoirs. "There seemed to be a lot of Nip snipers firing all around the place and the snap of the high-velocity small-caliber Jap rifles sounded as though some of them were not over a hundred yards away."[10]

With an almost superstitious belief in his own invulnerability, MacArthur showed no interest in the whistling bullets from the Japanese marksmen, inspecting the beach and troops further inland, before making his presence known to a larger audience. It happened at 2pm sharp, over the radio on a wavelength known to be broadcast to a large section of the Philippine population. "People of the Philippines, I have returned!" he said triumphantly, with only his slightly shaking hands revealing the depth of his emotions. "By the grace of Almighty God, our forces stand again on Philippine soil."[11]

In the following days, the GIs pushed further inland, fighting small groups of Japanese but never encountering what amounted to organized opposition. "The pockets of resistance were separated," said Bill Filter, a private with the 381st Infantry Regiment. "They didn't have say, one main line of resistance. There would be a pocket of 1,000 Japanese here, and 500 somewhere else, and up the hill, and through the valley, and up the mountain, and so forth.

It was isolated to the point where there was not one main line that had to be penetrated."[12]

News of the US invasion was received with a certain degree of bewilderment by the Japanese 14th Area Army, deployed to defend the Philippines. When the area army's chief of staff, General Muto Akira, was informed of the American landing, his reaction was revealing. "Very interesting," he said, "but where is Leyte?"[13] He had only just arrived in the Philippines hours earlier. Like the majority of the senior Japanese commanders in the theater, he was a complete newcomer, the product of a last-minute reshuffle in the senior ranks. Only the month before, Tokyo had sent an envoy to inspect the senior officers running the Philippines, and they had found men who had gone soft in the pleasant colonial atmosphere, devoting themselves to playing golf and reading for leisure instead of getting ready for war.[14]

Imperial General Headquarters had removed the senior commander in the Philippines and instead brought in a legend. General Yamashita Tomoyuki, the conqueror of Malaya who had spent the past several years in Manchuria, was ordered to the Philippines and arrived just days before the American invasion. He had insisted on bringing in new blood at the top, even if, like Muto, they had little knowledge of even basic facts concerning the Philippines. Even so, they were quick learners, as they were soon to show.[15]

The invasion of Leyte was the chance the Japanese Navy had been waiting for. The assembly of hundreds of enemy warships presented the opportunity for the great battle that would deal a blow so devastating to the American foe that he would settle for a negotiated peace. The Japanese admirals were fully aware of the risks involved, and that many of their ships would be sacrificed with their crews in the battle against a superior enemy, but not unlike their mood when attacking Pearl Harbor nearly three years earlier, they saw no alternative to this move, potentially fateful as it might be. It confirmed a Japanese pattern of entering into dilemmas where even suicidal options seemed unavoidable.

Vice Admiral Kurita Takeo, heading one of the strike forces being prepared for an assault on the Americans at Leyte, put the situation in stark terms. "Would it not be a shame to have the fleet remain intact while our nation perishes?" he asked rhetorically, addressing his division commanders on board his flagship, the heavy cruiser *Atago*, on the eve of battle. "You must remember that there are such things as miracles. What man can say that there is no chance for our fleet to turn the tide of war in a Decisive Battle?"[16]

Besides the logic of seeking the ultimate battle with the Americans, it was vital for the Japanese Navy to hold on to the Philippines and prevent the Allies from gaining control of the archipelago. Much had been made of the navy's dependence on oil from Southeast Asia, which meant that if it withdrew to Japanese waters in case of an American conquest of the Philippines, it would be cut off from its fuel supply. On the other hand, if it decided to remain in southern waters near the Indonesian oil fields, it would be unable to receive supplies of ammunition and arms produced in the Japanese home islands. "There would be no sense in saving the fleet at the expense of the loss of the Philippines," said Admiral Toyoda Soemu, commander of the Combined Fleet.[17] Thus began what many scholars have described as the biggest naval battle in history.

The scene had been set for the battle of Leyte Gulf, the greatest naval battle in history. By October 22, three Japanese strike forces were converging on Leyte, preparing to attack the invasion fleet from different angles. Kurita's central force, the largest, was approaching from waters near Singapore and had set its course to make its way through the Philippines archipelago in order to reach Leyte from the north. The southern force, led by Vice Admiral Nishimura Shoji, was also arriving from the Singapore area and was getting ready to assault Leyte from the south. It was expected to combine with a separate fleet, sailing in from Japan. Finally, as bait to draw away the American carriers, a northern force built around four aircraft carriers commanded by Vice Admiral Ozawa Jisaburo was heading for the Philippines from the northeast.[18]

Kurita's fleet was detected in the early hours of October 23 in the South China Sea by the American submarine USS *Darter*. The radar operator on board the submarine picked up a massive signal at a distance of 33,000 yards. "It's probably rain," he said, but within a minute he corrected himself, "No, it's ships… lots of them."[19] The captain, David McClintock, messaged the observation to his superiors, and along with the submarine *Dace*, he followed the towering Japanese warships until dawn. Then he decided to strike, firing off his torpedoes against the *Atago*, Kurita's flagship. "I took a quick look around through the periscope before we went deep to avoid the depth charges, and this heavy cruiser was afire and going down by the bow. She was finished."[20]

Atago was indeed doomed, and Kurita had to leave the burning ship and move with his staff to *Yamato*, the world's largest battleship, before continuing onwards towards Leyte. The deadly encounter with the submarines was only the beginning. While passing through the Philippine archipelago on the following day, October 24, Kurita's central force was attacked in almost uninterrupted fashion by carrier-based American planes. The US pilots

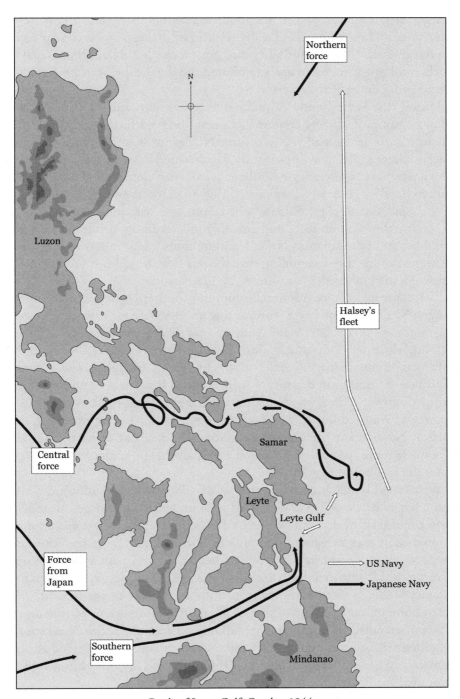

Battle of Leyte Gulf, October 1944.

focused their attention on the *Musashi*, the *Yamato*'s sister ship, and battered it mercilessly throughout the day. By the end of the day, it was clear it could not be salvaged. "My responsibility is so great it can't even be compensated by death and I must share *Musashi*'s fate," said the ship's captain, Kato Kenkichi before going down with his vessel.[21]

During the same hours, Admiral Bill Halsey received information that Ozawa's group of aircraft carriers had been observed further north. At this juncture an order he had received from Nimitz prior to the battle assumed special salience: "In case opportunity for destruction of a major portion of the enemy fleet is offered, or can be created, such destruction becomes the primary task."[22] Halsey had welcomed this order, eager to avoid a repetition of the June situation off Saipan, when Spruance had stuck to the task of protecting the invasion force and arguably missed an opportunity to destroy a sizable part of the Japanese Navy.[23] Within hours, Halsey was heading north with most of his ships, gambling that Kurita's fleet would not pose a serious threat. He had taken the bait offered by the Japanese.

That same night, Vice Admiral Nishimura's southern force was entering the Surigao Strait south of Leyte, confronting an assembly of Americans vessels. US motor torpedo boats were lying in wait under the cover of darkness, carrying out a series of attacks on the much larger Japanese ships without inflicting serious damage.[24] After midnight, in the early hours of October 25, it was the American destroyers' turn. Richard Rowe was a gunnery officer on the destroyer USS *Remey*, which made a night attack on the approaching Japanese. "We fired our fish, laid a smoke screen as we were executing that classical Naval maneuver known as 'getting the hell out of here,'" he said. "We made more speed after firing our fish than she did under full speed trial when she was brand new."[25]

What would later become known as the Battle of Surigao Strait, a part of the larger Battle of Leyte Gulf, was now underway. It proceeded under a black tropical night sky, and by sunrise most of the Japanese fleet was crippled or sinking. It was a textbook example of "crossing the T," as the American vessels were positioned in a line perpendicular to the Japanese line of ships, allowing the US side to unleash a series of massive broadsides. "The devastating accuracy of this gunfire was the most beautiful sight I have ever witnessed," said Roland Smoot, commander of one of the participating destroyer squadrons. "The arched lined of tracers in the darkness looked like a continual stream of lighted railroad cars going over a hill. No target could be observed at first; then shortly there would be fires and explosions, and another ship would be accounted for."[26]

By daybreak on October 25, it was clear that the Surigao battle was a decisive victory for the Americans, but there was no time to celebrate. In the very minutes when Nishimura's southern force was being defeated, a new crisis formed as Kurita's central force approached the Leyte invasion area from the north. With Halsey's powerful force up north fighting Ozawa's carriers, a slender line of ships was guarding the invasion area, concentrated near the island of Samar. Quartermaster Michael Bak, on board the destroyer USS *Franks*, had just been eating breakfast at 7am, when the loudspeaker announced, "General quarters, general quarters, man your battle stations. Enemy fleet is on the horizon." None of the crew could believe his ears. "I ran to the bridge and looked out," Bak said, "and I saw what looked like toothpicks on the horizon, right across the horizon—many, many ships."[27]

The Japanese, too, were surprised. After making its way through the San Bernardino Strait during the night, Kurita's central force had expected to encounter mostly transports in Leyte Gulf. "We had no information of the presence of [the US] task force east of Samar," said Koyanagi Tomichi, Kurita's chief of staff, in post-war interrogations. "We were quite taken aback when we met [the American] force off Samar on the morning of the 25th and some people even said they were Japanese carriers."[28] Kurita soon recovered from the surprise and, believing he had chanced upon the main US force, ordered a full-scale attack.

Although the defending fleet off Samar consisted of a cluster of escort carriers and destroyers far inferior to the attacking Japanese, the Americans joined the battle with death-defying, if not suicidal, fervor. Lieutenant Commander Robert Copeland of the destroyer USS *Samuel B. Roberts* made no effort to hide the odds: "This will be a fight against overwhelming odds from which survival cannot be expected. We will do what damage we can."[29] Bill Wilson, a gunner's mate on the destroyer, described the hectic battle that followed: "We fired our five-inch guns," he said. "The barrels were cherry red, two feet."[30]

The confused encounter became almost personal, according to a sailor on board the carrier USS *St. Lo.* "One of the Japanese ships got close enough to our ship... that I could see the sailors over there."[31] The air was filled with planes that sometimes, in split seconds, made the wrong decisions and shot at their own side. A crew member of one of the participating destroyers experienced a near miss when an American plane came dangerously close and nearly strafed the vessel: "Then the captain gave orders, shoot to kill—anybody that came down on us, shoot. It didn't matter who it was. I think once we may have shot down one of our own guys."[32]

The American losses were significant. The USS *St. Lo* was hit and sank within 30 minutes. At a point when the Japanese could have potentially won this part of the battle, they suddenly decided to withdraw. Kurita was not aware how close he was to prevailing, and he was concerned that American reinforcements were on the way. The defenders were as surprised as they had been in the morning when they first eyed the Japanese fleet, but this time pleasantly so. "They left us when they could have had a kill. They could have just dropped us all, in my opinion," said Michael Bak.[33]

Left in the ocean where the two fleets had fought it out were clusters of survivors, among them Alfonso Perez of the USS *St. Lo*. "We had some black guys that were stewards, and... I noticed that when we got in the water there was no difference. We were all buddies. When we were aboard ship they were separate and apart," he later recalled.[34] Among other survivors, the divisions prevailed. Richard K. Rohde, radioman on the destroyer escort USS *Samuel B. Roberts,* was floating in the water with an injured leg, and tried to get onto a raft filled with junior officers. "Somebody hit me so hard in the face, just knocked me back into the water," he said. "Survival of the fittest, and that was a tough lesson for me to learn. Anyway, I didn't try to get on that raft again. They weren't giving up their seats for anything."[35]

The water was also full of Japanese survivors. William McDowell, a radio technician on the destroyer USS *Bennion*, described the futile attempts to salvage them: "The Japanese that we went down [and] tried to take prisoners wouldn't have anything of us. They were in the water but wouldn't come up where we could haul them onto the ship."[36] Meanwhile, the Japanese who had made it back to safety now looked back at one of the most abysmal defeats in the history of their navy. Both Halsey and Kurita had failed, but Kurita's failure was more fateful for his side. Rear Admiral Koyanagi Tomiji later recalled an old tenet: "Battle is a series of blunders and errors. The side that makes the least will win and the side that makes the most will lose." He added, with bitterness, "The truth of this maxim was never more apparent than in the battle of Leyte Gulf."[37]

★ ★ ★

The escort carrier USS *Santee* had just launched a dozen aircraft in the morning of October 25 off Samar when a Japanese plane appeared in the distance and headed straight for its bulking hull. The crew on board the carrier watched incredulously as the plane moved closer and did not change course. "Pull out, you bastard, pull out!" a gunnery officer yelled instinctively.[38] Seconds later, the

Japanese pilot crashed through the wooden surface of the flight deck, leaving a gaping hole, and penetrated down to the hangar deck, where it exploded. Joseph Mika, a member of the ship's aviation fuel detail, was at the top of a ladder at the time of the blast. "It sort of knocked me off my fanny," he said.[39] Sixteen men were killed, and 27 injured.[40]

The crew of the USS *Santee* had just been exposed to a terrifying new weapon: the suicide pilot, or kamikaze, named after the "divine wind" which had destroyed the Mongolian fleet about to invade Japan more than six centuries earlier. It was an experience unlike any other even hardened veterans had been through. One described the uncertainty it entailed as similar to "being surrounded every minute of the day and night by a forest fire."[41] For sailors who were used to watching the enemy from miles away, it suddenly brought him uncomfortably close, and the war became more personal than at any time before. Richard Rowe, a destroyer gunnery officer, watched a kamikaze make a near-miss, passing just above the ship's two stacks. "He grins as he goes by and I can see his gold tooth," he said. "It was one of his front teeth."[42]

The use of "divine wind" pilot, who flew aircraft packed with explosives into Allied ships, was a measure of how desperate the Japanese commanders had become. "We can no longer win the war by adhering to conventional methods of warfare," Admiral Teraoka Kimpei wrote in his diary,[43] and following that logic, the kamikaze presented itself as the answer. Robert Ellinger, serving aboard the battleship USS *California*, saw the kamikaze as a brutally effective weapon, suddenly placing the Japanese at an advantage by utilizing the one area where they still had the upper hand—their willingness to die. "They sank ships. They damaged ships. They killed a lot of men," he said. "Before they would dive, you would try to shoot them down. This way they were coming at you. Their chance of hitting you were probably one out of seven. They didn't hit you all the time. Thank God."[44]

Admiral Nimitz later reflected in a post-war lecture on the kamikaze, telling an audience at the Naval War College how it was the one eventuality he had not foreseen: "The war with Japan had been re-enacted in the game room here by so many people and in so many different ways that nothing that happened during the war was a surprise, absolutely nothing except the kamikaze tactics towards the end of the war; we had not visualized those."[45] The Japanese, too, had not foreseen this weapon in pre-war planning, and it was a temporary measure introduced for the Leyte battle, which subsequently became permanent. In retrospect, many Japanese participants saw it as one of the first sure signs of imminent defeat. "The order [to use kamikaze] was nothing less than a national death sentence," said Yokoi Toshiyuki, commander of the Twenty-fifth Air Flotilla at the time. "Like every military order, it was issued in the name of the emperor and was, therefore, no matter how outrageous, not open to question or criticism."[46]

The young pilots who flew the kamikaze planes did not all volunteer for the missions, and they rarely lived up to their enemies' stereotypical ideas of brainwashed zealots, but often in their last letters home revealed a pensive, almost tender side. Hayashi Tadao, born in 1922 and a former student at the elite Imperial University of Kyoto, wrote a diary in which his Japanese was interspersed with literary quotes in French, German, and Latin. He dreamed of studying international politics and economics and helping to find a proper way for Japan in the modern world. "If I live, I shall accomplish this. If I die, well, it will turn out to be just a dream," he noted with a note of resignation in one of his last entries.[47] On the night before his final flight, he composed a poem which made no attempt to hide the sorrow of having to part with life:

Dusk, that most beautiful moment...
With no pattern
Millions of images
Appear and disappear
Millions of images
Beloved people.
How unbearable to die in the sky.[48]

Even so, the kamikaze pilots seldom questioned the mission they were made to undertake, despite the cost not only to themselves, but their loved ones as well. During his last visit home, Lieutenant Kishi Fumikazu was confronted by his sister, who described to him the anguish that his mother had to go through. "Ever since you joined up," she told him, "Mother has been setting meals before your photograph. She's given up drinking tea, and every evening she visits the shrine to pray for you." On the day of his departure, the ageing woman wrote on a Rising Sun flag which Kishi would carry into battle: "Happily Waiting for Returning Child." This did not move the young lieutenant. "Please don't worry about me," he wrote in his last letter home. "When you hear of my death, be happy for me, for I will have achieved my ambition." He was killed in the Philippines on October 24.[49]

The Japanese Navy was not alone in drawing flawed conclusions from the perceived victory in the battle over Taiwan. The Japanese Army, too, saw it as an opportunity to be seized. Abandoning its original plan to base its defense of the Philippines on a sustained struggle on the main island of Luzon, the army commanders now shifted to a focus on Leyte, expecting to stop the American attempt at reconquest there. "If the decisive battle in Leyte results in failure, it will upset the entire operation in the Philippines and the decisive battle in Luzon will be lost," they reasoned.[50] Consequently, in the days immediately after the American landing, large numbers of troops began crossing from Luzon to the harbor at Ormoc on the west coast of Leyte.

Initially, it would almost seem as if the Army were vindicated. The American air arm was not available to a sufficient extent at Leyte, seemingly confirming the Japanese assumption that it had been significantly reduced, and several Japanese transport vessels made it across to the island. Some vessels did come under air attack and were sent to the bottom of the ocean, but a fair number of soldiers were able to get ashore, and all in all, the Leyte garrison was boosted by an estimated 45,000 men during the tense weeks after the American invasion.[51] As a result, the four US divisions that had landed on Leyte ended up facing a stronger foe than they had expected, and the battle for the island evolved into a protracted struggle neither side had anticipated.

Ultimately, the battle for Leyte was an endeavor by the Americans to reach Ormoc and stop the reinforcements, and correspondingly a Japanese bid to prevent them from getting to the harbor. Fierce battles raged in the hills and jungles west of the region of Carigara, where the Japanese made a determined stand, taking advantage of the terrain in a manner reminiscent of the German Army's use of the bocage in Normandy for defensive purposes. The stalemate was only broken in early December when an American amphibious force was able to land on the west coast of Leyte, near Ormoc.[52]

The Japanese Army was not ready to give up Leyte yet. Also in early December, it launched one of its largest airborne operations of the late war period. Hundreds of Japanese paratroopers boarded transport planes on Luzon, each equipped with a small bottle of liquor with pre-printed instructions only to start drinking once they were in the air. Their target was, by a strange coincidence, the 11th Airborne Division, which was acting in a traditional infantry role on Leyte and guarding a key airfield. The American division's commander, Major General Joseph Swing, had finished supper and was sitting outside his tent in his underwear, hoping to catch some cool air, when he saw the Japanese transports pass overhead, and, shortly afterwards, dozens of parachutes opening up across the sky. "The 11th Airborne never had a more confusing night," wrote General Robert Eichelberger, in general command on Leyte. "The attack was, of course, a complete surprise, but the confusion of our troops was hardly a patch on the confusion of the Japanese; in the growing darkness it was hard to tell friend from foe."[53]

Most Japanese were killed on that night and during the following morning, and the last stragglers were hunted down over the next three days. Japanese resistance on Leyte was running out of steam, and even bold actions such as this airdrop could do nothing to change the inevitable. A letter found on a dead Japanese soldier expressed the desperate conditions faced by his army: "I am exhausted. We have no food. The enemy are now within 500 meters from us. Mother, my dear wife and son, I am writing this letter to you by candlelight. Our end is near. What will be the future of Japan if this island should fall into enemy hands? Our air force has not arrived. General Yamashita has not arrived. Hundreds of pale soldiers of Japan are awaiting our glorious end and nothing else."[54]

On December 26, after a campaign that had cost an estimated 56,000 Japanese lives and 2,900 dead Americans, MacArthur declared, "This closes a campaign that has had few counterparts in the utter destruction of the enemy's forces with a maximum conservation of our own."[55] In fact, months of "mopping up" remained. Eichelberger, the commander in Leyte, was at odds with MacArthur's practice, put on display here, of declaring victory in situations when a considerable amount of fighting remained, and soldiers were still risking their lives: "It seemed to me... ill advised to announce victories when a first phase had been accomplished without too many casualties. Too often... the struggle was to go on for a long time. Often these announcements produced bitterness among combat troops, and with considerable cause."[56]

The official history of the 11th Airborne Division provided a penetrating description of the hardship that filled the period after MacArthur's declaration of victory: "Through mud and rain, over treacherous, rain-swollen gorges, through thick wet jungle growth, over slippery, narrow, root-tangled, steep, foot trails, the soldiers pushed west to clear the Leyte mountain range of its tenacious defenders. It was bitter, exhausting, rugged fighting—physically, the most terrible we were ever to know."[57] The conditions were the same for their Japanese enemies, who at the same time received virtually no supplies and had to deal with symptoms of starvation when on a rare occasion they found something to eat. "Many instances occurred in which men vomited seven to ten times a day because they could not digest some of the food due to their weakened stomachs," Japanese Colonel Obakayashi Junkichi reported.[58]

Disease put a large number of American soldiers out of battle, and if it were not for the advances of medical science, the casualties could have been many times worse and led to permanent disability. Martin Mark, an infantryman with the 23rd Division, developed a severe case of jungle rot, ulcers caused by skin disease. He found out about his condition the hard way when a medic checked his feet: "He had taken his scalpel and cut open my bootlaces and pulled my boots off. They pulled my socks off, and the skin came with it." Mark was immediately evacuated to a field hospital, where a nurse fetched a jar with a black ointment, which she smeared on his feet. "What the hell is that?" he asked. The nurse replied, "This is supposed to save your life. They call it penicillin."[59]

On October 18, Subhas Chandra Bose, the head of the Japanese-backed Indian government-in-exile, was standing on a five-foot-high platform, reviewing a military parade 14 miles outside the Burmese capital of Rangoon. Just as the all-female Rani of Jhansi Regiment was passing by, Allied aircraft appeared over the treetops ringing the parade ground and started strafing the mass of soldiers assembled. Antiaircraft batteries immediately returned fire, and shrapnel from one of the guns whizzed past Bose, hitting a soldier next to the Indian leader in the base of the skull and killing him instantly. Determined not to lose his cool in front of the soldiers, Bose walked slowly towards the edge of the parade ground and sat down under a tree to wait out the attack.[60]

In a radio broadcast later the same day, Bose called the ongoing war with the Allies and their sophisticated weaponry "a fight between the human spirit on the one side and steel and armor on the other."[61] Everything indicated that steel and armor were winning, and Bose was quietly preparing for the inevitable. During a visit to Tokyo shortly afterwards, he met with the Soviet ambassador to Japan, Jakob Malik, hoping to establish a channel of communication with Moscow. Bose also spoke to his "American friends" through a number of radio broadcasts, trying to create understanding for his army and depicting it as an anti-imperialist force: "We are helping ourselves," he said. "We are helping Asia."[62] Bose knew his Japanese masters were facing defeat, and he was already bracing for a post-war world dominated by Soviets and Americans.

Bose was typical of the many Asians who had decided to side with the Japanese. Few had acted out of a pro-Japanese attitude, and many had simply been nationalists hoping to rid their countries of Western colonizers. The soldiers of the Indian National Army, or INA, saw themselves as opponents of British colonial rule and mostly considered their association with the Japanese Army as a means to an end. That became clear earlier that year when the INA had taken part in the Japanese offensive into northern Burma. "Once they were near the border of India everyone in the INA was fighting for Indian freedom," according to a Japanese war correspondent.[63] That offensive had failed, and the ambition of re-entering India on the back of a victorious Japanese Army had been exposed as an impossible dream. Now the members of the INA, and others like them across Asia, had to reconsider their choices and brace for an uncertain future.

Nowhere was this as clear as in China, where the sense of acute crisis was exacerbated by a sudden death. In the afternoon of November 10, 1944, the head of the Japanese-backed collaborationist government, Wang Jingwei, succumbed to multiple myeloma at Nagoya Imperial University Hospital in central Japan.[64] Wang, 62, had been weak for years, possibly due to the long-term effects of two earlier assassination attempts. His failing health was seen as symbolic of the declining fortunes of the collaborationist movement that he headed, and by the same token his death was a devastating blow from which the movement never recovered.

Wang had been a complex figure. Some saw more than a hint of ambition in his decision to lead the puppet government in Nanjing. "He lusted to become the top leader even if he had to betray his country," said one former ranking aide to Chiang Kai-shek.[65] Others saw him as an alternative to Chiang's Nationalists and Mao Zedong's Communists with a genuine model for China in an impossible situation. Zhou Fohai, Wang's second-in-command, had famously said that "the War of Resistance is meant to save the nation. Peace is also meant to save the nation."[66] Li Shengwu, minister of education under Wang, voiced a similar sentiment when he was put on trial after the war, arguing that Wang's "peace movement" was in the nation's best interests: "Most men of resolve said that if Mr. Wang really could protect the nation's position, penetrating deep into the enemy's rear area, pursuing the task of saving the country, it could well be of modest benefit to the War of Resistance."[67]

The regime which Wang had governed from the capital of Nanjing did not seek to hide the fact that his decision to defect from Chiang Kai-shek early in the war had been a controversial one and not supported by all Chinese. "Mr. Wang," according to one of his propagandists, "has not hesitated to follow many difficult paths so that the masses might prosper. He has thrown his own body to hungry tigers, not only giving up his life, but also his reputation." This act of self-sacrifice had turned him into "a Bodhisattva," the propagandist claimed, referring to the Buddhist concept of a person who has reached the highest stage of enlightenment but stays behind to help his fellow human beings.

The Buddhist metaphors contributed to a personality cult which the Nanjing government, with discreet Japanese support, had attempted to foster in the population. Many did not subscribe to it, but some did. This became clear when Wang's body was flown home to China, and curious onlookers were lining the streets of Nanjing amid heightened security. When Wang was laid to rest a few days later, there were groups of school children and youth groups who had clearly been commandeered, just as members of the Japanese and collaborationist militaries were present, but there also seemed to be members of the public who had not been forced to attend. Still, the choreographed nature of the event was unmistakable, as police officers zealously ensured people maintained a respectful silence and removed their hats when the funeral procession passed.[68]

The problem with focusing so much attention on Wang was that it made it impossible for his successor, the left-leaning politician Chen Gongbo, to step into his shoes. Chen only assumed the title of acting president, but more important, he possessed no independent power base. This was why he had been picked as a compromise candidate among rival factions in the first place, but it came at a cost. He soon found himself alone in Nanjing, nominally wielding power over all Japanese-occupied China, but in reality ruling little more than his own desk. While he sat, increasingly isolated, in his capital, the powerholders rushed back to their respective provinces to consolidate their power there, hoping to obtain bargaining chips which they could use in negotiations with Chiang Kai-shek once Japan had been defeated.[69]

The collaborationist regime was not just falling apart at the elite level, but also lost whatever backing it might have enjoyed from the war-weary population at the outset. Wang Jingwei had been the driving force behind a mobilization campaign meant to unite people in the big cities in open shows of loyalty to the regime. The campaign, known as the New Citizen Movement, promoted anti-communism and selfless dedication to the collective, while also propagating Pan-Asianism, a thinly disguised reference to the role China was expected to play under future regional leadership under Japan.[70] By late 1944, without Wang, this campaign was dead, while the population was anxiously awaiting peace and what it might bring. With the demise of the leader, according to a citizen who lived through it all, "the spark which kept the Peace Movement alight was gone."[71]

The sun rose on a clear sky over Saipan in the morning of November 24, meaning a week of anxious waiting was over. The crews of the XXI Bomber Command, in the smooth metallic hulls of their new B-29 Superfortresses, were told they were a "go" for their raid against Tokyo, beyond the horizon at a distance of 1,500 miles. It was the first such mission from the Marianas, after sorties from China had to be reduced because of the Ichigō offensive, but it had been agonizingly slow in coming. Each morning for the past seven days, the airmen had crawled into their giant machines, pumped up with adrenalin, only to be told again and again that their mission had been called off due to wrong wind directions and low-hanging clouds. This had frustrated not only the crews but also the two dozen war correspondents assembled to record the world historic event—the opening of the strategic bombing campaign against Japan waged from the Central Pacific.[72]

Now it was the real deal. The 110 Superfortresses took off at a dizzying pace, filling the morning air with their ear-deafening roars. "The giant planes dog-legged in the sky to form patterns of nine or twelve as they headed northwestward toward the most heavily guarded target in the Far East," the Associated Press correspondent reported.[73] The objective was the Musashino plant in northwest Tokyo, about 10 miles from the Imperial Palace, and believed by intelligence to be the producer of a large portion of Japan's total output of combat plane engines.[74] Underlining the significance of the raid, in the cockpit as co-pilot of the lead plane, the *Dauntless Dotty*, was Major Robert K. Morgan, who had previously piloted the legendary *Memphis Belle* deep into the skies over Germany.[75]

The mission proceeded in less than perfect fashion. Seventeen B-29s had to abort the mission on the way to Tokyo, and six reached the Japanese capital but were unable to carry out the bombing due to mechanical failure. The rest, bombing from altitudes in excess of 27,000 feet, were struggling with strong winds and a cloud cover hiding the target. No more than one in four attempted to bomb the Musashino plant, while the rest unloaded their cargo randomly over urban and dock districts. As a result, only one percent of the building area inside the factory compound was damaged, along with 2.4 percent of the machinery. Losses on the part of the B-29s were light, but they got a taste of the ferocity of the Japanese pilots. A Superfortress was lost after a fighter rammed, kamikaze-style, into the tail of the plane.[76]

It was a modest beginning, but the introduction of the XXI Bomber Command in the skies over Japan marked a new chapter in the war not least because of its primary weapon, the B-29 Superfortress. To many contemporaries, it seemed a visitor from the future. Originally built primarily for use in the European theater of war, the B-29 arrived too late to be of any importance there and instead was reassigned to the Pacific. It was a technological marvel for its time and a showcase of how far military aviation had developed in the course of a war which, in its early stages, had seen biplanes in significant operational roles. The crew in a B-29 flew in a pressurized cabin, protecting them from the thin, icy air outside, and an analog computer calculated the lead the gunner had to take into consideration when firing at attacking aircraft, as well as the effect air density and speed had on the bullets' trajectory.[77]

The Japanese were well aware of the danger they were now facing. Prince Higashikuni, the commander-in-chief of the Home Defense Headquarters, received news of the B-29 plane via foreign wire reports, and immediately realized its war-changing potential. "We had nothing in Japan that we could use against such as weapon," he said later. "From the point of view of the Home Defense Command, we felt that the war was lost and said so. If the B-29s could come over Japan, there was nothing that could be done."[78] Soon, the Japanese defenses were reduced to empty symbolic gestures, meant more to beef up morale in the terror-stricken population than to actually stem the shining fleets of B-29, which soon started arriving on a daily basis, with the relentlessness of a natural calamity. "Apparently the brass felt better when antiaircraft guns could be heard firing during an air raid," a Japanese eyewitness said. "The sound conveyed the impression that something effective was being done to deal with the air attacks."[79]

Japan seemed an unusually easy objective for strategic bombing. The Committee of Operations Analysts, an assembly of high-IQ mathematicians, engineers, and physicists charged with picking targets for the offensive, pointed out that Tokyo, Osaka, and four other Japanese cities accounted for a bigger share of the nation's industry than the 25 largest German cities combined. "No other industrial nation is dependent upon so small an area for so substantial a portion of its manufactured products," the committee emphasized. Consequently, the benefits of a strategic bombing campaign against Japan were likely to far outdo those of the offensive carried out against the Third Reich, according to a scientific report forwarded to the Army Air Forces: "Estimates of economic damage expected indicate that incendiary attack of Japanese cities may be at least five times as effective, ton for ton, as precision bombing of selected strategic targets as practiced in the European theater."[80]

Precision bombing was a relative term, since the committee pointed out that the same six Japanese cities were also home to nearly half of all Japanese workers in high-priority industries. Moreover, Japanese industry was decentralized to the extent that much basic production was farmed out to the homes of the workers, as described by an American scientist who toured the burned-out Japanese cities after the war: "Standing in the ashes of a substantial portion of the burned homes are various types of machine tools like lathes, drill presses, etc. Here family groups were manufacturing repetitive parts like nuts, bolts, or coils which were delivered to the manufacturing centers for use in the assembly of military weapons. In the area we examined, approximately one fifth of the homes showed evidence of such activities."[81] In other words, every Japanese home was a potential target. This would have severe implications for the coming months.

While the Marianas were becoming the main staging ground for the XXI Bomber Command's strategic air offensive against Japan, the XX Bomber Command continued its air raids from bases in China, albeit at a reduced pace. The targets were not just the Japanese home islands, but also occupied territory elsewhere. One target which took a heavy toll in late 1944 was the central Chinese city of Wuhan, home to a large foreign community before the war and occupied by Japanese forces in bloody fighting six years earlier.[82] US Major General Claire Lee Chennault, the founder of the famed Flying Tigers and now the commander of the Fourteenth Air Force, played a key role in the execution of the attack. Faced with the unrelenting success of the Japanese Ichigō offensive, he had been pushing since June for a bombing raid on Wuhan, the main Japanese staging area, but had failed to get the necessary backing from Stilwell. Only after "Vinegar Joe" was pulled out of China did Chennault get the go-ahead from his replacement, Lieutenant General Wedemeyer.[83]

Chennault was given responsibility for the overall planning for the mission, which was to target Wuhan's main warehouse district along the Yangtze river front. He wanted the B-29s to drop only incendiaries, whereas Curtis LeMay, the commander of the B-29s in Asia, preferred to use high-explosives. The result was a compromise in which four in five Superfortresses carried incendiary bombs. The 84 bombers, supported by 200 planes from the Fourteenth Air Force, attacked on December 18 in seven waves, ten minutes apart. The first waves, according to Chennault, left a thick blanket of smoke over Wuhan. As a result, when the last waves arrived, visibility was zero, and few of the aircraft were able to drop their bombs even within the city limits. On the ground, however, the mission had a huge impact, Chennault explained, while only hinting at the collateral damage: "Fires burned for three days, gutting the docks, warehouse areas, and large sections of the foreign quarters."[84]

Altogether, over 500 tons of bombs or incendiaries fell on the city, destroying nearly 300 acres of warehouses and industrial property.[85] According to Chinese records, about 20,000 people were killed or injured. "The horror of the bombings had a severe impact on the people's morale, and their situation was indescribable. Fearing for their lives, the residents gradually fled from [Wuhan], and eventually more than one third of the city's population had left," according to a local historical record. The Japanese exacted a brutal revenge on the American pilots they caught alive. A Chinese record describes the fate of three downed airmen: "They pulled off their uniforms, tied them up, and dragged them through the streets, beating and kicking them on the way, in an extremely bloody spectacle. In the end, the Japanese soldiers dragged the American aviators to a Japanese temple, where they hanged them and burned the bodies."[86]

Early in the afternoon on December 14, the air-raid siren started wailing over Camp 10-A near Puerto Princesa bay on the Philippine island of Palawan, and the 150 American prisoners were ordered into narrow shelters dug into the ground near their barracks. To the surprise of the emaciated inmates, no airplanes appeared. There was not even the distant sound of aircraft. Bewildered and worried mumbling spread among the prisoners, as they saw that their Japanese prison guards, fully armed, were forming a ring around their shelters. Then, a gruesome scene unfolded.[87] "I saw five soldiers go up to one of the air-raid shelters and throw buckets of gasoline into the entrance," Japanese superior private Sawa Tomisaburo, who was watching from a distance, said in post-war interrogations. "This was followed by two men who threw lighted torches into the opening."[88]

A hellish inferno erupted. Flames engulfed the shelter and trapped the prisoners inside, as agonized cries filled the air. In the other shelters, the prisoners sitting closest to the entrance saw everything and could only wait in sick horror until it was their turn. Some managed to get out but were cut down by Japanese bullets or killed with bayonets or rifle butts. Others were lucky enough to escape all the way out of the camp and make it to the bay, but several were caught on the beach by Japanese guards and killed on the spot. One was discovered by a patrol armed with a gasoline bucket and a torch. He begged desperately: "Please shoot me, please don't burn me! I don't want to burn!" His pleas were ignored. Only 11 survived the carnage by hiding and eventually disappearing into the countryside.[89]

Intelligence about the horrific massacre at Camp 10-A eventually reached American lines and confirmed rumors that the Japanese were preparing to kill their prisoners rather than allowing them to be liberated by the advancing Allied armies. Several POWs were told by their guards that this was indeed the fate that was in store for them. The journal of a camp in Taiwan captured after the war described "extreme measures" to be undertaken against the prisoners: "Whether they are destroyed individually or in groups, or however it is done, with mass bombing, poisonous smoke, poisons, drowning, decapitation, or what, dispose of them as the situation dictates. In any case, it is the aim not to allow the escape of a single one, to annihilate them all, and not to leave any traces." This murder was to take place in all cases "where escapees from the camp may turn into a hostile fighting force."[90]

Conditions in Japanese prison camps had been dismal from the outset, and they only worsened as the war dragged on. Jay Rye, an infantryman of the US Army captured during the Japanese conquest of the Philippines in early 1942, was among those lost inside the tropical camp hell. Being worked to breaking point and surviving on a starvation diet, he relied on the weevils in the dirty rice he was fed for extra nutrition. Disease was rampant, and the dead were tossed into shallow pits and covered by a thin layer of dirt. After heavy rains, arms and legs would stick out of the mass graves. "Sometimes they would let you cover them and sometimes they wouldn't," Rye said later. Arbitrariness was part of the daily terror, and the behavior of each individual guard was hard to predict. "Today he would be nice, tomorrow he'd kill you, so you couldn't picture the Japanese."[91]

Escape was virtually impossible, since no white man could disappear for long outside the perimeters before being discovered. Still, a colonel made the attempt and was gone for a few days, causing the other inmates to believe that he had made it to freedom. Then one day, he was brought back in, covered in bruises from a fresh beating at the hands of the Japanese. The camp commander prepared a firing squad, as the colonel pleaded desperately for his life, arguing he should not be shot since he had only performed his duty as an officer by trying to escape. The camp commander, who understood English, pulled out his sword and decapitated the man. "You see their theory?" Rye said. "He did what he wanted, didn't shoot him, chopped his head off." Later, to deter escape attempts, the Japanese divided all prisoners into groups of ten. If one of them went missing, all in the group would be killed.[92]

Futamatsu Yoshihiko, an engineer who helped oversee the construction of the Thai-Burma Death Railway, freely acknowledged the brutality routinely meted out against prisoners, putting it down mainly to the overall harsh behavior among the Japanese themselves: "In the Japanese Army there is absolute compliance with orders given by those of higher rank and it is the custom to levy corporal punishment on the spot to men of lower rank. The soldiers and auxiliaries practised the same principles on the prisoners on the job and one can imagine that corporal punishment was added, directly in person, when a prisoner did not comply with orders and commands."[93]

Conditions were only aggravated by the fact that the camps were located in areas where poverty and hunger became ever more pronounced due to the war. In an incident that may be unique throughout all of Japanese-occupied

Asia, civilians in an impoverished part of Korea tried to break *into* a camp for Western prisoners in an attempt to find food. "100 [K]oreans threw a riot outside the camp gates, tried to get in: the guard was turned out with fixed bayonets, took ½ hour to disperse them. One presumes poor devils are starving," Alan Vernon Toze, a British non-commissioned officer, wrote in his diary.[94]

The exact plight of the prisoners was largely unknown to their families at home, since the Japanese authorities did not allow representatives of the International Committee of the Red Cross to visit camps south of Hong Kong, in areas where a large proportion of the camps were located. Combined with the fact that the Japanese government did not provide detailed lists of POWs, many had, in the words of one historian, "disappeared behind a wall of silence."[95]

Despite the lack of concrete information about conditions for Japan's prisoners, rumors of the treatment meted out to the captives gradually reached the Allied societies and caused considerable anger. Japanese media shrugged off Allied allegations of abuse, dismissing it as mean-spirited Western propaganda. "Taking up such a petty problem as the treatment of captives and internees, the British and American authorities and press are making a great fuss and are despising the Japanese as enemy of humanity and as a barbarous and cruel nation," a journalist at the English-language newspaper *Nippon Times* wrote in 1944.[96]

By contrast, the treatment of the relatively few Japanese prisoners that ended up in Allied camps was generally characterized by a humane approach which at times even went beyond the requirements of the Geneva Convention. This was partly in a vain hope that, in return, Allied prisoners in Japanese hands would be treated less severely. "The Japanese prisoners of war," one contemporary observer noted, "were being treated with far greater consideration than American soldiers who happened to be black."[97]

When the Swedish head of the International YMCA visited camps for the Japanese in the United States in 1944, he found a Sunday menu consisting of soup, chicken, and ice cream, and upon his return home he told local journalists that the facilities he had inspected were "the cleanest he ha[d] seen anywhere in the world."[98] Another YMCA representative made a visit to a different facility and noted with satisfaction that the prisoners were fond of the colored crepe paper and thin wire that his organization had donated to allow them to make artificial flowers in the traditional Japanese way, and listed a few objects that still needed to be supplied, including incense sticks for Buddhist rites.[99]

There is evidence that the mild treatment had a puzzling effect on at least some of the Japanese captives, as they had failed to become dead heroes, placing them in roles they had not been prepared for. "They were better than model prisoners," wrote American anthropologist Ruth Benedict. "Old Army hands and long-time extreme nationals located ammunition dumps, carefully explained the disposition of Japanese forces, wrote our propaganda and flew with our bombing pilots to guide them to military targets. It was as if they had turned over a new page; what was written on the new page was the opposite of what was written on the old, but they spoke the lines with the same faithfulness."[100]

In other cases, the lenient conditions appeared to cause the Japanese prisoners to become arrogant and conspicuously uncooperative. In one camp, their complaints, passed on via an English-speaking spokesman, were never-ending: "They did not want to work with American women in the camp laundry," in the words of a modern historian, "they resented being housed with three Marshall Island natives; they demanded coal for the barracks stoves instead of the wood made available by the camp authorities; they wanted more books and dictionaries; they did not want American personnel present in their barracks during Saturday morning cleaning; and on and on." The scorn of the Japanese even extended to their Axis partners, and in one camp that also housed Germans, the two groups of prisoners mostly ignored each other if not acknowledging their presence with obscene gestures.[101]

In Australia, the humane policy towards prisoners may have contributed to much more serious consequences. In August 1944, a total of 359 Japanese managed to break out from their camp near the small town of Cowra in New South Wales. Over the next few days, all escapees were rounded up, but not without considerable bloodshed. More than 230 of the inmates ended up dead, either killed by Australians or by other Japanese prisoners. Some also committed suicide. "They did not understand the Articles of the Geneva Convention," wrote E. V. Timms, a novelist who as an officer took part in guarding the Japanese at Cowra, "and our strict adherence to its terms merely amused them and further convinced them of our moral and spiritual weakness. They read into our humane treatment of them a desire to placate them, and this they felt sure sprang from our secret fear of them."[102]

Whatever leniency the Japanese experienced at the hands of Allied captors took place outside the combat zone. Those captured in battle could only be reasonably sure of mild treatment if they were lucky enough to make it back to the hinterland, and this was far from sure. Killing prisoners was a practice that emerged early in the Pacific War, motivated partly by the experience of seeing Japanese appearing to surrender, only to blow themselves and their captors up with hidden grenades. It was a vicious cycle, since the Japanese soldiers' determination to fight to the last man may have been partly inspired by knowledge that survival was extremely unlikely in any case. This was one of the ways in which the war in the Asia Pacific became particularly brutal.

A crewmember of an American bomber spent a break between missions to visit a temporary encampment used by the Marines to hold prisoners. He only saw two Japanese behind the barbed wire and asked a Marine, "Where are the rest of the prisoners?" The Marine answered, "We have all we wanted here."[103] Aviation pioneer Charles Lindbergh, who spent several months in the Southwest Pacific in 1944, encountered similar attitudes. After witnessing a skirmish in which a Japanese was reportedly brought back alive, he inquired about details from an American colonel who insisted it could not possibly be true. "Our boys," he explained, "just don't take prisoners."[104]

CHAPTER SIX

The Long Haul

January–March 1945

Few in the Asia Pacific area entered into 1945 believing the war would end within the next twelve months. Many thought that the worst was still in store. "We may be separated most of the time for the next two or three years," Admiral Raymond Spruance wrote from Pearl Harbor in a letter to his wife, whom he had hardly seen since the war began. "I can see no predictable end at present."[1] Not far away, Admiral Nimitz held a New Year's press conference, promising "an unhappy 1945 for the Japanese," but also issuing a document which stated ominously that "the decisive battles, the greatest battles, the hardest battles of the war in the Pacific are still to come."[2]

The same day, the Canadian magazine *MacLean's* ran a feature titled "Forecast for 1945," containing predictions by a number of prominent observers about the progress of the war in the year ahead. While they were generally optimistic about the likelihood of peace in Europe, with one even expecting a German capitulation by April, they were generally much more cautious when it came to Japan. "The end of the war against Japan is too far away to foresee yet," opined Hugh Templin, a newspaper editor. Max Werner, a military analyst, was slightly more upbeat: "Japan will be beaten on the sea and in the air and weakened on land." Several of those asked believed that a Soviet entry into the war in East Asia would be decisive.[3]

The troops in the Asia Pacific ushered in the year in a somber mood. There was "a minimum of joy and jollity on the combat fronts," according to General Robert Eichelberger, commander of the Eighth Army in the Philippines.[4] Millions of men and women were scattered across the region, wondering whether the coming year would be their last. "We just felt it was going to be a long haul," said Michael Bak, on board the destroyer USS *Franks*. The invasion of the home islands in particular, expected at some point in 1945, would bring more fighting and more suffering, and not necessarily a quick end: "I didn't know, and I don't think anybody aboard ship had any feeling, other than it was going to be a long, drawn-out war."[5] Admiral Halsey's New Year message to his men was characteristically grim: "Keep the bastards dying!"[6]

In Japan, Prime Minister Koiso Kuniaki struck an impossibly optimistic note in his New Year's address. "This year, we will definitely expel the enemy from the region of Greater East Asia and win victory," he said. Sticking to the same assumption of America's fundamental mental weakness that had sustained Japan's war effort since 1941, he continued, "Now that they have seen how costly the present war is in respect to human resources, the American public has realized the senselessness of sending out their beloved fathers, brothers, husbands and sons to the bloody battlefields."[7]

Many Japanese, whether out of loyalty to their government or because they sincerely believed in their cause, did their best to boost morale. Yamanaka Ryōtarō, a teacher who had accompanied his students to the countryside, spent January 1 preparing his class for the hardship ahead, holding up the example of the kamikaze pilots, who had recently shown the way in the Philippines: "As my words for the new year, I gave an admonitory lecture saying that we should rise up and greet the year of decisive battles and do what we do with the spirit of the divine wind special attack units."[8]

Others with a more complete understanding of Japan's precarious situation vented their quiet despair. In the morning of January 1, Kase Toshikazu, a high-ranking official in the Japanese foreign ministry, enjoyed fine weather on a stroll through Tokyo but also noticed how a pre-dawn air raid had hit the district of Ueno and was coloring the sky an uncanny and unnatural red. Returning home, he wrote in his diary: "Poor helpless people rendered homeless on New Year's Day! This is the year of decision. This year will see the end of war both in Europe and Asia. Sad though it is, we must face realities squarely. We have lost the war."[9]

During their meeting in Hawaii the previous summer, President Roosevelt and General MacArthur had discussed the potential cost of invading Luzon, the key island in the Philippines, where the capital Manila was located. "Douglas," the president had said, "to take Luzon would demand heavier losses than we can stand. It seems to me we *must* bypass it." Confidently, MacArthur had replied, "Mr. President, my losses will not be heavy, any more than they have been in the past. The days of the frontal attack are over. Modern weapons are too deadly, and direct assault is no longer feasible.

Only mediocre commanders still use it. Your good commanders do not turn in heavy losses."[10]

Now was MacArthur's time to show that he could indeed wrestle the most populous island in the Philippines back from the Japanese while avoiding excessive losses. However, many of his soldiers did not expect to survive the upcoming campaign. "The enemy's strength on Luzon was known to be heavy; his suicidal fanaticism, the last ditch of the defeated, was fully comprehended," recalled Sergeant Vincent L. Powers, who served at MacArthur's headquarters. "It was not out of fear or pessimism but in the light of cold reality that many of us who were going [checked] our last Will and Testament."[11]

If the invasion fleet at Leyte had been the biggest in history, the one approaching Lingayen Gulf north of Manila in early January 1945 was its equal.[12] It consisted of nearly 1,000 ships, as well as 3,000 landing craft, and 280,000 men. As historian William Manchester points out, this was more than the United States had deployed in the invasions of North Africa, Italy, or Southern France, and more than the entire Allied force used to take Sicily. In short, according to Manchester, the invasion of Luzon was "the climax of World War II in the Southwest Pacific."[13]

The fleet, passing south and west of Luzon, exposed itself to intense attacks by Japanese airplanes, primarily kamikazes. Nervous crews on board the ships fired wildly against the approaching low-flying suicide planes, often killing or maiming men on neighboring ships. After one day of particularly lethal friendly fire, Vice Admiral Jesse B. Oldendorf, the commander of the invasion fleet's support force, criticized the "indiscriminate, promiscuous and uncontrolled shooting" in a statement to the crews on his ships. "Ammunition was wasted, death and injury to shipmates inflicted, and material damage caused to our ships," he wrote in his stern message. "All hands are enjoined to make certain that their guns are fired at the enemy and not at their shipmates."[14]

By contrast, the landing itself in Lingayen Gulf went ahead with virtually no opposition, and most men managed to wade ashore without being shot at. XIV Corps took up the right half of the invasion area, closest to Manila, and was charged with moving towards the capital. Its flank were to be covered by I Corps, on its left. The advances made on the first day of the invasion, according to XIV Corps's after-action report, "far exceeded the wildest dreams of those who had planned the operation."[15]

Official Japanese news outlets put on a brave face. "The battle for Luzon—that is, the battle for the Philippines—has now entered its main stage," Tokyo radio reported. "The battle in which 300,000 American officers and men are doomed to die is about to begin."[16] Behind the scenes, however, the Japanese leaders were deeply worried, and none was more worried than Hirohito. As early as January 6, when the American fleet was reported near Lingayen Gulf, he had remarked that "the war situation in the Philippines was becoming increasingly grave," and some days later, once it was clear that the Americans had secured a foothold on Luzon, his frustration exploded into scathing sarcasm: "Your plan sounds good, as usual; but so far you have failed to execute your previous plans. Are you sure about [your plans] this time?"[17]

The Japanese commander on the Philippines, General Yamashita, did indeed have a sound plan ready for the defense of Luzon. It involved holding on to three mountainous areas on the island and making the Americans pay as dearly as possible for every yard of territory they conquered. Still, the immediate Japanese reaction to the invasion was disorganized and hurried, due to multiple pinprick operations carried out by Philippine insurgents, combined with US naval and air movement in the southern part of Luzon, suggesting that American operations were planned there as well. "Japanese forces on the island, harassed by guerillas and by air, drove north, south, east, and west in confusion, became tangled in traffic jams on the roads, and generally dissipated what chance they might have had to repel the landing force," George Marshall, the US Army chief of staff, wrote later in a report.[18]

Still, after the initial speedy advance out of the invasion zone, XIV Corps moved southward towards Manila at a slower-than-expected pace. The commander of the Sixth Army, the German-born General Walter Krueger, was concerned about the need to secure the left flank before risking his forces in a dash toward the capital, but in his memoirs, he also blamed the sluggishness partly on local civilians: "A multitude of Filipinos—men, women and children—on foot, on bicycles, in pony-drawn carromatas and carabao carts, streamed south along the highways toward Manila, close on the heels of the advancing troops." This interfered seriously with the advance and with the movement of ammunition and other supplies, he argued. "But since [MacArthur] had directed that the movement of Filipino civilians was not to be interfered with, this could not be avoided."[19]

Towards the end of January, US forces landed north and south of Manila Bay in preparation for a second offensive in the direction of the capital. The 11th Airborne Division, disembarking in the south, also found itself held up by the local population: "There was a tremendous welcome," wrote Eichelberger, who accompanied the division. "Filipinos lined the streets and gave away such precious and hoarded food stocks as eggs, chickens, bananas, papayas. There was a village square and a bandstand, and a lot of cheering and chatter."[20] Soon, however, the serious business began. The airborne division was faced with some of the toughest Japanese opposition on all of Luzon. The pre-invasion deception had almost worked too well, leading the Japanese to believe that the major American thrust would come from the south, and the access to the Philippine capital from that direction was consequently exceptionally well defended.[21]

The units approaching Manila from Lingayen Gulf also moved at a slowing pace. In places where organized Japanese resistance was encountered, such as Clark Field north of the capital, the troops were bogged down for days. At this point, MacArthur gave an impromptu pep talk to Major General Verne Mudge, the commander of the recently disembarked 1st Cavalry Division. More than 3,000 American internees were kept at Manila's Santo Tomás University, now transformed into a prison camp, MacArthur pointed out. Their lives were at risk, and they must be saved before the Japanese massacred them as had happened elsewhere. Whether or not it was a means to motivate the troops, MacArthur made it the main purpose of rushing to the capital. "Get to Manila!" he told the division commander. "Go around the Japs, bounce off the Japs, save your men, but get to Manila! Free the internees at Santo Tomás!"[22]

Just hours after MacArthur's order, early on February 1, the 1st Cavalry Division sent its Flying Column straight for Manila, a 100-mile trek down Highway 5. Any Japanese machinegun position or other obstacle along its route caused only a brief delay. Tanks would roll up and blow it away before the entire column continued. Japanese survivors retreating into the surrounding countryside were allowed to escape. There was no time to chase them down. "The Japanese would try to stop us," said Fred Faiz, a machine gunner with the column. "We went right through them and kept on going. We had to get to Manila."[23]

Within 48 hours of its departure, the Flying Column was a mere 15 miles from its objective. In the evening of the following day, on February 3, it crossed into Manila, and picking up two Filipinos who acted as guides, they headed straight for Santo Tomás University. At 8:30 pm, a medium tank nicknamed the *Battling Basic*, crashed through the gates of the compound. Brief firefights broke out in the dark with Japanese guards, but the Americans soon got the upper hand.[24] Faiz was among the soldiers fanning out among the former university buildings. One of the first inmates he saw was a little old man, who hugged him and said, "What took you so long?"[25]

Marines wade ashore at Cape Gloucester, New Britain, shortly before New Year 1944. (National Archives)

Deception was a key skill in jungle warfare. Here, the Japanese at Cape Gloucester have arranged a group of scarecrows to look like a machine-gun team. (National Archives)

Marines beat back a Japanese counterattack in the jungles of Cape Gloucester in January 1944. The man in the middle handles an M1917 Browning machine gun. (National Archives)

American medium tank crosses Suicide Creek at Cape Gloucester after a bulldozer has paved the way across. (United States Marine Corps)

Marines land at Kwajalein atoll on February 1, 1944, immediately seeking whatever cover from enemy fire they can find on the beach. (National Archives)

Soldiers of the 7th Division use flame throwers to clear out a Japanese block house on Kwajalein Island in early February 1944, while others wait with rifles ready if survivors emerge from the blaze. (National Archives)

Men of the 4th Marine Division storm a Japanese blockhouse on Namur Island, part of Kwajalein Atoll, February 1944. (National Archives)

A severely injured Marine receives plasma during the battle for Namur Island, Kwajalein Atoll. (National Archives)

Allied commanders: Admiral Chester Nimitz points at a map of the Western Pacific during a meeting in Hawaii in 1944. Seated from left are General Douglas MacArthur, President Franklin D. Roosevelt, and Admiral William D. Leahy, the president's chief military advisor. (US Navy)

Japanese commanders: Emperor Hirohito at a conference with senior officers. Navy officers are seated on the left in the photo, and Army officers on the right. (Mainichi Shimbun)

Near Imphal in the spring of 1944, a Sikh signaller receives reports from patrols reporting on Japanese positions. (Library of Congress)

Troops of Merrill's Marauders and the Chinese march side by side in Burma, February 1944. (United States Army Signal Corps)

A Chinese infantryman advances through the devastated city during the Burma campaign, flanked by two American allies. Chinese personnel received training and equipment from the United States in anticipation of major battles in China at the end of the war. (United States Army Signal Corps)

Japanese troops made rapid advance southward through the central Chinese provinces during the Ichigō offensive, spring of 1944. (Private collection)

TBMs, SBDs and F6Fs on the flight deck of aircraft carrier USS *Lexington* during pre-invasion raids on Saipan, June 1944. (National Archives)

US Navy aviator Alexander Vraciu holds up six fingers to signify his kills during the "Great Marianas Turkey Shoot" in June 1944. (United States Navy)

US Marines in the first wave on June 15 have just disembarked on Saipan and keep as low as possible. A burning landing craft can be seen in the background. (National Archives)

Marines in a foxhole during a lull in the battle on Saipan, July 1944. (National Archives)

Marine landing craft moves towards the island of Tinian, near Saipan, on July 24, 1944. (National Archives)

At the end of the Tinian battle, a young Japanese girl from the island's civilian population emerges from the jungle and receives a cup of water from a Marine sergeant. (National Archives)

Marine tanks and infantry advance along a road on jungle-covered Guam island, July 1944. (National Archives)

Marines persuade a lone Japanese survivor to give himself up at the end of the Guam battle. During the fierce Pacific battles, the Japanese defenders usually preferred death to surrender. (National Archives)

Two Marines rest during a brief lull in the fighting for Peleliu island, September 1944. The man to the right clutches a 30-cal. machine gun. (National Archives)

US Marine during action on Peleliu Island. The battle was one of the bloodiest of the Pacific campaign, although after the capture of the island it was generally considered to be of little strategic use. (National Archives)

The *Yamato*, one of the two largest battleships ever built, is hit by a bomb near its forward gun turret during the battle of Leyte Gulf, October 1944. (Naval History and Heritage Command)

Service crew load drop tanks on SB2Cs on board the USS *Lexington* prior to a search mission during the Leyte Gulf battle. (Naval History and Heritage Command)

The USS *Belleau Wood* is burning aft following a hit by a kamikaze in October 1944. Suicide pilots emerged in force during the battle of Leyte Gulf, initially as a temporary measure but, following their success, they became a permanent weapon wielded by the Japanese commanders. (National Archives)

Japanese kamikaze pilots prepare for battle by tightening an auspicious scarf, or *hachimaki*, around their heads. The suicide pilots were initially volunteers, but as the war dragged on, a growing number were ordered to fly to their certain deaths. (Naval History and Heritage Command)

Emaciated Australian and Dutch prisoners of war held in a Japanese camp in Thailand. The four men are suffering from the tropical disease beri beri. (Australian War Memorial)

Crew of the battleship USS *New Jersey* look on as a Japanese prisoner of war is shaved, deloused and bathes himself, late 1944. (National Archives)

Wang Jingwei in the uniform of the east Chinese puppet regime that he headed. (Private collection)

Subhas Chandra Bose, the separatist leader who sought Japanese backing for his endeavor to rid India of British colonial power. (Private collection)

Marines have just disembarked from their landing craft on Iwo Jima in February 1945 and press themselves against the island's volcanic sand before moving inland. (United States Navy)

Flamethrower operator of the 9th Marines runs under fire on Iwo Jima. Flamethrowers, sometimes carried by armored vehicles, were used by both sides in the Pacific War as an efficient means of clearing enemy fortifications. (United States Marine Corps)

American soldiers from the 25th Division advance on the Philippine island of Luzon, passing the body of a Japanese adversary. (United States Army Signal Corps)

Japanese forces surrender to US and Philippine soldiers during fighting in the devastated capital of Manila. (Library of Congress)

Two Marines move along a ridge under enemy fire during the battle of Okinawa, May 1945. (National Archives)

Men of the US Army's 77th Division on Okinawa listen to a radio broadcast announcing the end of the war in Europe. Reports of the collapse of Hitler's Reich aroused little enthusiasm in the Asia Pacific as the combatants expected hostilities to continue for months, if not years, more in their part of the world. (National Archives)

Two British soldiers move through the ruins of a Burmese village on the road to the city of Mandalay, 1945. (Imperial War Museums)

Chinese soldiers meet up in southwestern China, comparing equipment. The man to the left has benefited from supplies from the American ally. (United States Army Signal Corps)

Nuclear cloud over Nagasaki, August 9, 1945. (Office of War Information)

Japanese civil and military officials arrive for the surrender ceremony on board the battleship USS *Missouri* in Tokyo Bay, September 2, 1945. Foreign Minister Shigemitsu Mamoru, who was greatly bothered by his artificial leg before and during the event, is seen in the front row with a cane. (National Archives)

The sky over Tokyo Bay is filled with Allied aircraft on September 2, 1945, in a show of force that leaves no doubt that Japan has been defeated. (United States Navy)

General Douglas MacArthur and Emperor Hirohito at their first meeting in Tokyo, September 1945.
This photo served to underline that the Japanese ruler had renounced his divine status and came as
a shock to many of his subjects. (United States Army)

Chinese Communist leader Mao Zedong, left, and his nationalist rival Chiang Kai-shek meet in China's wartime capital of Chongqing in September 1945. Shortly afterwards they were on opposing sides in a bloody civil war. (Private collection)

Image of defeat: A Japanese soldier walks through the ruins of Hiroshima in September 1945, a month after it has been leveled by a nuclear blast. (National Archives)

Some of the Japanese guards barricaded themselves inside a building with a number of prisoners as hostages and were allowed to evacuate with their weapons in exchange for the lives of the internees. Others were not so lucky. A Japanese guard who had tormented his prisoners for years was shot in the stomach during a brief skirmish and was the object of a gruesome revenge: "Now groaning and writhing on the ground," according to a contemporary account, "he was seized by the legs and dragged to the main building clinic, internees kicking and spitting at him, one or two men even slashing him with knives, and some women burning him with cigaret[te]s as he was pulled past them."[26]

At the same time, soldiers of the 37th Division were also advancing rapidly into Manila, likewise urged on by an impatient MacArthur, and eliminated whatever resistance they met. This was when the going got hard. The Japanese defenders, mostly sailors led by Rear Admiral Iwabuchi Sanji, withdrew to the south of the capital, preparing for a desperate fight to the end. "We are very glad and grateful for the opportunity of being able to serve our country in this epic battle," Iwabuchi said. "Now, with what strength remains, we will daringly engage the enemy. Banzai to the Emperor! We are determined to fight to the last man."[27]

The day after Santo Tomás was freed, the 37th Division reached Old Bilibid prison, where 1,400 military and civilian internees were being kept. Six GIs appeared at the front gate, trying to smash it open, but found it sturdier than they thought. "How the hell do you get in this place," they shouted. "How the hell do you get out," the prisoners yelled back. "We've been trying three years."[28] The soldiers hailed from Ohio, the "Buckeye state," and were surprised to be spoken to in German by some of the liberated prisoners, who were confused by their M1 helmets, adopted by the United States after their capture. "Germans were all right, they thought, for judging from the shooting going on outside the Japs and Nazis were no longer on good terms. Rescue was rescue, no matter the source," a veteran of the 37th Division reminisced. "But they were overjoyed to learn that their rescuers were from the Buckeye State and not from Berlin."[29]

The 11th Airborne Division also moved towards Manila from the south but still met with determined opposition and some of the most formidable hardware prepared by the Japanese in expectation of the assault. At Nichols Field, a US military airfield established before the war, they were shelled by five-inch naval guns, removed from warships and placed in strategic positions. Being forced to halt, a company commander messaged back to headquarters, "Tell Bill Halsey to stop looking for the Jap fleet. It's dug in on Nichols Field."[30]

In parts of the city, the fight proceeded Stalingrad-style, with protracted combat building for building, floor for floor, room for room. When soldiers of the 1st Cavalry entered into Manila Hotel, they were met with a hail of bullets from Japanese positions on the stairs leading to the upper floors. Deadly combat ensued, as the Americans worked their way up, while the Japanese counterattacked from one floor to the next. One group of defenders held on to the mezzanine floor for 24 hours, and it was three days before every Japanese in the building had been killed, leaving it in American hands.[31]

Shortly afterwards, Eichelberger moved into the annex of the hotel, taking in the view of Manila. "I could see the city of Manila gleaming whitely in the sunshine. I could see Corregidor, and the hook of the Cavite peninsula, which curves into Manila Bay. In another direction I could see Balayan and Batangas Bays on the sea, and, inland, Lake Taal in the crater of an extinct volcano and the shimmer of Laguna de Bay," he wrote in his memoirs. "It was strangely like a homecoming. But soon tall plumes of smoke began to rise in Manila, and at evening the tropical sky was crimsoned by many fires. The Japanese were deliberately destroying the magical town which had been traditionally called 'the Pearl of the Orient'."[32]

The almost complete devastation of Manila, including the picturesque Intermuros district dating back to the 16th century, took place despite MacArthur's express wishes to spare the city and its people. He had told Kenney, the commander of his air corps, to avoid bombing the city from the air: "You would probably kill off the Japs all right, but there are several thousand Filipino civilians in there who would be killed, too. The world would hold up its hands in horror if we did anything like that."[33] However, deliberate Japanese arson, a kind of urban scorched-earth tactics, combined with artillery fire on both sides to lay waste to the city. "Every beautiful public building is in ruin, and there is no roof on any building in the Intramuros," Eichelberger wrote in a letter to his wife. "It is all just graveyard."[34]

It bore a resemblance to the fate that had befallen Warsaw the year before, and the same could be said of the senseless killing of civilians. Just as the most brutal units of the German SS somehow found time to massacre the population of the Polish capital, the Japanese, too, went on a bloody rampage among defenseless men, women, and children. "Crazed with alcohol, Japanese officers and men raged through the city in an orgy of lust and destruction that brought back memories of their conduct at the capture of Nanking several years before, when their actions had horrified the civilized world," Kenney wrote later.[35]

One scene out of many took place on an afternoon in the middle of the battle at Manila's Red Cross building. Suddenly a squad of Japanese soldiers entered and began shooting and bayoneting everyone they found. "A soldier shot a young mother with her 10-day baby, along with... the baby's grandmother," said Modesto Farolan, the acting manager of the Philippine Red Cross in later testimony. Farolan himself narrowly escaped death by hiding under a desk and only emerged hours after the Japanese had left.[36] Japanese soldiers also attacked Manila's Spanish consulate, which had become a refuge for numerous Spanish citizens as well as Filipinos. The Japanese shelled the building, then sprayed it with machine-gun bullets, and finally set it on fire. Fifty people were killed.[37]

More than 100,000 civilians died in the battle for Manila. The last Japanese resistance in the city was overcome in early March, after a month of bloody fighting. At the same time, the US forces took back Corregidor, the small, fortified island at the entrance of Manila Bay, in an operation that combined parachute and amphibious assault. It was a moment of immense poignancy for MacArthur since it was from its South Dock that, three years earlier, he had boarded a boat for safety, leaving behind only a vague promise to return. That promise, implausible as it might have sounded at the time, was now fulfilled. "The capture of Corregidor is one of the most brilliant operations in military history," he said. "I see that the flagpole still stands. Have your troops hoist the colors to its peak, and let no enemy ever haul them down."[38]

The battle for Manila was over, but the battle for the Philippines continued. In the period from Christmas 1944 until the end of the war, Eichelberger's Eighth Army had 52 D-days in the archipelago. During one particularly intense 44-day period, his troops carried out 14 major landings and 24 minor ones, for an average of one landing every 36 hours. "There was never a time, during this action-packed interlude, when some task force of my command was not fighting a battle," he later wrote. "And most of the time, hundreds of miles apart, separate task forces were fighting separate battles simultaneously."[39]

For the soldiers involved, the strategic value of the targets, gained at the cost of the blood and sweat of exhausted men, was not always obvious. "Most of the fighting is in inconspicuous little actions, which nobody hears about—mopping up," said Roscoe B. Woodruff, commander of the 24th Division. "In Europe when we advance, we really capture something. Out here we just capture another island, important enough though it may be, that looks much like all other islands. As one doughboy remarked after we had cleared out a small objective—'Well, there's another half million coconuts'."[40]

★ ★ ★

There were no coconuts on Iwo Jima. In fact, there was very little on the Japanese-controlled island apart from volcanic ash, making it unusually inhospitable even in a region where natural conditions often made human habitation next to impossible. What Iwo Jima did have was proximity to Japan, located 800 miles south of Tokyo, and it had flat terrain suitable for airstrips. The presence of Japanese aircraft on the island meant that American bombers heading for Japan from the Marianas had to undertake a significant detour instead of going straight for their targets. That was not the only reason why Iwo Jima would prove valuable in US hands. While its eight square miles made it too small as a base for strategic bombers, it could accommodate fighter escorts for the bombing mission, just as it would enable emergency landings by bombers too damaged or otherwise unable to make it back to the Marianas.[41]

General Kuribayashi Tadamichi, the general commanding the defenses on Iwo Jima, had deep knowledge of the enemy he was facing. Having served as military attaché in Washington DC, he had spent years in the United States, like Admiral Yamamoto Isoroku, who had masterminded the attack on Pearl Harbor. Similar to the admiral, he also had no illusions about the enormous

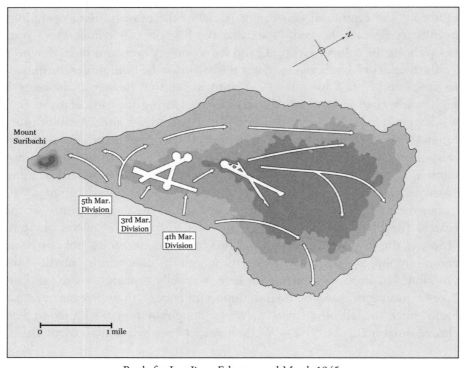

Battle for Iwo Jima, February and March 1945.

power of the adversary. It was "the last country in the world that Japan may fight," he had written to his wife.[42]

Likewise, he had no illusions that he could hold on to Iwo Jima indefinitely, or even that he or any other Japanese on the island would survive, for that matter. However, they could make the enemy pay as dearly as possible for its possession. All civilians had been evacuated in 1944, and by early spring 1945 the island, with its dominant feature, Mount Suribachi, had become a honeycomb of heavily protected and concealed positions, underground living quarters and interlocking tunnels. Twenty thousand defenders were lying in wait, preparing for a subterranean fight to the death, when the invasion fleet arrived in mid-February.

The men on board the ships off Iwo Jima, from the 3rd, 4th, and 5th Marine Divisions, were struck by the tiny size of the island. "It was just so closely compacted. The Japs just had no place to go and they just stuck it out and fought," said Marine Colonel Edwin Pollock.[43] A war correspondent compared it to a miniature Japanese garden, adding that "its stones and rocks were like those contorted, wind-scoured, water-worn boulders which the Japanese love to collect as landscape decorations."[44] The Marines had asked for ten days of uninterrupted naval shelling of this "landscape garden", but the Navy, stretched thinly across the Western Pacific, gave it only three. What the fire support lacked in length of time it seemed to make up for in intensity, and even Kuribayashi from his headquarters deep underground, messaged back to Tokyo, "We need to reconsider the power of bombardment from ships; the violence of the enemy's bombardments is far beyond description."[45]

Still there was plenty more bite left in the Japanese defenses, as the Marines were to find out when they embarked on their landing in the morning of February 19. As the first wave moved towards Iwo Jima on board their landing craft, and the black beach came closer with no sign of the enemy, the Marines silently prayed that the Navy's guns had indeed done their work. "Then all hell breaks loose," said combat cameraman Norman T. Hatch. "The beach comes under all kinds of fire and boats are being blown up and that kind of thing."[46]

After Marine Arthur Talmadge jumped off his Higgins boat, the first thing he saw was a dead Marine floating in the water. "Not very enthusiastic to go on," he remarked laconically.[47] Ralph Simoneau, in the first wave as part of a 60-mm mortar section, found himself standing inside an Amtrak, waiting for orders to hit the beach. "That was really kind of unnerving to be caught there. Because at least if you can dig in a little bit or lay prone you can feel safe. But when you are standing in this coffin, as it were, it was a little scary."[48] Once he was allowed to get out and hit the beach, he found Marines shellshocked by the violent Japanese fire: "There were guys that were just frightened out of their wits… they would sit in that foxhole and they would just be trembling like they were freezing."[49]

Even after the first waves had secured a foothold on the beach, it continued to be a killing zone. The volcanic sand caused the Marines, loaded with heavy packs of ammunition and equipment, to sink in to their ankles, while vehicles got bogged down and were unable to move. "It was just littered with our dead and knocked out machinery, halftracks, Higgins boats, tanks couldn't get up the sand because of the grit on the beach. Everything was full there and it was just a mess," said Marine Robert Amstutz. "I didn't see anything to shoot at. I hunkered down between a knocked-out halftrack and a dead Marine."[50]

Meanwhile, off the island, Marines were waiting for their turn to land, some of them impatiently. "Boy, we need to get in there," one of them said. "Ain't nobody getting hurt. I don't see nobody getting hurt." Later that afternoon, a boat arrived from the beach area with 36 wounded. "That changed their minds right quick, you know," another Marine remarked.[51] The injured brought in gave just an inkling of the hellish scene on the beach, which war correspondent Robert Sherrod wrote about with remarkable candor: "About the dead, whether Jap or American, there was one thing in common. They died with the greatest possible violence. Nowhere in the Pacific war have I seen such badly mangled bodies. Many were cut squarely in half. Legs and arms lay 50 feet away from any body. In one spot on the sand, far from the nearest cluster of dead men, I saw a string of guts 15 feet long."[52]

The Marines gradually made their way inland, but the fighting did not become any less intense. For Simoneau, the Marine in the mortar section, it became a nightmarish battle with an unseen enemy, always hiding in the shadows, appearing only for a few brief seconds to shoot and then disappear again. "You are shooting at shadows. You are shooting at noise," he said. "You would take fire from caves and what have you, but you never saw anybody. You never had anybody in your sights. It was completely different than what you ever imagined that combat would be like."[53]

Adding to the ghostly feel of the island, the volcanic ash was heated from underground streams. Marine Colonel Edwin Pollock remembered how one of his fellow officers had brought a bottle of Scotch whiskey. "We were sleeping on the ground, on the sand. He put his bottle down on the side of his bed and when he woke up the next morning and lifted up the bottle, the bottom fell out of it, and all his whiskey. He couldn't figure out what had happened. It was the heat from the sand, that had broken the bottom of the bottle."[54]

Alvin Orsland, a Marine rifleman, was assigned to a burial detail immediately upon arrival, helping to inter men who had been killed a few days earlier. He noticed first-hand how quickly he became accustomed to the carnage surrounding him. "We would pick up fellows by the arm and all of a sudden you had an arm. We would pick them up by the legs, and you might have a leg," he said. While he was shocked, a group of Marines which had been doing the same job but for two days longer were completely unfazed. "They were able to sit there and eat the old C Rations and K Rations and we couldn't eat a thing. [We thought] these guys are inhumane. But, you know, the second day we were eating right along with them."[55]

Orsland watched from afar when on the third day after the landing, a Marine patrol succeeded in reaching the top of Mount Suribachi and planting a flag. The sight of the Stars and Stripes caused a wave of optimism to spread across the island where Marines were fighting for their lives. "It was crazy," said Orsland. "We figured it was all over with. Everybody screaming and hollering. It was quite a celebration. We, obviously, didn't know what was ahead, nobody did, and I have a strong suspicion that our commanding officers felt the same way. Little did they know."[56]

In fact, more than a month of fighting remained before the Marines had eliminated the last opposition. Often the Marines dealt with caves full of Japanese by simply blowing up the entrances and sealing them off. A Marine described entering into one such cave later on: "In this, strewn, body-to-body just like dominos on top of one another, you'd find Japanese bodies that had suffocated and just collapsed right there."[57] Atrocities were committed on both sides. Amstutz remembered entering into a cave with eight to ten injured Japanese, some of them on stretchers, who had given up the fight. "I suppose they thought we were going to take care of them. Lord, we didn't have enough body bags and we couldn't get our own wounded off part of the time. [Two other Marines] just shot them. I just walked away but they just shot them. They didn't take very many prisoners."[58]

After weeks of intense combat, some Marines got desperate to leave the battlefield. Orsland witnessed how a fellow Marine in his unit managed to pull it off. One morning he came up to him and said, "Orsland, I think it is time for me to get out of here." Orsland replied, "You can't get out of here." He said, "You see that little bush up ahead there? I'm going to crawl up there and I'm going to get my butt up just high enough and I'm going to get a nice crease. I been watching guys going by there and they are getting their wounds right in there." The Marine was gone for half an hour and then crawled back. He showed Orsland how he had been grazed by a Japanese bullet exactly where he wanted it. "Well, I got her, I'm getting out of here. I'm going home."[59]

Nearly all 20,000 Japanese soldiers on the island were killed. A total of 26,000 Marines became casualties, including 6,800 who lost their lives. "A lot of boys died that shouldn't have died. We got slaughtered there," said Michael Long, Marine, who carried a 50-caliber machine gun. "They was waiting for us and they set us up. They laid down like they were going to give up easy, they all hid underneath the ground and on the crevices and stuff and then they bounced on us and nobody had a chance. They slaughtered us for a while until we got the upper hand then. Finally, we gained the upper hand and we took over the war, we killed them."[60]

The first B-29 made an emergency landing on March 4, at a time when the last Japanese defenders were still offering resistance from their underground positions. But many of those involved were left with the feeling that they had paid a steep price and questioned if it was worth it. "I don't think Iwo Jima should have been taken, because of the cost to take it," said Charles Adair, a US Navy amphibious expert. "And I don't think the value was there. I don't think it was needed, and if every plane that landed on Iwo Jima that had to critically were added up, and the pilots were added up, I'll bet they wouldn't anywhere near total 25,000. That's a contrary opinion!"[61]

Duong Thieu Chi, assistant of the governor of the Indochinese province of Nam Dinh, did a fair amount of traveling in his official capacity, even in the critical year of 1945, but he always avoided eating at restaurants and streets stalls. He could not be sure if the meat that was served was not human flesh. Famine ravaged large parts of northern Indochina, and cannibalism was rampant. Duong was sent to investigate two cases. In one of the cases, a murderer devoured his victims and sold off the flesh he could not finish himself. In the other, two parents, driven to madness by hunger, had killed their own child and eaten it.[62]

The famine lasted for five months in early 1945 but its causes could be traced back to the year before, and similar to the mass starvation that had struck British-ruled India earlier in the war, it was the result of both natural calamities and official policies. Drought and insect attacks caused the spring harvest in 1944 to drop steeply below expectations, and the following autumn devastating typhoons cut down the agricultural output dramatically.[63] The worst effects of the hunger disaster could have been mitigated if rice had been sent to the north from southern regions, where the crops were more plentiful. However, American bombing had destroyed bridges, railroads, and other infrastructure, and anyway both the Japanese army and the French colonial authorities, who were still in charge despite the presence of large Japanese forces, prioritized the transportation of their own military forces over vital food supplies for the civilian population.[64]

Between one and two million people died as a result of the 1945 mass starvation in Indochina. This overall figure covered vast regional variations, and in the worst hit areas of northern Indochina, society teetered on the brink of collapse.[65] The hamlet of Luong Phu, an example among thousands, had been considered prosperous by neighboring communities in the pre-war years. Out of a population of 1,379, nearly 600 died from famine and accompanying conditions. One family serves as an illustration of the range of calamities striking the population: it lost two members to epidemic diseases, one who died from eating an unripe papaya, and one who died from corporal punishment after having stolen rice.[66]

A French witness described the miserable scenes played out in Indochina in the spring of 1945: "To behold these human forms more hideous than the ugliest of the animals, to behold these corpses curled up at the roadside, having as clothes and shrouds only some stalks of straw, one is ashamed of mankind."[67] Some hunger-stricken peasants simply locked themselves up at home and waited to die. Others hit the roads and started wandering, often ending up in the big cities. A resident of Hanoi wrote in his diary about his impressions after walking through streets littered with starving beggars coming in from the countryside: "Sounds of crying as at a funeral. Elderly twisted women, naked kids huddled against the wall or lying inside a mat, fathers and children prostrate along the road, corpses hunched up like fetuses, an arm thrust out as if to threaten."[68]

The food scarcity also affected those inhabitants of Indochina who were not directly pushed to the limit by starvation, but still saw a precipitous drop in the standard of living due to steep prices in rice. The result was that the French colonial authorities became even more unpopular than before. The fact that the French administration had helped prevent the kind of mass conscription of forced labor that had happened in other parts of Japanese-controlled Asia mattered less.[69] To many Indochinese it made a much deeper impression to see sharply dressed Japanese officers walk the streets of the major cities, in humiliating contrast to the often flabby-looking French colonial troops.[70]

Therefore, there was widespread anticipation of better times when on March 9, 1945, the Japanese Army in Indochina took over control from the French colonial authorities in a swift coup. French officers were taken into custody, and their soldiers ordered to lay down their arms. Those who resisted were met with trademark brutality. A few French garrisons opposed the Japanese move, and in some cases extended firefights took place. At the end of the battles, French prisoners were bayoneted or beheaded.[71] Defeated foreign legionnaires were forced to watch as Japanese soldiers hauled down the French flag, tore it to shreds, and stamped it into the ground.[72] Rapes of French women were commonplace.[73] Duong Thieu Chi, the official who had witnessed instances of cannibalism, was shocked to see a senior French colonial official be thrown to the floor by a Japanese captain and then beaten bloody with the hilt of a sword.[74]

The new Japanese rulers took steps to improve the food supply, for example by handing out grain from public granaries under much publicity, and also ensured a fairer distribution of rice where it was needed.[75] However, they were less enthusiastic about nationalistic sentiments in the population, who suddenly believed that colonialism might be a thing of the past, resulting in mass gatherings and strikes. "The defense of Indochina against the enemy outside the country will be completely ineffective if domestic order is not perfectly maintained," the Japanese military authorities warned in a statement.[76] The people of Indochina gradually came to understand that their new masters were perhaps not all that different from the old ones.

At the same time as Indochina was boiling over, another deadly cocktail of starvation and growing violence was developing in the former Dutch East Indies. The Dutch-Indonesian author Elizabeth Vuyk, who was allowed some freedom of movement due to her Asian ancestry, witnessed a female beggar lying in front of a bakery, barely surviving: "She lies on a piece of old matting, another strip of it bound around her waist, around her enormous swollen belly. Her arms and legs are sticks and her face bloated from oedema, so that her eyes appear to be deeply sunken. The child is a skeleton clawing like an animal at the empty flaps of skin that are her breasts."[77] The woman was just one example of a tragedy of almost unfathomable proportions. It is estimated that as many as 2.5 million people died from famine during the war years, with the vast majority of fatalities taking place in 1944 and 1945.[78]

It was the disastrous result of a steep drop in the production of vital crops, which had characterized the entire Japanese occupation. Rice output fell by one third during the period, and soybeans were down by 60 percent. The only product that stayed at prewar levels was quinine, extracted from the Cinchona-tree, which the Japanese needed to fight malaria.[79] Unlike India and Indochina, the starvation in the East Indies was almost exclusively man-made and rendered all the more tragic by the fact that the densely populated island of Java had been self-sufficient in rice, and even able to export some, before the war.[80]

One factor behind the late-war disaster was the recruitment of able-bodied men for forced labor, reducing the manpower available for the farms.[81] Even more important was the collapse of the transport system, mostly based on a fairly dense networks of railroads. The Dutch had blown up bridges and destroyed part of the infrastructure as they withdrew in 1942, and the situation was further exacerbated by the Japanese occupation authorities as they cut down rail transport due to fuel shortages and reserved a large part of the remaining rolling stock for military uses.[82]

Although the causes were complex, unlike the situation in Indochina, the growing hardship resulted in an increase in anti-Japanese sentiment among Indonesians. A Japanese technical expert employed at an East Indies harbor heard from a local contact that "people there spoke openly about the arrival of the Americans and when the Dutch would be back here again." The Indonesian population also took an anti-American song propagated by the Japanese and changed the lyrics so that it became targeted at the Rising Sun symbol of Japan: "Destroy the red ball! Come soon, America!"[83]

Those in the East Indies unfortunate enough to be called up as labor for the Japanese forces suffered especially from malnourishment or starved outright. By 1945, emaciated and sick laborers dying or already dead were no longer an uncommon sight in the cities. The countryside was hard hit too, and the lack of food was to a great extent blamed on the Japanese, who requisitioned provisions from farmers, often paying with cash which was normally useless in an economy ravaged by inflation. A popular slogan in circulation reflected the sentiment perfectly: "The Japanese must die—we are starving!"[84]

On February 14, the unhappiness with the Japanese occupation exploded into violence on Java. Mortar rounds began falling around Hotel Sakura, which served as the living quarters of Japanese officers in the city of Blitar in the eastern part of the island. At the same time, machine-gun fire was directed at buildings occupied by the Japanese secret police, the Kempeitai. A revolt, long in the planning phase, was underway, and the perpetrators were soldiers whom the Japanese themselves had trained, members of PETA, short for Pembela Tanah Ayer, or Defenders of the Fatherland.[85]

The rising was triggered by a series of grievances, including a requirement that the Indonesians were to salute any Japanese soldier or officer, regardless of rank, but again lack of food was one of the prime motives. In one of the incidents prior to the rebellion, three PETA officers had been dining at a restaurant in Blitar when they saw a column of trucks arriving from Gayasan, a construction site outside the city limit where forced labor was employed: "They were being dumped like living corpses from transport trucks near the Blitar station. The three men in the restaurant were stunned for a moment by the ghastly scene. 'From Gayasan' were the only words they could utter."[86]

In the course of the short-lived rebellion, the mutineers killed a number of Japanese and Chinese. Rather than seeking to suppress the rising with brute force, the Japanese military appealed to the ringleaders and brought about a negotiated end to the rebellion. It was testimony to the constraints that the Japanese Army was under, forcing it to conserve its forces whenever necessary. At the same time, however, it reflected fundamental differences with Japan's Axis partners, especially Germany, which would have responded to the same type of challenge with extreme violence.[87] The Japanese Army could be remarkably pragmatic when it needed to.

Michael Bak, the quartermaster on board the destroyer USS *Franks* who had expected a long war at the beginning of 1945, suddenly changed his views and became more optimistic in March. He was at sea, and he witnessed a fleet of B-29 Superfortresses for the first time. "We saw many, many B-29s—they filled the whole sky—and started going toward Japan. It was just an awesome, awesome sight. That's why we had no fear. That's why we thought maybe, seeing those planes going toward Japan that the war would be ended sooner. I never heard of a B-29 until we first saw them in the sky and it was a nice feeling."[88] In Japan, the liberal journalist Kiyosawa Kiyoshi watched as row after row of B-29s flew towards the center of Tokyo, getting a similar impression of American might. "The B-29s were flying at low altitude, and their silver wings were revealed in the searchlights as they flew at a leisurely pace," he wrote in his diary. "The B-29s were clearly outlined against the sky and indeed pretty."[89] Second Lieutenant Kohatsu Satohide, a fighter pilot whose job was to intercept B-29s, remembered seeing the giant silhouettes of the Americans bombers against the sky and feeling increasingly hopeless. "Our fighters were so small," he said. "It was like an eagle versus a sparrow."[90]

That same month, the US strategic bombing offensive against Japan entered into a new, more sinister phase. The daylight precision bombing against previously selected industrial objectives that had been attempted in the early part of the offensive had proven of less value than originally anticipated. The alternative was indiscriminate area bombing of industrial and residential areas. It was introduced by General Curtis LeMay, a veteran bomber commander who had built up a fearful reputation in Europe, for the first time on March 9, 1945. A total of 1,667 tons of bombs were dropped over 15 square miles, consisting of some of the most densely populated parts of Tokyo.[91]

Normally, bomber crews during World War II were shielded by distance from witnessing the carnage they caused. However, the bombings of Tokyo and other major Japanese cities were so massive, and conducted at such as low altitude, that a visceral feeling was unavoidable. Philip Webster, co-pilot on the B-29 *Sentimental Journey,* described one mission over the Japanese capital: "It was bright enough to read a newspaper, just from the light of Tokyo burning," he wrote in his diary.[92] American airman Chester Marshall recalled a sweet smell permeating through to the cabin of his B-29. Someone asked, "What is that I smell?" and a fellow crew member replied, "Well, that's flesh burning." Many years later he still recalled the sickening feeling. "I couldn't eat anything for two or three days. You know it was nauseating, really."[93]

On the ground it was hell on earth in the evening of March 9. "The drone of the planes was an overwhelming roar, shaking earth and sky," an eyewitness said. "Everywhere, incendiary bombs were falling."[94] Ray "Hap" Halloran, an American B-29 navigator who had been shot down earlier and was now kept prisoner at a horse stable, could follow the bombing mainly from the sound of men, women, and children running by outside screaming, and the howl of the firestorm created by the incendiary bombs. "My guard just tied my hands and my feet. I could not move. I was just there waiting to burn. That was a bad, bad thing," he later recalled. "I heard B-29s crash. Two of them pretty close by. I heard the fire while I could not see out the front door. The stable was just solid red glare."[95]

Many Tokyo residents survived by sheltering in firebreaks and rivers, even though in the smaller canals, the water was brought to the boiling point by the heat. Panic struck many who were trapped by the blaze and tried unsuccessfully to dash through the flames.[96] A woman carried her baby on her back as she fled her home, and while she herself survived, the child disappeared in the nightly inferno, leaving only gruesome signs on the woman of what had happened. "Where [the child's] legs had touched her body there were horrible burns. Her elbows, where she was probably holding him to keep him from falling off, were burned so that you could see the raw flesh."[97]

The official toll from the night, which was the most destructive on any Japanese city during the war, was 83,793 dead and 40,918 wounded, and it took 25 days before all the dead had been removed from the ruins.[98] An official at the Home Affairs Ministry reported the situation: "People were unable to escape. They were found later piled upon the bridges, roads, and in the canals… We were instructed to report on actual conditions. Most of us were unable to do this because of horrifying conditions beyond imagination."[99] A Tokyo radio broadcast stated that "the sea of flames which enclosed the residential and commercial sections of Tokyo was reminiscent of the holocaust of Rome, caused by the Emperor Nero."[100]

Exaggerating the casualty numbers, LeMay wrote later in his memoirs that "we scorched and boiled and baked to death more people in Tokyo on that night of March 9–10 than went up in vapor at Hiroshima and Nagasaki combined."[101] He himself believed he might have been prosecuted as a war criminal if the United States had lost the war, but put his view on the matter bluntly: "There are no innocent civilians. It is their government and you are fighting a people, you are not trying to fight an armed force anymore. So it doesn't bother me so much to be killing the so-called innocent bystanders."[102]

Halloran, the downed B-29 navigator, survived the bombing on March 9 and 10, and some days later he was taken to Ueno Zoo north of the Imperial Palace and placed inside an empty cage. "I think they were really putting me there on exhibit. I don't know. They tied my hands, took all my clothes from me," he said. "They tied me to the bars and then the people could come by and see. I think the message was, 'Do not fear these B-29s. They are not super people, look at them. Look at this one before you'."[103]

Despite propaganda efforts such as these, it was unavoidable that some Japanese would start thinking they were up against an unstoppable enemy, since night after night following the March 9 firebombing, the home islands were targeted by new waves of B-29s visiting the same kind of horror on other parts of Tokyo, and other major cities. The fact that the giant American machines met very little resistance fed into growing discontent which was directed at the rulers.

A Yokohama resident vented these emotions: "I did not receive any help from the government or anyone else. We just had to look after ourselves; nothing was given to us. I felt bitter toward the government and wished we had never started the war."[104] Obata Tadayoshi, one of Japan's influential elder statesmen, had now come to the conclusion that the idea of "sure victory" still propagated by some the press, should really be replaced with "sure death." "Our leaders should frankly reveal the real state of affairs, while their people on their part must be ready for any emergency."[105]

Eight days after the raid on March 10, Hirohito, who had said as late as the previous month that he believed the war was still winnable,[106] inspected the streets of Tokyo. The sight that met him reminded him of the World War I battlefields he had visited in Europe as a young man, and it was worse than the devastation he had witnessed in 1923 after the greatest earthquake in modern Japanese history had leveled major parts of the capital. "It pains me deeply," he told an aide. "Tokyo has become scorched earth."[107]

Many high-ranking Japanese were ready to fight to the bitter end, but some were not, and they were quietly pinning their hopes on the emperor, the only individual with the ability to stop the bloodshed, waiting for the opportune moment. Perhaps that moment was approaching. Foreign Minister Shigemitsu Mamoru wrote a private memorandum to himself, taking a hard look at Japan's situation: "From His Majesty I have already heard about his personal wishes that Japan must take necessary measures to conclude the war at the appropriate time—even at the expense of [having to make] territorial concessions; and now is the time that we should examine this matter thoroughly."[108]

CHAPTER SEVEN

Sunset

April–June 1945

In the morning of April 1, *Yamato*, one of the two largest battleships ever built, was moored at no. 26 buoy in the Japanese port of Kure, waiting for minor repairs. The men were going about their routine duties when, without warning, they were startled by a metallic voice over the ship's loudspeaker, "Commence sailing preparation from 0815; weighing anchor at 1000!" The rumor spread like wildfire: the Americans had landed on the island of Okinawa, 600 miles to the south. The officers and sailors scrambled to get ready. Roll calls were taken to ensure no one was left ashore, since missing a ship going into battle was punishable by death. Amid the hectic activity, a mood of exhilaration spread through the ship. Despite its size, *Yamato* had seen limited action during the past more than three years of war, and its huge guns had fired at enemy vessels only once, during the battle of Leyte Gulf. Now was finally the chance to make a difference. *Yamato* with her crew of more than 3,000 men left Kure at 10am sharp.[1]

While the *Yamato* was getting underway, the American invasion fleet, assisted by a much smaller force from the British Royal Navy, was already unloading troops by the thousand onto the 70-mile-long island of Okinawa. It was a necessary stepping stone on the road to Tokyo, assuming that Japan would fight to the bitter end, the way Germany was doing in Europe. A memorandum from Nimitz's headquarters listed the arguments why Okinawa was needed ahead of the final assault on the home islands: "Okinawa gives us: 1. A base for supplying bomber and fighter cover for invasion of either China or Japan or both. 2. A good anchorage and naval supply base within 400 miles of the coast of Japan. 3. A forward staging area. 4. An important base for furthering the war of attrition, in which sustained heavy bombing and air-sea blockade are our major weapons."[2]

Marking the culmination of a war that had seen previous records of naval warfare successively broken, the US-led fleet at Okinawa was the biggest ever assembled.[3] It consisted of over 1,500 ships and vessels of various forms and sizes, and it carried more than 80,000 Marines and nearly 100,000 soldiers into battle.[4] On L-Day—"L" stood for "Love"—the fleet disembarked two Marine divisions and two Army divisions on a seven-mile stretch of beach on the western side of Okinawa. An observer wrote about the demonstration of American might in downright poetic terms: "The approaching landing waves possessed something of the color and pageantry of medieval warfare, advancing relentlessly with their banners flying. In the calm sunlight of the morning, it was indeed an impressive spectacle."[5]

Prior to the invasion, the usual air and naval bombardment had taken place, only even more ferocious than what had been targeted at earlier islands. The diary of a Japanese superior private suggested what it was like to be at the receiving end, describing a full day of near-continuous air raids. "While some fly around overhead and strafe, the big bastards fly over the airfield and drop bombs. The ferocity of the bombing is terrific. It really makes me furious," he

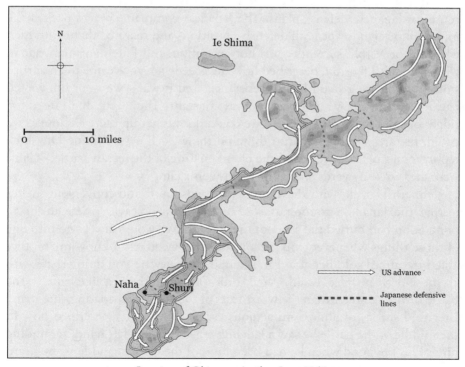

Invasion of Okinawa, April to June 1945.

wrote. "What the hell kind of bastards are they? Bomb from 0600 to 1800! I have to admit, though, that when they were using tracers this morning, it was really pretty."[6]

The landing on the first day proceeded with minimal bloodshed. Al Adkins from the 6th Marine Division had tried to be shot at when landing both in the Marshalls and on Guam, but when he set foot on Okinawa, nothing happened initially. "We were startled. We didn't know what happened. We came in and went on about our business," he said.[7] This was the result of Japanese tactics similar to those employed at Peleliu and Iwo Jima, which discarded most attempts to fight the invader on the beach and instead exact a steep price from camouflaged and fortified positions. The Americans were aware of that. "Our landings in Okinawa have gone better than our wildest dreams could have led us to expect," Spruance wrote to his wife, but acknowledged that it was unlikely to stay that smooth. "There are many thousands of Jap troops on Okinawa and undoubtedly they will put up a stiff fight and have to be killed."[8]

Spruance was exactly right in his prediction. As the soldiers and Marines moved inland, they closed in on the ancient castle of Shuri, which was at the center of Japanese defense plans. The Japanese commanders had packed the mountainous landscape with defensive positions and manned them with men who had been told surrender was not an option. Bill Filter, an infantryman with the 96th Division, described how the speedy advance came to an abrupt stop: "We hit their main line of resistance, and it was—we went up, we fell back. We went up, we fell back. It was constant. They were dug into those ridges of solid rock," he said. "All we could do was get up there as close as we could, fire artillery directly into those portholes."[9] The 1st Marine Division's report for a single day reflected the bloody nature of the seesaw battle: "Gains were measured by yards won, lost, then won again."[10]

Kenneth Harrell, with the 1st Marine Division, found convenient shelter during the Japanese counterattacks, in the form of caves where the local population had buried the ashes of their dead. "We would always go into one of those things whenever we'd get a real big heavy attack. I know my mother asked me after I told her about it, she said, 'What were you doing there with all those dead people?' I said, 'Well, I didn't want to be just like 'em'."[11] The battle turned deadlier than the worst fears of the men participating, and many later told stories of almost miraculous escapes. Bill Filter described how in the middle of the battle he saw a ladybug crawl onto his left hand, reminding him of his boyhood when he had been fond of the insects. Suddenly he heard the whine of a mortar shell approaching. "I hugged the earth, and it was a dud. Yes, it hit and skidded, and just went bumpity-bump-bum-bump down the mountain, and never exploded. That's where the ladybug luck came in."[12]

The battle for Okinawa lasted weeks, even months. It was not until the end of June that organized Japanese resistance ended, and the bodies of the Japanese commander and his chief of staff were found with what a war diary described as "indisputable evidence of hara-kiri."[13] Some of the last combat took place near Oroku Naval Base, where last remnants of the defenders were still fighting a desperate battle in early June. General Lemuel Shepherd, the commander of the 6th Marine Division, described how Okinawa eventually developed into numerous battles-within-the-battle: "Despite the powerful converging attack of three regiments, the advance was slow, laborious, and bitterly opposed. The capture of each defensive locality was a problem in itself, carefully thought out planning and painstaking execution."[14]

In the end, as elsewhere in the Pacific, it was American material superiority, supported by a well-oiled logistical apparatus reaching all the way back to the US west coast, which determined the outcome, but it was more than that. It was also an expression of the confident expertise in handling sophisticated state-the-art machinery which the US Army had gained through more than three years of war. Robert Neiman, a Marine tank officer, watched one of the last advances during the battle of Okinawa, marveling at the smooth operation of the American military machine: "The 8th Marines' attack went like clockwork. It was really a pleasure to watch fresh, well-trained marine fire teams at work. The fire teams went out—some men rushing, some providing covering fire—and then the tanks came rolling through. You could see that everybody knew everybody else. They went right on through their objective with hardly a pause, and with relatively minor casualties. Bing, bing, bing—just like clockwork."[15]

Off Okinawa, parts of the invasion fleet were facing dangers comparable to those endured by the invasion army. Kamikaze attacks, which had been used in significant numbers during the battle of Leyte Gulf the year before, reached a massive scale during the battle of Okinawa. Arthur Aicklen, a machinist on board fleet oiler USS *Taluga*, was onboard when the vessel took a direct hit from a suicide plane. "I ran up to the boat deck. And some fellows were going over the side when I was climbing and they were screaming. They were on fire... The whole starboard side of the bridge was gone, and that's where the kamikaze hit," he said. The pilot had been hurled out of his cockpit and was lying amid the destruction he had caused. "He had his little rabbit fur cap on lying there and all his intestines, everything was lying out on the deck."[16]

Kamikazes contributed to making Okinawa the deadliest of any campaign the US Navy participated in during World War II.[17] "One of the most effective weapons that the Japanese developed, in my opinion, was the use of the suicide bombers. The suiciders hurt the Navy badly at Okinawa," Admiral Richmond K. Turner, one of the senior naval commanders in the battle, said in a speech delivered after the war.[18] A total of 32 vessels were sunk during the battle, and 368 were damaged, mostly due to kamikaze attack. Over 4,900 sailors were killed, and roughly the same number injured.[19]

The toll could have been even higher if the invasion fleet had not introduced new tactics in the form of a system of destroyers patrolling along the outer perimeters, performing picket duty and informing the main body of the fleet when kamikazes were approaching. According to Noel A. M. Gayler, a naval aviator, the fighters dispatched to shoot down the incoming enemy planes were usually highly effective, but even so, some managed to slip through and steered their plane towards the first ship they saw. "What is remarkable is that so many missed," he said. "When you think about it, to drive an airplane into a ship is the simplest thing in the world. There's no reason why you should miss, nor is it a question of flinching at the last moment, because you're just as dead if you dive in the water as if you dive into a ship."[20]

The naval officers involved in the Okinawa operation advocated a greater effort to target the kamikaze aircraft on the ground, before they even took off, but were not satisfied with the results. Halsey asked Spruance how successful American planes based in the Philippines had been in eliminating targets in Taiwan, hoping that they had been targeting aircraft earmarked for suicide missions. "They've destroyed a great many sugar mills, railroad trains, and other equipment," Spruance replied, with a touch of sarcasm in his voice. Halsey blew up, "Sugar mills can't damage our fleet! Why the hell don't they destroy their *planes?*"[21]

The battle for Okinawa became unusually gruesome because of the large number of civilian casualties. The American drive across the Pacific had begun at Tarawa in late 1943 where there was virtually no one except the combatants themselves. On Saipan the following year, the US forces came across a sizable number of civilian settlers and were forced to watch in horror as many of them obeyed the orders of the military authorities and committed suicide rather than surrender. Okinawa was similar, but even more densely populated, with nearly half a million people, mostly of Okinawan descent, different both ethnically and culturally from the Japanese.[22]

The Americans got a hint of what was in store even before the invasion of Okinawa proper. In late March, soldiers of the 77th Division seized the Kerama islands, about 20 miles to the west, and witnessed how old men cut the throats of small children and young girls rather than give themselves and their families up. "We yelled at them to stop, but it did no good," a GI recalled.[23] When invading Ie Shima, another island near Okinawa, American soldiers again were witnessing how war exacted an awful toll among the young and innocent, according to a modern unit history: "For two days, the naked body of a young baby had lain in the road in front of the 2nd Platoon's night defensive position and each day the men had seen it. Just looking at the body had deeply affected the men. On the third day, they were devastated when they saw it crushed beneath the threads of a tank moving forward to attack."[24]

On Okinawa, dead civilians were everywhere. A Marine later recalled that the first dead person he saw on the island was a woman. "You just shot everything that moved. You had to. Because the Japanese would dress like them at times and so you couldn't tell who was what. And at night you'd just kill anything that moved. It was a tragic, tragic thing. Lots of people killed," he said.[25] Another Marine remembered coming across a circle of GIs near a road. They were "quite animated" and he assumed they were playing a game of craps. "Then as we passed them, I could see they were taking turns raping an oriental woman. I was furious but our outfit kept marching by as though nothing unusual was going on."[26]

The *Yamato* never made it to Okinawa. Commanded by Vice Admiral Itō Seiichi, it sortied Japan's Inland Sea on April 6 accompanied by a light cruiser and eight destroyers and was seen off with a message from Admiral Ozawa Jisaburō, the commander-in-chief of the Combined Fleet, to "render this operation the turning point of the war."[27] The battle that lay before it ended up in almost the exact opposite fashion, as perhaps the worst anticlimax in the Japanese Navy's history. Signals intelligence, read like an open book by the American codebreakers, had alerted the US side to the plans to deploy the ship,[28] and it was sighted by a reconnaissance plane in the morning of April 7.[29]

The crew aboard the *Yamato* spotted the first American planes over the horizon at 12:32, and over the next two hours, the battleship and its accompanying ships were subjected to wave after wave of relentless attacks by American airplanes and, given no aircover, it could do little despite its impressive anti-aircraft armament. The ship was already listing dangerously when the final attack set in at 14:00, and twenty minutes later, the deck was nearly vertical.[30] When all hope was out, Vice Admiral Itō shook hands with his staff officer and walked alone into his cabin. He was never seen again.[31]

The *Yamato* disappeared under the waves shortly afterwards. Only 23 officers and 246 men, or roughly one in ten, survived.[32]

In retrospect, it was clear that the *Yamato* had been headed for Okinawa, but when it became apparent in early April that it had left Kure harbor, this set off much more fantastical speculation among Allied intelligence operatives about its ultimate destination, according to Captain Joseph Muse Worthington of the US Navy: "Intelligence reports indicated she was sailing but we did not know whether she would head south for Okinawa or head east. There was a very strong indication she would head east for San Francisco in hopes of making a raid on the United Nations Conference that was just opening up for the President."[33] Similar reports of a planned Japanese naval attack on the upcoming UN meeting reached Admiral Halsey, who was in the United States at the time and was placed in command of a Mid-Pacific Striking Force aimed at meeting the Japanese assault if it were to materialize.[34]

As it turned out, Franklin D. Roosevelt never made it to San Francisco for the conference, which opened at the end of the month. After having won the election in November and embarked on an unprecedented fourth term in office, he died on April 12 in Warm Springs, Georgia, from an intracerebral hemorrhage, aged 63. To those who had seen him in person during his last months, it was hardly a surprise. Submarine skipper Lawson P. Ramage was received by Roosevelt in the White House in early 1945 and was appalled by his appearance: "I didn't recognize the man. His face looked like it was about two inches wide. His profile was still good, but he was just wasted away, and it didn't look as if he had any legs in his pants. He looked like he was just kind of set up in the chair, which he probably was. A very sick man."[35]

To soldiers and sailors spread across the Asia Pacific, who had known nothing about the president's poor health, news of his death was a shock. Marine Ralph Simoneau was in Camp Tarawa when the report reached him. For many of the young men, he was the only president they had ever known. "I think he was probably the most liked president that we ever had by most everyone. That was really devastating. I don't think there was a dry eye in the camp at that time."[36] Marine Raymond Strohmeyer was fighting on Okinawa when he heard the news and did not spend much time talking about it. "We were too busy fighting," he said. "We didn't even know who was vice president. I didn't know who would take his place."[37]

By this time, Harry S. Truman had already taken over as president and assumed the vast and heightened responsibilities entailed at a time of global war. He soon made it clear that he was not deviating from his predecessor's non-negotiable demand for complete Japanese capitulation. "The longer the war lasts, the greater will be the suffering and hardships which the people of Japan will undergo—all in vain," he said, shortly after assuming the presidency. "Our blows will not cease until the Japanese military and naval forces lay down their arms in unconditional surrender."[38]

The report of Roosevelt's death gave rise to one of the most bizarre official Japanese statements of the entire war. At a time when Japanese cities were being firebombed by American planes on a nightly basis, incinerating men, women, and children; when Japan was preparing to defend the home islands to the last person; and when it was making plans to execute all Allied POWs, the country's new prime minister, Admiral Suzuki Kantaro, publicly extended his condolences to the people of the United States. "I must admit that Roosevelt's leadership has been very effective and has been responsible for the Americans' advantageous position today," he said. "For that reason I can easily understand the great loss his passing means to the American people and my profound sympathy goes to them."[39]

Time magazine reacted with disbelief, describing it as a reflection of the "unfathomable" character of the Japanese.[40] The surprise was not made any less by the fact that the Japanese press gave up on any easy propaganda gain from the president's death, instead quoting former Ambassador to the US Nomura Kichisaburō, the man who had carried out negotiations in Washington at the time of the Pearl Harbor attack, as saying that "America's war policy will not be affected."[41] It was indeed a challenge for the contemporary American public to make sense of the sentiment, and even at a distance of eight decades it remains mysterious.

The original Japanese report provides some of the answer, describing the premier's reaction as indicative of high exalted moral character and arguing that it was "not strange coming from a man of large caliber as the new Premier is."[42] Indeed, it may reflect a pragmatism with deep roots in Japanese culture, originally meant to nip vendettas in the bud. "Japanese people make an effort to forgive an offender after his death or after he receives punishment," according to a modern Japanese observer. "It is the wisdom which developed in long history in order to cut off the chain of hate."[43]

While the Japanese premier's statement on Roosevelt's demise was meant to project a magnanimous attitude, propaganda leaflets dropped over American positions on Okinawa a few days later, were of a more unforgiving nature:

"The dreadful loss that led your late leader to death will make you orphans on this island. The Japanese special attack corps will sink your vessels to the last destroyer. You will witness it realized in the near future."[44] This was wishful thinking and recognized by the Americans as such.

The same was true for the main Japanese propaganda outlet meant for the US troops—the nightly broadcast by "Tokyo Rose," the nickname used for a range of English-speaking Japanese women appearing on Japanese radio trying to appeal to American servicemen with popular music and reports about US defeats. "Rose would tell us we were risking our lives, getting killed by their soldiers and airmen, while back home our wives and girlfriends were going out with guys," recalled Marine officer Robert M. Neiman. "This was a big laugh, but we listened because the music was good."[45] Michael Bak, on board the destroyer USS *Franks*, recalled being allowed to listen to the broadcasts: "I believe the *Franks* was reported sunk three times by 'Tokyo Rose'. They mistook us several times for a cruiser."[46]

The real situation became clear to the Americans by listening to internal Japanese communication via Magic, getting a first-hand impression of the desperate conditions stretching the Japanese war economy to breaking point, and sometimes beyond. Noel A. M. Gayler, a naval aviator, recalled listening to messages on supply difficulties and frantic requests: "We received some remarkably revealing disclosures of how close to being on the uppers the Japanese were. For instance, we saw proposals to make aviation fuel out of pine root oil and sort of desperate measures like that. We picked up a lot of that."[47]

Even more tangible evidence that the Japanese military was exhausted came in the form of skies gradually emptying of its planes. "I don't want to be flippant about it," said Gayler, "but there weren't enough Japanese to go around. The most dangerous thing was people diving on the same pilot."[48] American submarines experienced a similar challenge, as a dwindling part of the Pacific was even reasonably safe to Japanese military and commercial shipping. "The oceans out there that had been ours early in the war were no longer ours," said submarine captain Roy S. Benson. "There were less and less areas where we could go and try to find some targets."[49]

Mexico entered into the fray in a modest way. In the spring of 1945, 201st Squadron, a group of pilots known as the "Aztec Eagles" flying P-47 fighters, was deployed in the Philippines. "The Mexican flag conquers gloriously on the Philippine front," the *El Nacional* newspaper boasted.[50] The pilots were used mainly for close tactical support of ground operations, and at the same time made a name for themselves because of rowdy off-duty escapades.[51] The deployment, which ended abruptly due to serious losses of pilots and planes, had mainly symbolic impact, since it served to underline the common cultural heritage of Mexico and the Philippines as former Spanish colonies while also indicating that Japan was not just fighting the United States and a few other English-speaking countries.

Back home in Japan, the military tried to put a positive spin on events, attempting perversely to turn even downright defeats into minor victories. "Something like Iwo Jima is simply nothing more than an electrical spark, and the war begins now," a colonel was overheard saying.[52] The Army also held overly optimistic views of the general situation. "While Japan is still occupying large tracts of enemy land, the enemy only has laid a small hand on Japanese territory," the war minister, General Anami Korechiga, said at a senior Cabinet meeting. "Our conditions for peace with the United States and the United Kingdom should reflect this reality."[53]

Despite the deep discrepancy with the actual situation, the Japanese Army's perspective, and the way it was reflected in the official propaganda, seemed to be generally believed by the population. There had been no great enthusiasm in December 1941, when war with the United States broke out, but if many Japanese had been apathetic when the war began, now that the war was about to end, they were curiously slow to face the stark realities. By late 1944, only about 10 percent were certain that Japan would be defeated, a figure that exceeded 20 percent only in the spring of 1945.[54]

Just as the Japanese leaders had entered the war with little faith in the American public's stomach for a long, bloody war, now they seemed to have perhaps too much confidence in the Japanese people's ability to withstand hardship. Indeed, as the material superiority of the enemies was becoming ever more obvious, it was expected of the Japanese that they would make up for that shortcoming with a more robust fighting spirit. A doctor in Hiroshima, which had been left largely intact from major bombing, described the general mood: "It is without doubt the truth that the Japanese fought this war relying on the gods, rather than on machines... The leaders taught that Japan is guarded by the gods, even if it does not have planes, guns and battleships. Therefore, if you fight with all your might you will win."[55]

Still, some Japanese started questioning quietly if even the best morale in the world would be enough. "When air raids got severe, and there was no opposition by our planes and factories were destroyed, I felt as if we were fighting machinery with bamboo," a middle-aged machinist said. "Also, the food rationed to us was not enough to keep us working. We could hardly stand it. The government kept telling us that we would defeat the United States forces after they landed here, but as my house was burned down and I had no food, clothing, or shelter, I didn't know how I could go on."[56]

The German diplomat Erwin Wickert, who spent the war years in Tokyo, noted a stark contrast between the lofty official language and the actual feelings among ordinary Japanese. "Radio, newspapers, and public speakers went on about the Japanese spirit, about sacrifice and victory. Everywhere you heard the same exalted vocabulary, but not among the people itself. It had grown tired." While the government ordered the total mobilization of society for the war efforts, the majority of the Japanese were busy making ends meet at a time when rationing meant sugar was a luxury that could only be enjoyed a few times a year and a sack of potatoes on the black market cost more than 60 times the official price. Crime rates also soared amid a general collapse in morals.[57]

The one Japanese who had perhaps the most complete view of the situation at the front was also the one who could stop the bloodshed. In the crucial months of spring 1945, Emperor Hirohito appears to have fundamentally changed his views on the right course for his empire. While he had previously refused to even consider the Allied terms for surrender, especially the call for total disarmament and punishment of those in the Japanese leadership found responsible for the war, shortly before the fall of Germany in early May, he acknowledged that both demands could be unavoidable. "Not only that, on the contrary, he is now even thinking that the sooner we act, the better," his advisor Kido said. "We have to wait for an opportune moment, but I think that the time for us to ask for the emperor's decision [to end the war] will come in the near future."[58]

The battle of Okinawa left Hirohito in no better mood. He acknowledged that both the Army and the Navy had fought to the utmost to delay the enemy advance, but he believed they had done too little in terms of coordinating their efforts. "It was a completely stupid, stupid battle… I thought if we were defeated in this last decisive battle, unconditional surrender would be inevitable," Hirohito said after the war, reminiscing over his thinking in the crisis spring of 1945. "After Okinawa there could be no expectation of a decisive naval battle. The one ray of hope I thought was to strike a blow against the Americans and British at Yunnan [province in southwest China] together with Burma operations."[59]

Even as Hirohito was pinning his hopes on Burma, he was in the process of losing control of that country. Following the debacle of the failed Japanese

Imphal campaign the year before, the British forces had been on the offensive since early 1945, reclaiming the former colony in a series of aggressive strikes which not only yielded huge swathes of territory but also left in its wake huge numbers of Japanese casualties. The suicidal ferocity that the Japanese displayed throughout, fighting to the death even for the possession of the tiniest hamlet, demanded the grudging respect of their enemies. "If a British regiment had fought against such odds as they had fought, the story would live forever in their history, but it was not unusual for the Japanese to fight like this," a British veteran wrote, inspecting 200 Japanese killed to the last man in the defense of a small village standing in the path of the British advance.[60]

Bill Slim, the commander of Commonwealth forces in Burma, initially planned to attack the Japanese forces in the Shwebo plain, between the Chindwin and Irrawaddy rivers. Instead, the Japanese pulled back east of the Irrawaddy, digging in to make the British pay dearly for their advance inch by inch. Slim's forces, consisting of British, Indian, and African troops, crossed the river on several occasions during January and February. Mountbatten was present during a major crossing operation in the middle of February, when two divisions made it to the other side encountering little resistance. "The casualties in the crossing have, up to date, been surprisingly light when you think that the successful crossing of the Irrawaddy with sufficient British troops will mean the end of the Japanese Army in Burma," he wrote in his diary.[61]

The British-led troops showed an initiative honed through years of training and fighting during the advance after crossing the Irrawaddy. Captain William Rhodes-James, the commander of a company of Ghurkas, was riding on a Grant tank until the bullets started to bounce off the armor. "We found the Japs dug in, the tanks seemed to hypnotize and cow them. My men sorted them out, while the tanks stopped."[62] The strategic town of Meiktila was reached in early March and wrestled from the Japanese army in a series of brutal battles.

Slim witnessed the savage combat resulting from the Japanese Army's ability to turn every existing obstacle into a veritable fortress. "Where every house was a strong point, every water channel had its concealed bunker and every rubble heap its hidden machine or antitank gun, fighting was costly and progress slow," he wrote. "There was hand-to-hand fighting as savage as any yet experienced in a theater where close combat was the rule rather than the exception."[63] The Japanese defenders were killed in huge numbers. In one area measuring 100 by 200 yards according to a modern unit history, a total of 876 Japanese bodies were counted. The last 50 Japanese soldiers jumped into the lake and drowned or were killed in the water.[64]

The Japanese willingness to fight to the last man was widely seen as a sign of fanaticism but could also occasionally have other causes. After more than three years of war, the hostilities had become personal for the combatants, and prisoners were not often taken. Major John Randle, commander of a company of Indian soldiers, described how during an advance, a soldier in front of him was shot by a Japanese. His comrades went mad, attacking a company of over 120 Japanese with bayonets, grenades, and tommy guns. Randle attempted to take a few prisoners, but an Indian captain under his command told him, "It's no good, you're wasting your breath." One of the last Japanese to die was the company commander. The victorious Indians handed his sword to Randle. "We were on a high, adrenalin running, all steamed up. My chaps were in a bloodlust."[65]

From mid-April the race for Rangoon was on. The advance towards the Burmese capital became not just an effort to overcome Japanese resistance but also a contest against time, as Slim aimed to reach the capital before the monsoon was to make movement infinitely harder. The British had near-complete air superiority. Pilot officer Harry Morrell remembered roaming the Burmese countryside at will in his Beaufighter, looking for prey. "We were highwaymen, anything that moved we hit," he said. "The big prize was a train. If there were no trains about, we attacked the stations, or the engine sheds."[66]

The Japanese commanders in Rangoon were initially prepared to turn the city into a meat grinder, fighting for every house. "We have over a million troops in Southeast Asia, and we will throw every soldier into the battle," the chief-of-staff of the defending army said menacingly.[67] In the end, they decided otherwise, pulling most of their forces out of the capital prior to the arrival of the enemy. This did not, however, spare the city. In the interregnum between the Japanese departure and the Allied arrival, a period of lawlessness ruled in the streets, characterized by looting and random violence.

The British colonial flag which had flown over Rangoon before the war had been captured by the Japanese troops who occupied the city in 1942. When those same troops were transported across the northern Pacific to fight in the Aleutians, they had brought the flag with them. There, the Americans had seized it, and at the Quebec Conference in August 1943, the US side had handed it back to the British. Now, finally, it was hoisted again over the liberated city of Rangoon.[68] A few days later, Mountbatten moved in, finding a room at Government House where there were still booklets with titles such as *How to Learn Japanese*.[69]

Meanwhile, the British-led troops continued their pursuit of the retreating Japanese forces. The momentum hardly lessened despite the capture of the

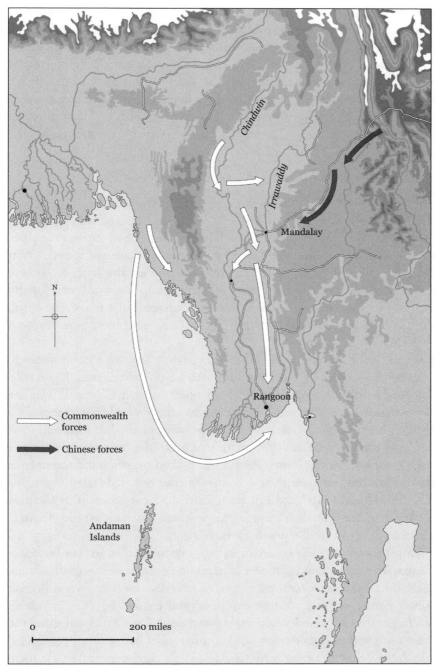

Liberation of Burma, 1945.

capital; it carried on in an unabated fashion at a time when Hitler's Germany had collapsed, and the weapons went silent in Europe for the first time in nearly six years. For the men fighting in Asia, this meant little. Lieutenant Colonel Hugh Pettigrew of the 17th Indian Division near Rangoon received a message from a dispatch rider saying the war in Europe was over. Pettigrew called out to a sergeant, "I've got a message here. The war in Europe is over." The sergeant replied, "Very good, sir," saluted, turned to a group of men standing nearby, and said, "The war in Europe is over. Five-minute break."[70]

By the spring of 1945, China had become a sideshow. It was the only part of the Asia Pacific where Japan still held the main initiative and mostly held the upper hand. The year before, the Japanese Army had proven capable of driving deep inside Chinese-held territory, eventually threatening even Chiang Kai-shek's capital of Chongqing. The only area where the Japanese side was decisively disadvantaged was in terms of airpower. In the words of a Japanese officer, if it had not been for the American Fourteenth Air Force, the heirs of Claire Chennault's legendary Flying Tigers, "we could have gone anywhere we wished."[71]

Even so, until the last weeks of the war, while few were yet informed of the destructive power of the atom about to be unleashed over Japan, plans were being made for major US-led land operations in China. Wedemeyer, the new senior US commander in the China theater, laid tentative plans for a massive three-pronged attack on the large parts of the battered nation still under Japanese control, once the cessation of hostilities in Europe had freed up enough troops. General George Patton was picked to command the northern offensive, heading for Beijing and Tianjin. If the war had lasted longer, and if "Old Blood and Guts" had not been killed in a car accident in Germany, it could have seen him in charge of huge American tank armies driving at breakneck speed across the north Chinese plain.[72]

Chiang's forces were to play an important role in the planned land offensives in China. To this end, Wedemeyer initiated a comprehensive reorganization of the Chinese armed forces, based on 36 new divisions, known collectively as Alpha Force, which would be equipped and trained by the US side and have a large corps of American advisors attached.[73] Work on establishing these divisions was still only underway, and combat units had still not received the required 23 weeks of training, when in April 1945, the Japanese Army launched a major offensive into Hunan province, heading for Zhijiang, a major forward base run by the Fourteenth Air Force 270 miles southeast of Chongqing.[74]

Despite their lack of preparedness, several Chinese divisions rushed into battle, reinforced by battle-hardened compatriots flown in from the Burma front. Over the next month and a half, fierce battles raged in Hunan province, but Zhijiang remained in Allied hands. Close coordination with US pilots offering tactical support was a major benefit for the Chinese infantry. "Napalm bombs were especially effective as antipersonnel weapons, since they not only penetrated the foxholes but their heat drove enemy soldiers from nearby positions to expose themselves to the fire of the Chinese ground soldier," according to the official US history.[75] Japanese officers later acknowledged that the main reason for their defeat had been their underestimation of the efficiency of the Chinese troops, despite warnings from their intelligence services that the enemy had improved both in terms of equipment and tactics.[76]

The victory at Zhijiang could not conceal the fact that the Chinese Nationalist forces under Chiang Kai-shek had suffered enormously after eight years of war. The battle for Zhijiang had cost 18,000 casualties, three times as many as the Japanese losses. The previous year, attempting to stem the Ichigō offensive, Chiang's troops had sustained a staggering 750,000 casualties.[77] Chiang's manpower pool was being bled dry, and even though the Chinese leader had succeeded in making a reasonable impression on Wedemeyer, it was hard for Nationalist China to shake off a reputation of being a cesspool of corruption, even though the US armed forces themselves were deeply involved. In one notorious incident, an American pilot flying the Hump supply route across the Himalayas from India to China, parachuted out with 10,000 dollars in gold bars and was never seen again.[78]

While Chiang was in a severely weakened state in 1945, the Communist forces in the north of China under the command of Mao Zedong, holed up in the remote town of Yanan for over a decade, had strengthened both in relative and absolute terms. Prior to early 1944, the Communists had been subjected to vicious "burn all, kill all, loot all" campaigns by the Japanese, and the Nationalists, too, had planned an offensive to finally rid itself of its red rival.[79] Both threats to the Communist survival receded when the Ichigō offensive instead caused the Japanese and the Nationalists to turn their full attention to each other, and while Chiang's forces were decimated in the south, the Communists grew their military capabilities. From June 1944 until April 1945, the number of troops under Communist control nearly doubled from 474,000 to 910,000.[80] In the words of a Japanese historian: "The Ichigō offensive was a disaster for both the Japanese army and the Nationalists. The only winners were the Communists."[81]

At the same time, the Communists were winning friends in parts of the US diplomatic and military establishments, just as many American journalists compared them favorably with the Nationalists. Since the middle of 1944, the US government had maintained a small permanent presence in Yanan, nicknamed "Dixie," since, according to an American diplomat, "it was rebel territory."[82] The purpose of the small group of American envoys, known as the "Dixie mission," was to probe Communist intentions and determine whether an alliance with Mao was feasible and desirable.

The first impressions that the Communists made on their American guests were overwhelmingly positive. Some of the reports they sent back to Washington even suggested that Yanan was akin to an egalitarian paradise. "To the casual eye, there are no police in Yanan," John Service, the head of the "Dixie mission," wrote in a confidential report. "There are also no beggars, nor signs of desperate poverty." Mao himself also struck his American interlocutors as approachable and sociable, even though he was spoken of with respect, if not veneration.[83]

The "Dixie mission" was unable to follow the internal discussions among the Communist leaders, but behind closed doors Mao showed a clear understanding that after two decades in the wilderness, including moments when his movement had been on the verge of annihilation, he had now reached a position of strength that might constitute his one and only chance at grasping national power. Previously, failure had meant death to large numbers of Communists, even close friends and relatives. He could not afford to fail again. "This time," he said on several occasions, "we must take over China."[84]

In the course of six years of war, more than half of it focused in Asia, the Australian Army had made a name for itself both among friends and enemies. "They are not the kind of soldiers we are," an American military journalist said. If British or American troops were faced with a Japanese strongpoint, he argued, they would use artillery and aircraft to soften up the target before going in themselves. "The Aussies don't do that. They fix bayonets and charge. Now they have a lot of fatalities this way, but damn it, after they get this reputation among the Japanese, the Japanese see those bayonets, they get the hell out of there."[85]

By 1945, however, Australia's fearsome warriors had been relegated to a sideshow, fighting pockets of Japanese resistance in northern New Guinea and Bougainville. The combat was often ferocious, and feats of great heroism were performed. Still, much less was at stake now than in the early war years when the Japanese juggernaut had rolled down the Pacific and ground to a halt on Australia's doorstep. While the war had begun on an existential note, with Australian soldiers fighting against what they thought was the threat of a Japanese invasion, by the end of the conflict, it maintained soldiers in the field mainly in order to ensure that its voice would be heard during peace settlement negotiations.[86]

During the last year of the war, Australia's divisions were placed in theaters where their contribution would necessarily be of secondary importance with little strategic impact.[87] In the words of Australian historian David Horner, "the harsh fact is that if Australian forces had conducted no more offensive operations after 1944 there would have been no change in the outcome of the war."[88] To a large extent this was the result of machinations by MacArthur to prevent Australian troops from taking part in the liberation of the Philippines, partly because he feared that they would later be mobilized for a British plan to advance into Indochina, an approach known as the "Middle Strategy."[89]

The troops sent to fight and possibly die in theaters of no vital importance were growing increasingly frustrated. The men of the 6th Division, in the Aitape area in northern New Guinea lamented being "first rate troops given a second rate job."[90] The troops were more than happy to express their dissatisfaction. When the commander-in-chief of the Australian Army, General Thomas Blamey, inspected Lae on the east side of New Guinea, he saw a group of engineers stripped to their waists, clearing a large pile of stores from the beach. What's going on, Blamey asked, and received the flippant reply, "Well if you don't know, who does? You organized it."[91]

While frustration characterized the Australian ranks, the prevailing mood among their Japanese enemies left in the South Pacific was desperation. Cut off from any kind of seaborne supplies, Hirohito's soldiers found themselves short of even the most basic necessities. "There were no clothes, no shoes, no blankets, no mosquito nets, no tools, no ammunition, no medicine, and there was, of course, a shortage of food but bravely and tenaciously our troops continued their garrison efforts, with no sleep and no rest," wrote Japanese Lieutenant General Yoshihara Kane. "In fact they showed their aggressive morale by daring infiltrations. But the number of sick and wounded increased sharply, so that the responsibilities of the fit troops became heavier."[92]

Beyond New Guinea, the Australian Army developed plans to retake Borneo and its oil fields, one of the main raisons d'être of Japan's original offensive in late 1941. Landings were scheduled for three locations on the large island, but by spring 1945, the Allied advance had reached so far that a full-scale operation had lost any justification.[93] Eventually, only one of the three landings went ahead, and troops of the 7th Australian Division landed at Balikpapan in July. Fighting continued until the end of the war, at the cost of 229 Australian lives. According to two modern Australian historians, "it was an exceptionally high price to pay for an operation that had absolutely no strategic or operational purpose."[94]

Some Japanese units were left in situations where they might begin to ask if they had been forgotten by history. The 5,000-strong Japanese garrison on Mili atoll, part of the Marshall Islands, was passed by in the Allied drive across the Central Pacific and was isolated totally during the last two years of the war. The soldiers and sailors on the island received only scattered reports about the progress of the war from Japanese, American, and Australian broadcasts. Messages sent from the Japanese Army and Navy were useless, because the garrison's codes were out of date. "The main occupation was making gardens to provide food," said Lieutenant Commander Tokuno Hiroshi of the Japanese Navy, who spent 25 months on the island as executive officer until the Japanese surrender. "We were very assiduous in building fortifications until June 1944 then we gave up the idea. We felt it was more worthwhile to grow food than to build fortifications."[95]

Although the soldiers were never involved in ground combat with enemy troops, the war was anything but a vacation for them, and only about half survived to be taken prisoner at the end of the war. Life was harsh on the islands left to "wither on the vine." In late 1943, the atoll was subjected to heavy bombing by American B-24s. Out of 1200 men hit by bombs, only 100 recovered. "The high percentage of deaths was due mainly to lack of medical supplies and proper food," Tokuno said. "Another 1200 deaths resulted from other causes such as lack of food, eating poisonous fish, diseases such as beri-beri, dysentery. Nobody escaped." The garrison exacted a gruesome revenge on a B-24 crew of five who were shot down and baled out near the atoll. They were all killed.[96]

CHAPTER EIGHT

The End

July–September 1945

Okinawa was a victory for the United States, but it was also an eye-opener. It brought home to the American people and their leaders how far the Japanese were willing to go to defend their home soil. A senior US Navy intelligence officer summed up the situation after the capture of the island: "The Japanese gamble for Empire has failed... Of the fighting forces, only the Army remains relatively strong... The Japanese are defeated but we have not yet won the victory."[1] At a meeting with his strategic planners at the White House on June 18, President Harry S. Truman said despairingly he "hoped that there was a possibility of preventing an Okinawa from one end of Japan to the other."[2]

That hope was felt even more fervently by the millions of ordinary Americans whose close relatives were poised to take part in the biggest invasion in the history of mankind. The anguish was expressed eloquently by an unidentified woman in a letter to Secretary of the Navy James Forrestal: "Please, for God's sake, stop sending our finest youth to be murdered in places like Iwo Jima. It is too much for boys to stand, too much for mothers and homes to take. It is driving some mothers crazy. Why can't objectives be accomplished some other way? It is most inhuman and awful—stop, stop."[3]

The pleas were, of course, in vain. Military necessity dictated that the war against Japan be carried out to the end. The planned invasion of Japan, codenamed "Downfall" was to take place in two stages and eventually involve more than a million men and the largest armada in world history. It would become bloody. Art G. Anderson, a Marine intelligence officer, recalled the somber mood as he and his comrades prepared mentally for the upcoming battles: "We were all counting on this being the last invasion for all of us. It would be suicide going into the main island. We were awful powerful apprehensive."[4]

In Japan, there was a parallel war-weariness as the near-daily bombing raids on major cities had a dramatic impact on expectations of eventual victory. More and more Japanese were coming to the realization that they might actually lose, and they placed the blame not with Emperor Hirohito, who was beyond reproach, but the people in the ruling elite who served him. "Criticism of weak air raid defenses, location of the Japanese fleet, of the advance of the military in the political and economic fields, inability of the government officials to act, are gaining strength," a secret police report said. Some Japanese were now wishing for peace, but others were calling for more capable people to be put in charge, the report added: "They want renovation in internal politics, even in military government. Such a trend of thought also is gaining strength."[5]

Even so, there was a Japanese determination to fight to the last man, woman, and child. In the words of the US officers planning the final conquest of Japan, the invasion would be opposed "not only by the available organized military forces of the Empire, but also by a fanatically hostile population."[6] It bore similarities with the attitude of some feudal lords towards the "Black Ships" nearly a century earlier. Resistance was equally futile and likely to end in death, and yet perhaps a majority of Japanese saw no alternative. A post-war survey suggests the rationale behind this suicidal mood, showing that 68 percent of the population expected "brutalities, starvation, enslavement or annihilation" at the hands of Allied victors, while only four percent believed they would receive good treatment.[7] "I was prepared to fight till the last ditch. I was even willing to give up my children and fight till the death," a Japanese housewife said.[8]

In a sign of the near-total mobilization of Japanese society ahead of the expected Allied invasion, even overweight sumo wrestlers, so far exempted from military duties because of their participation in the morale-boosting sports, were drafted for the effort to prepare defenses. As had been the case in Germany, where pre-adolescent members of the Hitler Youth had been recruited for the hopeless fight against the invading armies, Japan's young were not spared either. Ten-year-old schoolgirl Nakane Mihoko recorded in her diary that a teacher, Yoshikao-sensei, had taught her and her classmates how to fight the invading enemy with spears: "Yoshikado-sensei said, 'They're still there. Spear them! Spear them!' and it was really fun. I was tired, but I realized that even one person can kill a lot of the enemy."[9]

Rear Admiral Takata Toshitane, the deputy chief of Military Affairs at the Navy Ministry, knew the situation was desperate, but that there might be a way out. "Our one hope was that, if we could destroy the invasion fleet when it came to actually land in Japan—although even then we could not actually win the war—we could hold out indefinitely for any number of years."[10] To this end, the Japanese military planners were expecting to employ kamikaze units in unprecedented numbers, and they were devising tactics that would allow the suicide pilots to take off despite intensive American efforts aimed at destroying Japan's airfields. "We believed that by taking advantage of weather, heavy overcast, and intervals between bombing raids, we could repair the airfields enough to keep them serviceable. Also we could use stretches of beach along the coast," said Lieutenant General Kawabe Torashirō, deputy chief of staff of the Japanese Army.[11]

The Allied forces preparing the invasion were keenly aware of the kamikaze threat, but only after the war were they informed about the full extent of the Japanese program. A pilot in the US Navy remembered his emotions when, shortly after the end of the war, he toured a Japanese naval base and saw the prototype of a rocket-style device, which was to have been fired from catapults in caves, carrying a 5,000-pound warhead and a human operator. "I could understand somebody diving an airplane into a ship," he said, "but I could not believe that someone would start an entire development program like this. It was essentially a guided missile whose guidance system was going to be a human being. That's what they were doing."[12]

By the summer of 1945, Japan had lost command of the seas surrounding it. Once in possession of one of the world's most powerful navies, the empire now had to concede that its control ended at the water's edge. The US Navy roamed at will within sight of major cities, and no point in Japan, from the humblest fishing village on the northern island of Hokkaido to the innermost quarters of the Imperial Palace in Tokyo, was beyond the reach of carrier-based American airplanes. "What is left of the Japanese Navy is helpless," Admiral Halsey said self-assuredly in a message to the American public. "My only regret is that our ships don't have wheels, so that we can drive the Japs from the coast, we can chase them inland."[13]

Halsey was on a mission he had been pining to undertake with his Third Fleet for months, carrying out a sustained campaign against the Japanese islands from inside its home waters. The first major mission was on July 10, when hundreds of planes scoured the area around Tokyo for airfields and aircraft to destroy. "The pilots were quite disappointed over the lack of Jap planes in the air," Henry O'Meara, an aviator from the carrier *Yorktown* said later.[14] Five days on, Halsey's planes attacked shipping supplying the main island of

Honshu with coal, cutting Japan's capacity in half within a few hours of heavy raids.[15] "Pretty soon we'll have 'em moving their stuff by oxcarts and skiffs," said Ralph Wilson, Halsey's operations officer.[16]

On the same day, Halsey's fleet shelled the Nihon Steel Company and the Wanishi Ironworks in the city of Muroran in southern Hokkaido. During the one-hour-long bombardment, the ships fired 860 rounds of 16-inch shells, sailing as close as 28,000 yards from the target.[17] To carry out the mission, the fleet had to enter Uchiura Bay, "right into the enemy's jaws," as Halsey put it. "We were landlocked on three sides," he recalled. "It was a magnificent spectacle, but I kept one eye on the target and the other on the sky."[18] His concern was unwarranted. No Japanese planes attacked. Still, Noel A. M. Gayler, a naval aviator now performing staff duties, considered the entire Muroran raid a waste, seeing it as Halsey's attempt to carve out a role for the battleships, borne out of reluctance to let all the credit go to the aviators. "Admiral Halsey decided that it was time for the battleships to get into the act," he said. "Being intolerant as young officers are likely to be, I thought it was a terrible fiasco, but at least the battleships had their day in the sun."[19]

American submarines, starved of targets, also moved into the Sea of Japan, and often had to expend ammunition on cargo-carrying sampans because there was little else to sink. The crew on board the USS *Barb* even ventured on land for new targets, after observing a railroad running alongside the coastline on southern Sakhalin island. A demolition party was sent ashore and hastily placed explosives. The submarine had still not left the area when a train passed by and triggered the charges. "Engine wreckage flying, flying, flying up some 200 feet," the submarine's commander later wrote, describing the moments after the explosion. "Cars piling up, into and over the wreckage in front, rolling off the track in a writhing, twisting maelstrom of Gordian knots."[20] Subsequent reports suggested that 150 passengers, including women and children, had been killed in the derailing.[21]

During the last weeks of the war, a growing number of submarines were involved in rescue missions for airmen shot down in the waters near Japan.[22] "When a big strike of air was going to be done anywhere, certain submarines would be assigned to the air-sea rescue job and the people in the planes would know where those submarines were going to be," said Roy S. Benson, commander of the submarine USS *Trigger*.[23] On one occasion, the 10-member crew of a downed B-29 was picked up by the USS *Tinosa* as it was on its way into the Sea of Japan, not away from it. "When the aviators learned of *Tinosa*'s destination they were unanimous in their desire to be put safely back in their rubber boats," wrote Wilfred Holmes, a Navy codebreaker. The *Tinosa* managed, however, to find a submarine returning to base from a mission, willing to transport the crew members back.[24]

Japanese submarines, by contrast, played a much more limited role than they could have in resisting the American advance towards the home islands, and the reason was not just a lack of submarines, according to Commander Nakajima Chikataka, on the staff of the Combined Fleet, in post-war interrogations. "It was also very important for them to supply even isolated and ineffective bases because the Army, which was also a partner in the planning, would have refused to send additional strength to the South Pacific if the Navy had left men to starve."[25]

One Japanese submarine far from home was able to claim one last triumph over the mighty American enemy. Twenty-eight minutes before midnight on July 29, the *I-58*, commanded by Hashimoto Mochitsura, sent two torpedoes into the hull of heavy cruiser USS *Indianapolis* in waters west of Guam. It swiftly took in water, rolled over, and sank bow first. Up to 400 of the 1,199-member crew were killed in the blast or went down with the ship. Because it all happened so fast, the men only managed to release a few life rafts and floater nets, and most of the survivors had simply to stay afloat with the help of life jackets of often questionable quality.[26]

For many, the real terror was only beginning. Days went by before the US Navy was aware that the ship was missing, and meanwhile the sailors were drifting in the middle of the ocean, surrounded by sharks. "They stalked for hours, going around and around," said Seaman First Class Gus Kay. "Finally, they attacked—they pulled guys right out of the water."[27] More than half perished before they were rescued.[28] It was the horrific end of a ship that had just completed a mission of world-changing significance. At the time when it was struck by the torpedoes, the USS *Indianapolis* was on its way to the Philippines after having delivered to the island of Tinian components of a new bomb with unfathomable destructive potential, about to be used against Japan.

Hiroshima, an ancient castle city in western Japan with a population of a quarter million, had miraculously escaped most of the devastation that the American bombers had visited on other major populations centers. For months, the B-29s had just passed by Hiroshima without dropping a single bomb. The residents grew complacent, even if they considered it very odd that they were spared, and they came up with a range of theories. "We kept thinking that Hiroshima would not be bombed at all," one of them said later. "There were rumors that some relative, perhaps the mother, of President Truman was here, and therefore Hiroshima was not to be bombed." Others sensed instinctively that there must be a much more sinister reason, and they were right.[29]

At 2:45 on August 6, the *Enola Gay*, a B-29 bomber piloted by Colonel Paul W. Tibbets, took off from a runway on Tinian, accompanied by two other B-29s carrying photographic and measurement equipment. Ahead was six and a half hours of flight across the Pacific. At about 9am, the target emerged in front of the plane—the nearly undamaged city of Hiroshima. After a short run-in, the *Enola Gay* opened its bomb port and released its cargo, a single bomb, from an altitude of 31,600 feet. Tibbets made a sharp 150-degree turn and nosed downwards to gain speed, reaching a distance of 15 miles by the time the bomb exploded 2,000 feet above the ground.[30] A sharp glare filled the plane, and it was subsequently hit by two shock waves. "We turned back to look at Hiroshima," Tibbets recalled. "The city was hidden by that awful cloud... boiling up, mushrooming, terrible and incredibly tall."[31] His co-pilot, Captain Robert Lewis, wrote in his logbook: "My God, what have we done?"[32]

Many survivors on the ground reported never having heard the blast. One reported a distant crackling as the only sound,[33] but between 70,000 and 80,000 people were killed in the minutes and hours after the detonation, victims of the explosion itself and the subsequent firestorm.[34] The testimony of an anonymous woman who was at her home with her baby and elderly parents at the time of the attack conveys the shock experienced by survivors: "My clothes were burned off and I received burns on my legs, arms and neck. The skin was just hanging loose," she said. "My mother and father came crawling out of the debris. Face and arms were just black. I heard the baby crying so I crawled in and dug it out from under the burning lumber. It was pretty badly burned."[35] The vice mayor of Hera village, a little more than seven miles south of Hiroshima, recalled the shock of seeing the wounded: "Everybody looked alike. The burns on the faces were horrible," he said. "They all looked like boiled lobsters."[36]

Father John A. Siemes, a German-born Jesuit priest and a professor of modern philosophy at Tokyo's Catholic University who had spent the war years in Japan, hardly recognized Hiroshima when the sun rose over the devastated city less than 24 hours later: "The bright day now reveals the frightful picture which last night's darkness had partly concealed. Where the city stood, everything—as far as the eye could reach—is a waste of ashes and ruin," he wrote. "Only several skeletons of buildings remain. The banks of the river are covered with dead and wounded and the rising waters have here and there covered some of the corpses. On the broad street in the Hakashima district, naked, burned cadavers are particularly numerous."[37]

Several of the crew on board the *Enola Gay* were not aware of the exact nature of the bomb they were carrying, but soon the whole world was to be informed of the revolutionary new weapon which had in an instant changed the way war was waged forever. "It is an atomic bomb," President Truman said, in a public statement sixteen hours after the explosion over Hiroshima. "It is a harnessing of the basic power of the universe. The force from which the sun draws its power has been loosed against those who brought war to the Far East."[38]

It was the first time Bak on the destroyer USS *Franks* heard the word "atomic bomb": "But I understood from the accounts that we heard by newspaper, radio, and ship's information that it was the most awesome bomb ever made, and that it killed many, many people in Hiroshima."[39] Buckner Fanning was a Marine waiting to take part in the invasion of Japan when he suddenly heard about the new "superbomb." "I didn't know what it was," he said. "I had had chemistry class in high school and knew what an atom was but I had never heard of an atomic bomb, nuclear fallout or radiation. For all of us our language was completely changed after that."[40]

Just three days later a second device was detonated over the city of Nagasaki, killing an estimated 30,000 to 40,000 people instantly. Everyone who witnessed the devastating power unleashed with the new bomb was in awe. "It was a living thing," wrote William L. Laurence, a correspondent flying on board the plane that dropped the device over Nagasaki, "a new species of being, born right before our incredulous eyes."[41] Among the industrial targets destroyed in the Nagasaki blast was a torpedo plant run by Mitsubishi. "This is where we made the first torpedoes, the ones dropped on Pearl Harbor at the onset of the Pacific War," said an employee at the factory. "In the end here's where we were stabbed to death. We fought a stupid war, didn't we?"[42]

The decision to drop the bombs was ultimately Truman's, and his alone. However, he was following the advice of an eight-member interim committee, which argued in favor of the use of the bomb without prior warning. One of the eight members, Undersecretary of the Navy Ralph Austin Bard, subsequently changed his mind, sending a letter to Secretary of War Henry L. Stimson, citing "the position of the United States as a great humanitarian nation" and arguing that Japan be given two to three days advance notice before the atomic bomb was actually dropped. The call was not heeded.[43]

Millions of young American fearing or perhaps even expecting to die in the upcoming invasion of Japan welcomed news of the bomb. "We were not too happy for the Japanese, but we felt very, very happy about the fact that the bomb was dropped and that we were doing a number on Japan," said Michael Bak. "Even though so many people were killed, we felt good about it.

I felt good about it, because I thought it was a way of ending the war sooner, and maybe not getting killed myself."[44] Garold Weasmer, a soldier with the 43rd Infantry Division in the Philippines, was skeptical that the bomb would be enough to force a Japanese surrender, having seen how any amount of bombing of islands in the Pacific had failed to get the Japanese defenders to give up. "We knew that no matter what that super weapon was it was still going to take us guys going in there. It might save us a few lives but we had never dreamed it was the enormous thing that it was."[45]

Some senior officials believed that, bomb or not, an invasion might never be necessary. The brutally efficient naval blockade was enough to force Japan into submission, according to both Nimitz and Spruance, supported in Washington by Admiral Ernest King.[46] This view was widely held, especially among naval commanders, who had seen at first hand the damage done to the Japanese economy and the nation's ability to wage war. By July 1945, Halsey estimated that Japan would surrender in October at the latest, arguing that the nation's shortages were "reaching the point of no-return, the point where collapse of his whole war machine would become inevitable."[47] That view was to be reinforced by dramatic events taking place along the northern fringe of the Japanese empire at the same time that a B-29 was carrying the second bomb to Nagasaki.

In the early hours of August 9, an army of 1.5 million Soviet soldiers supported by more than 5,000 tanks and self-propelled guns and nearly 4,000 aircraft invaded Manchukuo, the huge northeastern part of China which Japan had conquered thirteen years earlier and, in a sense, set in motion the events that eventually led to the Pacific War. Just hours before, the Soviet Union had declared war, making good on its promise to join in the effort to bring Japan to its knees as early as feasible following the victory in Europe. Joseph Stalin's battle-hardened Soviet troops, fresh from the triumph over Hitler's Reich in the spring of that year, moved with almost unbelievable swiftness, pushing aside most Japanese defenses. Some Soviet forces covered 280 miles in the course of the first three days of the offensive.[48]

The Soviet forces benefited from a massive Japanese intelligence failure. Although several Japanese units had observed troops movements across the border, the Japanese commanders in Manchukuo dismissed the warnings, insisting that the Soviet Army would be unable to redeploy its forces to East Asia so soon after the victory in Europe. The Soviet offensive would eventually come, they agreed, but no sooner than September or October, and more likely in early 1946. As a result, the Kwantung Army, the independent-minded unit that had been responsible for carrying out the defense of Manchuria through all the years, was caught flat-footed and consistently unable to put up an efficient fight against the invading forces.[49]

Yet, the Soviet generals could hardly believe the ease with which they moved forward. "The main forces of the Kwantung Army have as yet not materialized, been located or detected," Marshal Aleksandr M. Vasilevskii, commander-in-chief of the Soviet troops in the Far East, wrote to Stalin during the early stages of the offensive.[50] The fact was that once the Kwantung Army had recovered from the initial shock of the invasion, it swiftly moved south, abandoning any idea of trying to halt the Soviet masses at the border. Only in certain strategic areas did they stop to fight. In the city of Mudanjiang, five Japanese regiments kept resisting for two days in fierce house-to-house fighting before giving in to the superior Soviet firepower.[51]

Left behind in the Kwantung Army's rush to escape the Soviet juggernaut were more than 1.5 million Japanese civilians who had been sent as settlers and colonial administrators over the previous decade and a half to consolidate

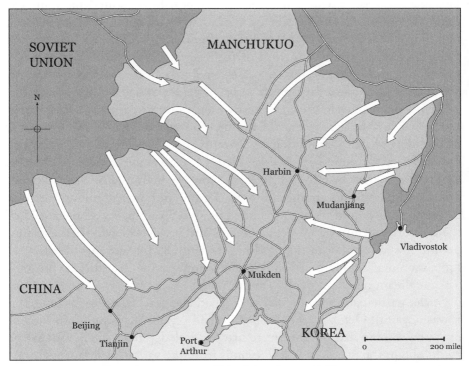

Soviet invasion of Manchuria, August 1945.

the empire's control of the region.[52] Japanese private Oguma Kenji was on a train taking his unit south when he passed through a city which had just been bombed by Soviet planes. The city's train station was crowded with Japanese families desperate for a ride to safety. "No civilian refugees boarded our train," he said. "I think almost all of them were left at the station."[53]

Instead, tens of thousands were forced to try to walk south, through rural areas filled with hostile Chinese bent on revenge and eager for loot.[54] The roughly 300,000 Japanese peasants who lived in isolated colonial farm villages spread across Manchuria suffered particularly in an ordeal of almost epic dimensions. Aoki Sachiko, a young woman, was attacked twice by groups of Chinese robbers. The first time, she was knocked unconscious and woke up, lying on the ground stark naked. Everything had been taken from her, even her clothes. She was rescued by her sister, and the two women continued their trek, only to be assaulted by robbers a second time. Her sister did not survive. She was struck with a sickle, and "blood ran like tap water over her body."[55]

Inevitably, the Soviet Army caught up with the refugees. Seven-year-old boy Torao Beniya was with a group who had sought shelter in the abandoned Japanese Sado Settlement and witnessed the horrific slaughter that unfolded then. The Soviet soldiers shot the lucky ones. They locked up others inside the buildings and set fire to them, and they threw children into the settlement's well. They raped women in front of their crying babies. While all this was taking place, they barbecued the last remaining horses in the settlement, drinking, singing, and dancing. It was a "banquet of hell."[56]

Many Japanese were driven to despair and committed mass suicide, often ordered to do so by their elders, the way their compatriots had killed themselves in the hour of defeat from Saipan onwards. In one of numerous instances, the leader of a group of refugees suddenly lost hope and ordered the whole group to take their own lives, leading the way by shooting his wife and child, and then himself.[57] In another instance, a group of Japanese soldiers decided to prevent a group of refugees from falling into Soviet hands, shooting all of them before moving on.[58] Whether at their own hands, killed by their enemies, or simply succumbing to the hardship, roughly 80,000 Japanese settlers, or more than one in four, perished in the invasion, paying the ultimate price for Tokyo's dream of a continental empire.[59]

Soviet participation in the defeat of Japan had been foreseen for long, but it was not until October 1944 that Stalin had promised to enter into the war in East Asia. He had done so in return for a pledge from his Allies that he could obtain the northern Kurile Islands from the vanquished Japanese. Part of the deal was also that the United States would provide military support for the Soviet forces.[60] Most urgently, they needed amphibious capabilities, and in what has been called the most ambitious transfer program of the war, the US Navy agreed to hand over a large number of American vessels and pass on the required skills to operate them. Eventually, nearly 150 ships were transferred, and 12,000 Soviet sailors received training in their use.[61]

The Soviet Union never ended up implementing any major amphibious campaign against Japan. The war ended too early for that, and the Soviet armed forces did not have the required capability, despite American aid. They carried out one island invasion, landing on Shumshu in the Kurils in late August, suffering heavy casualties. Although Stalin had briefly aired the idea of seizing the large northern island of Hokkaido, the plan never materialized, but if implemented, it could have been a bloodbath that would make Okinawa pale. In short, Japan was never in any real danger of being divided between the Western and Soviet victors, the way Germany was.[62]

The twin nuclear blasts and the Soviet invasion of Manchuria, coming nearly simultaneously, were a double psychological blow for many of the top decision makers in Tokyo. "I felt the atomic bomb struck me hard on one cheek, and immediately afterwards the Soviet declaration of war hit me with full force on the other cheek," said Kawabe Torashirō, deputy of the Army General Staff.[63] While most appreciated the disastrous consequences of the avalanche-like Soviet advance, not all of the military leadership agreed that the atomic bomb was a game changer. Marshal Hata Shunroku, the commandant of Hiroshima, was under the impression that the new weapon only had limited devastating power, and that troops hiding more than a foot underground were hardly impacted at all.[64]

Others had a clearer understanding of what they were up against. Admiral Ugaki Matome, commander of naval aircraft near the western island of Kyūshū, called the bomb "a real wonder," 20,000 times more destructive than the largest bomb dropped so far by B-29s over Japan, and yet he advocated continued war, guerrilla-style, making the enemy "taste the bitterness of prolonged conflict."[65] The minister of war, General Anami Korechika, actually welcomed the Wagnerian end of the Japanese nation. "Would it not be wondrous for this whole nation to be destroyed like a beautiful flower?" he asked.[66] Ironically, President Truman appeared to be more appalled by the effects of the nuclear attacks than the Japanese top brass, withdrawing a previous permission to the US military to use the bombs "as made ready," and ensuring that future bombs would only be used on his explicit order.[67]

The disasters hitting Japan in August had profound implications for Japanese politics. One group within the political elite had been arguing for months for the need to seek a tolerable peace, but had encountered stiff resistance especially from the Army. It is an indication of how desperate the Japanese leadership had been, even before the twin shocks, that former Prime Minister Konoe Fumimaro had suggested in July to travel to Moscow with an offer to provide a large number of Japanese soldiers as labor force for the war-ravaged Soviet Union in return for its mediation of a peace agreement with the United States and Britain.[68]

Now, the arguments in favor of peace were overwhelming. "I think that the atomic bombs alone could have allowed us to terminate the war. However, the Soviet Union's entry into the war certainly made it easier," Hirohito's close adviser Kido Kōichi told a historian after the war. Navy Minister Yonai Mitsumasa put it in stark terms, speaking to a confidante: "Perhaps the way I am putting this is inadequate, but I think that the use of the atomic bomb and the Soviet entry into the war are gifts from Heaven," he said. Like some other members of the military elite, he was worried that continued war could trigger discontent in the Japanese population, threatening the social order with the emperor at the top. "It is good fortune," he said, "that we can now save the situation without bringing such domestic affairs into the open."[69]

The Japanese government knew only too well that any peace with the Allies necessarily had to be on the basis of the Potsdam Declaration, named after the city near Berlin where the US, British, and Soviet leaders had met in late July and called for Japan's unconditional surrender. The Japanese Army still seemed to believe that the terms were negotiable, holding out for a peace not unlike the one Germany had achieved at the end of World War I, which had allowed German war criminals to be processed by their own courts. Hirohito's concerns were more narrowly focused on the imperial throne's ability to survive defeat and occupation.

Two days after the bomb over Hiroshima, the emperor made it clear that peace was the only option. "Now that this sort of weapon has been used, it is becoming increasingly impossible to continue the war," he told his advisors. Whether out of self-interest or an understanding of his importance for Japanese society, he argued that the only adjustment to the Potsdam Declaration worth insisting on was the maintenance of the imperial institution. Beyond that, he considered it futile to spend precious time trying to achieve a broader set of conditions, as was the Army's intention. "I hope you will take measures that will conclude the war as soon as possible," he said.[70]

The urgency reflected in the emperor's words only intensified with the bomb over Nagasaki and the Soviet entry into the war and, at a top leadership meeting that began shortly before midnight on August 9 and lasted into the early hours of August 10, the emperor made the point even more emphatically: "It is truly unbearable for me to see my loyal armed forces disarmed and see those who rendered me devoted service punished as war criminals. However, it cannot be helped for the sake of the nation."[71] Shortly afterwards, the Japanese government sent a message to its US counterpart via Switzerland, accepting the Potsdam Proclamation, but with the crucial addition that this was contingent on "the understanding that the said Declaration does not comprise any demand which prejudices the prerogatives of His Majesty as a sovereign ruler."[72]

The Japanese response came sooner than the US government had expected, and Secretary of War Henry Stimson, for one, was on the way to the airport for a vacation when news of the reply arrived. "That busted our holiday," he wrote in his diary.[73] He returned to the White House and a lengthy discussion on how to approach the Japanese request for a guarantee that the imperial system could continue. Opponents of the idea, including Secretary of State James Byrnes, feared the continued reign of the emperor could give rise to Japanese militarism in the future. Proponents, including Stimson, made the almost exact opposite argument. Only Hirohito had the authority to persuade Japanese troops scattered across the Asia Pacific to lay down their arms. Otherwise, the United States might be in for "a score of bloody Iwo Jimas and Okinawas," Stimson argued.[74]

Truman, together with a handful of aides, set about wording a reply to the Japanese message. It was highly ambiguous, saying merely that "the authority of the Emperor and the Japanese Government to rule the state shall be subject to the Supreme Commander of the Allied powers," adding that the ultimate form of government was up to the Japanese people to decide.[75] A demand that the surrender was to be signed by Hirohito himself was dropped from the draft, before it was sent to Tokyo via Swiss diplomatic channels.[76] The reply was obviously not a clear-cut answer to the Japanese request for a guarantee, and new heated discussions erupted in Tokyo. Some politicians were willing to accept it, even if it were to mean the end of the institution of the emperor, while others, especially in the Army, advocated continued fighting until the Americans had unequivocally committed themselves to the preservation of the throne.[77]

What the emperor himself was thinking at the time will probably forever be shrouded in mystery. However, the sources suggest that by now he had decided firmly on peace at any price. At a meeting on August 14, he argued in favor of accepting the American note. "It is natural to be unable to completely trust an enemy's conduct, even if it is through peaceful means. But compared with an alternative path that would lead to Japan's annihilation, if we can preserve our race, there is a hope for recovery... All of us now must bear the unbearable and tolerate the intolerable."[78] Subsequently, he told an aide: "Here, for the first time, I was given an opportunity to speak my own opinion freely... So I expressed my own convictions that I had been holding for some time and ended the war."[79]

An official announcement about the surrender had been prepared in advance, and sound technicians from the official broadcaster NHK arrived at the Imperial Palace that same evening, recording Hirohito's first attempt at reading the text. The emperor listened to the recording but was not satisfied. "It didn't go well. It seemed a little too quiet. Let's try it again," he said. The second recording was louder, but still with some stumbling. After briefly considering a third recording, the men assembled decided against it. The technicians stayed overnight with the recording within the Imperial Palace compound amid rumors of impending rebellion.[80]

Indeed, a minor rebellion did break out during the night, as firebrand officers opposed to surrender attempted a coup d'etat and stormed into the Imperial Palace compound and occupied the NHK building to prevent the recording from being played. Only after some bloodshed was the rebellion put down, and the following morning, the recordings were being carried off to NHK. Hirohito's subjects now heard their emperor's voice for the first time ever, being exposed to one of history's most remarkable understatements: "The war situation has developed not necessarily to Japan's advantage."[81]

Beginning with the attack on Pearl Harbor, Japan had been seeking a decisive battle with its enemies in order to deal a blow so shocking that they had to bow out of the fight. There was a certain irony in the fact that instead, after nearly four years of fighting, and several attempts at delivering the final devastating strike against the Americans, it was Japan itself which had to surrender after a series of genuinely paralyzing hits that put into question its ability to survive as a nation. A professor at Tohoku Imperial University in the city of Sendai, north of Tokyo, recalled how people reacted in disbelief to hearing Hirohito's words, having expected the emperor's broadcast to be a call for a fight to the end. "Everyone acted as though in a dream. We were just stunned."[82]

For several senior officers it was the ultimate dishonor, and it could only be atoned for in one way. Drunk on sake, War Minister Anami committed seppuku in his office, slicing open his stomach. "With my death," he said in a note left behind at the scene, "I humbly apologize for my great crime, believing our sacred land shall never perish."[83] Admiral Ugaki chose an even more dramatic departure. "I'm going to follow in the footsteps of those many loyal officers and men who devoted themselves to the country," he wrote in his diary before getting into the cockpit of a kamikaze plane and heading south in search of the American Navy looming over the horizon. There is no record of him hitting an enemy target, and he probably crashed into the sea.[84]

Throughout the occupied territories, reports of the defeat triggered a variety of reactions from the officers and men who had spent years fighting for Hirohito. Lieutenant General Tanida Isamu received the news in the isolated port of Rabaul. "I was practically laughing," he said later. "It all seemed so strange to me."[85] At the other end of the empire, in Manchuria, Japanese private Oguma Kenji was intensely frustrated when he first heard the news of the surrender. He could not fathom that Japan might lose a war. After twenty minutes spent in gloomy thoughts it occurred to him that it meant he could return to see his family, and his mood brightened. "You couldn't let that show, so I kept quiet about it, but I think everyone felt that way."[86]

Large numbers of Japanese troops were scattered across East Asia, many of them undefeated in battle and under the impression that they could have fought on if their emperor had ordered them to. The British officer Frederick Spencer Chapman entered the Malay town of Kuantan in early September and found the former occupiers in a defiant mood: "The Japs, who seemed to consider the cessation of hostilities as a mutual agreement rather than surrender, were very truculent and still went about the town fully armed."[87] In a prison camp in northeast China, some of the American inmates jeered at their former guards, but they were in a minority. "Most kept silent, feeling perhaps that jeers were inappropriate—we had been defeated by the Japanese in the early part of the war," wrote one of the prisoners, John J. A. Michel.[88]

From Indochina to Formosa, there was no authority to take over control from the Japanese army of occupation, and rather than leave local society to the random violence of unruly mobs, the Allies often let Japanese troops or militias patrol the areas that they had ruled with an iron fist until then. Mountbatten arrived near the town of Palembang on Sumatra, having been informed beforehand that the British Army had been forced to keep Japanese troops under arms to protect lines of communication and vital areas. "It was nevertheless a great shock to me," he said later, "to find over a thousand Japanese troops guarding the nine miles of road from the airport to the town, and to find them drawn up in parties of twenty, presenting arms, the officers saluting with swords which long ago should have been souvenirs."[89]

For the Allied troops who suddenly and unexpectedly found themselves victorious, peace was an unknown condition, and the first days after the Japanese surrender passed in a slightly unreal, dreamlike atmosphere. Michael Bak described how the crew onboard the destroyer USS *Franks* took their first faltering steps into peace. "We were able to put the running lights on aboard ship and be able to walk the decks with lights on. It was just a very strange, eerie feeling—it's no longer dark! You don't have to bump your feet into a hatch somewhere or feel your way around like we did in very dark nights."[90]

In the island of Bougainville, east of New Guinea, the soldiers suddenly got extremely cautious, Australian gunner Ken Cotter recalled. "War's everyday dangers had become routine but, with peace declared, nobody was prepared to take any risks for fear of becoming a casualty; all suddenly became reluctant to go beyond the perimeter's wire. Their main concerns were booby traps and 'wandering Jap raiding parties'."[91]

Peter Medcalf, a 20-year-old Australian infantryman also in Bougainville, sat down silently, listening over the radio to the sound of hysterical crowds in Brisbane, celebrating peace, until someone shouted, "Turn that bloody thing off!" Slowly Medcalf realized that they were all lost, and that the life they had come to know was over. "Killing and death had become part of us, we accepted the constant rain, the smell of rotting growth, the night sounds of the jungle. Now this was gone, could we become part of that strange other life we had almost forgotten?"[92]

One group of people was more lost than any other: the Asians who had cast their lot in with the Japanese and now had no way back. In Singapore, Subhas Chandra Bose, the leader of the Indian movement that had sought liberation from British colonial rule with Japanese help, now saw his project in ruins. Instead, he looked towards the future. "The roads to Delhi are many," he said in his last declaration to his soldiers, "and Delhi still remains our goal. The sacrifices of your immortal comrades and yourselves will certainly achieve their fulfillment."[93]

In a separate message to Indian civilians in East Asia he promised that "India shall be free and before long."[94] Shortly afterwards, he got on a plane to Bangkok, the first stop in a meandering journey by plane across East Asia, as he considered his options. On August 18, his plane landed briefly in Formosa and then took off again. Minutes later it crashed into the ground and burst into flames. Ground personnel rushed to the scene and watched in horror how one of the passengers had been turned into a human torch. It was Bose. He died shortly afterwards at a military hospital.[95]

Prior to the arrival of the first American forces in Japan, there was considerable worry that senior US officers might become the victims of assassination attempts carried out by dissidents in the Japanese military who would have liked to carry on the fight. Nimitz told a member of his staff, intelligence officer Edwin Layton, that he thought MacArthur would be in particular danger. Layton disagreed. "You're the one they would kill, not MacArthur, if they were to try such a thing," he said. The Japanese islands had been attacked by planes taking off from Nimitz's carriers, and their cities had been levelled by B-29s based on islands in the Pacific where Nimitz held command. Nimitz seemed convinced and asked Layton to accompany him at the surrender ceremony as his bodyguard. He made sure that Layton was a sufficiently proficient shot by taking him to a pistol range to retrain his "shooting eye."[96]

Naval aviator Noel Gayler was among the first Americans to set foot in the Yokosuka area near Tokyo. Visiting with a friend, initially he held his .38 in his hand, expecting that someone might shoot at him, but he soon relaxed. The two Americans, big and smelly after weeks at sea, hopped on an electric trolley, which was the only vehicle still running. It was full of Japanese but no one gave them a dirty look. They inched their way inside. A little old gentleman in a Western suit pulled out his calling card and gave it to them. They went to a resort outside the city and walked inside a big, good-looking building. "It turned out to be a school for little kids of privileged people in the Japanese society. When we got there, they invited the two evil-smelling, enormous conquerors to sit down on tatami mats, gave us tea, and had the little kids do their song and dance for us. Unbelievable."[97]

The formal surrender ceremony took place on board the battleship USS *Missouri* anchored in Tokyo Bay on September 2. Most senior officers who had played a role in the defeat of Japan were present. General Eichelberger flew in from the Philippines for the occasion, feeling that he was walking through the pages of history. "The ceremony aboard the battleship *Missouri* surely did nothing to dispel this compelling sense of drama," he wrote in his memoirs. "From the steel deck of the *Missouri*, as hot in the sunlight as the top side of a kitchen range, I could see in Tokyo Bay the gleaming might of the greatest armada of all time."[98] In a show of strength, US planes flew in circles over

Tokyo. "Some of my friends said it was the most dangerous mission of the war," a naval aviator said. "They all were supposed to fly over at 500 feet and just keep it going—1,200 airplanes from the fleet."[99]

The Japanese delegation, consisting of both officers and civilians, formed a bleak presence. On the civilian side, the delegation was led by Foreign Minister Shigemitsu Mamoru, in formal diplomatic attire including a top hat. Having lost one leg to a Chinese bomb during the previous decade, Shigemitsu had great difficulty getting on the battleship, and had to be lifted on board with a swing-like device. "If the memories of the bestialities of the Japanese prison camps were not so fresh in mind, one might have felt sorry for Shigemitsu as he hobbled on his wooden leg toward the green baize covered table where the papers lay waiting," wrote Homer Bigart, a correspondent for the *New York Herald Tribune*.[100]

Halsey also observed Shigemitsu, taking in all the details: "He took off his gloves and his silk hat, sat down, dropped his cane, picked it up, fiddled with his hat and gloves, and shuffled the papers. He pretended to be looking for a pen—an underling finally brought him one—but I felt certain that he was stalling for time, though God knows what he hoped to accomplish." Halsey got impatient: "I wanted to slap him and tell him, 'Sign, damn you! Sign!'"[101]

Halsey's hostility did not make an impression on the Japanese. Rather, they paid attention to MacArthur, and the short speech he made after the signing of the surrender. Captain Henri Smith-Hutton of the US Navy, who accompanied the Japanese delegation, noticed a remarkable change in the faces of those who understood English. "Especially when he said that the representatives of the Allied powers did not come to the ceremony in a spirit of distrust, malice and hatred. It seemed to me as though they didn't expect such generous treatment."[102]

They also listened intently when MacArthur went on to talk about what had been won at such cost in lives, and what mankind risked if no lesson were learned from the past: "Today the guns are silent. A great tragedy has ended. A great victory has been won. The skies no longer rain death, the seas bear only commerce, men everywhere walk upright in the sunlight. The entire world is quietly at peace. The holy mission has been completed... We have had our last chance. If we do not devise some greater and more equitable system, Armageddon will be at our door."[103]

CHAPTER NINE

"Peace"

September 1945 Onwards

In his fourth and last inaugural speech, held on January 20, 1945, less than three months before his death, Franklin D. Roosevelt had expressed the hope that the immense sacrifice suffered by the Allied peoples in their effort to defeat the Axis powers would not be in vain. "In the days and in the years that are to come we shall work for a just and honorable peace, a durable peace, as today we work and fight for total victory in war. We can and we will achieve such a peace," he had said.[1] Less than eight months later, after the formal end to hostilities on board the battleship *Missouri*, was the time to turn that vision into reality.

For Allied servicemen across Asia, it seemed a formidable task. Especially those who revisited places they had known before the war and witnessed the devastation brought about by years of conflict were close to succumbing to despair. Cecil King, chief yeoman on the aircraft carrier USS *Hornet*, who had left Manila in late December 1941, just before the Philippine capital was captured by the Japanese, could hardly recognize the city. It was, he said, "beat to death." And yet, there was an atmosphere of hope and of willingness to move on. "There was a feeling, just sort of recovering, and getting over the shock, and getting back to a normal way of life," he said. "It was a bustling place. It was really a feverish activity."[2]

Retribution was in most cases part of the process of returning to peace, although it was implemented with varying degrees of severity across the region. China followed a remarkably lenient course, and only a tiny fraction of the Japanese and collaborators were punished when set against the enormous crimes that had taken place on their watch. In the Philippines, MacArthur confirmed the death sentence of General Yamashita Tomoyuki for his ultimate responsibility for the crimes committed by his troops during the US invasion in 1944. "The soldier, be he friend or foe, is charged with the protection of the weak and unarmed," MacArthur stated. "It is the very essence and reason for his being. When he violates this sacred trust, he not only profanes his entire cult but threatens the very fabric of international society."[3]

The most extensive war crimes trial in the region was the Tokyo Tribunal, resulting in seven death sentences and 16 sentences to life in jail. Jim Sansom, a prison guard at Sugamo Prison, knew several of the prisoners on death row. He taught them how to play gin rummy and gave former Prime Minister Tōjō pointers about how to win. He also attended the hangings. Some of the condemned yelled "Banzai!" before their execution. Only one showed fear and was whimpering on the way to the gallows. "I think I felt sorry for him," said Sansom. "Well, I didn't feel sorry for him for what he had done. He was there and that was that. But he knew he had done something that he shouldn't have."[4]

After up to four years of war, there was a pervasive desire among Allied personnel to escape out of uniform and return to the life that had been left behind. Marine Arthur Liberty described the situation after his unit arrived back in Baltimore. They received a final physical checkup, and after that, a Marine recruiting officer gave a talk, explaining how each of them would get 90 days' leave, receive a 300-dollar bonus, and be promoted to the next rank if they agreed to reenlist. The Marines all said, "Noooo! We want to go home."[5]

Robert Ellinger, a sailor in the US Navy, recounted a strange experience he had after returning stateside. "We would be walking down the street and somebody would say 'you guys just got back, didn't you?' We'd say, 'How do you know?' 'Well, when you walk aboard a ship, your legs spread out and you use them for balance. Then you get on land and you are still walking the same way'."[6] They shared a special bond, and in a more general sense, the men who had been at war were a band of brothers, and no outsider would ever completely understand what they had been through.

This held true many years later. "It's amazing how the current generation has no idea of what the feeling was back then. They never will, because I don't think a war like that will ever happen again," said Michael Bak, who had spent the war on board the destroyer USS *Franks*.[7] Ralph Simoneau, a Marine who had been on Iwo Jima, found it relatively easy to deal with the memories of battle. He never saw it as his mission in the war to kill other people. "Our job was to go from Point A to Point B and your adversary or the enemy did not want you to go from Point A to Point B so he tried to stop you," he said.

"I don't carry any scars from that. A lot of people can't quite understand that, that you can go through this and not have these scars."[8]

America thanked its soldiers by giving them an education many of them would never had have access to otherwise. There had been precursors to this even before the war in the Pacific had ended. While in Guam in 1944, Major John Ellis of the Marine Corps took part in a program to teach basic academic topics to his men. "One of my officers had a PhD in education and we did set up an education program. A lot of these kids had not graduated from high school," he said. "We were very proud of that program."[9] At the same time, a similar philosophy was implemented on a much grander scale in the form of the GI Bill, short for the Servicemen's Readjustment Act, which mandated a number of benefits for veterans, most importantly training that could help them in their civilian lives. A total of 2.2 million veterans ended up attending college.[10]

Bill Filter was one of them. He started classes in Ohio after being discharged from Walter Reed Hospital. He was 22 and had been in the Army since he was 18. Now he was determined to put his time in the Pacific behind him. "It just rolls off of you like a bead of sweat," he said. "We didn't want to talk about the war. We didn't want to talk about combat. We didn't want to talk about the Pacific Islands, and France, and Germany. Nobody wanted to talk about it. We wanted to have a good time. We wanted to go to football games. We wanted to drink beer, chase women, the whole works."[11]

On August 15, 1945, after Emperor Hirohito's voice was heard over the radio, Tokyo Imperial University professor Yabe Teiji stepped out into his garden, with its flourishing sweet potatoes and cucumbers, to bow in the direction of the Imperial Palace, struggling in vain to hold back his tears. "Though mortifying in the extreme, the Potsdam Declaration has been accepted, and with it, unconditional surrender. The time for endurance begins today," he wrote in his diary. "What fate awaits us I do not know, but I am determined to live as a righteous patriot, leading the way to Japan's revival."[12]

That revival looked a distant prospect in the early autumn of 1945. Japan had lost the fruits of half a century of colonial expansion. It had to relinquish Taiwan and Korea, and its sphere of influence, which had included the vast territory of Manchuria, was now rolled back to the water's edge. Hirohito was allowed to stay on as emperor, but he had to give up his divine status, and he appeared in an iconic photo, very ungodlike in his bespectacled humility, standing next to MacArthur, who looked twice his size.

In a sense, the complete and utter defeat that Japan experienced in 1945 was no surprise, not even to the nation itself. Japan had been warned. Admiral Harold Stark, chief of naval operations in 1941, had spoken to the Japanese ambassador Nomura Kichisaburō in remarkably frank terms: "If you attack us we will break your empire before we are through with you."[13] Japan had entered into the war, knowing from the outset that it would be the underdog, and its strategic objectives were similarly limited. A scenario of Japan occupying the western part of the continental United States, as described in alternative history novels such as *The Man in the High Castle* by science fiction author Philip K. Dick, was never considered within the realm of the possible by Japan's commanders.

Yet, the Japanese fought with a wild determination belying their moderate goals. "Of all the major combatants," historian H. P. Willmott states, "Japan alone did not aspire to final victory but nevertheless fought with a totality and finality unequaled by countries intent on securing the unconditional surrender of their enemies."[14] Japan had suffered massive bloodletting on the battlefronts. More than two million soldiers lost their lives,[15] and especially during the last year of the war, the well-known expectation of Japanese soldiers to take a large number of enemies with them before dying was turned on its head. In the period from March 1, 1944 to May 1, 1945, for every American soldier losing his life in battle, 22 Japanese were killed.[16]

Casualties at home were also staggering, and more than half a million men, women, and children had been killed in the massive bombing raids on the major cities concentrated during the last year of hostilities.[17] American servicemen were exposed to the enormous destruction in Japan, with survivors living in rubble extracting whatever usable materials they could find to build new homes. "It was just desolate, and bombed out," a sailor said. "We saw nothing but ruins, and how people lived in that ruin is beyond me. Why didn't they end the war a lot sooner?"[18]

The Japanese population was apprehensive at first. The official propaganda had been spreading horror stories of the abuse that was to be expected from the victorious Allies, and the first Americans did indeed encounter a great deal of nervousness, especially from the women: "You'd see a woman run out on the sidewalk and grab her kids and up the stairway they'd go with these kids, you know. The women and kids disappeared as you come down the street."[19]

For 16 remarkable days after the Japanese Empire had surrendered on September 2, 1945, the American occupation authorities did not impose censorship on the media, and the newspapers could report on the behavior of the country's new masters in an unobstructed fashion. Criticism of the behavior of the newly arrived GIs was rife. "There was a fair amount of crime in the first two or three days" after the Americans set foot on Japanese soil, the *Asahi Shimbun* reported on September 7. For example, on one day in late August, American troops had, among other things, stolen a Japanese sword and several bicycles, and robbed a beer truck. More sinisterly, according to the same paper, they had also carried out two rapes and attempted two others.[20]

Indeed, reports of sexual violence emerged as soon as the occupation began. On September 1, two American soldiers in a truck allegedly abducted a 26-year-old woman in Yokohama and took her to temporary barracks. "There altogether 27 of the American soldiers violated her in turn and rendered her unconscious," stated the complaint that Japanese officials subsequently sent to US authorities.[21] Similar incidents occurred in parts of Japan occupied by Commonwealth force. The Australian intelligence officer Allan Clifton visited the hospital bed of a young woman in Hiroshima who had been raped by 20 of his countrymen. "The moaning and wailing had ceased and she was quiet now," he wrote in his memoirs. "The tortured tension on her face had slipped away, and the soft brown skin was smooth and unwrinkled, stained with tears like the face of a child that has cried itself to sleep."[22]

There is little doubt that a significant number of rapes did take place during Allied rule of Japan and it appears that the problem was particularly serious in the early days of the occupation, when a state of some chaos reigned. The American authorities had not yet deployed military police in Japan, and General Robert Eichelberger, one of the senior commanders of the occupation force, had to rely on armed Japanese gendarmes for his personal security.[23]

The extent of the issue is a matter of continued debate. According to one oft-cited statistic, in the prefecture of Kanagawa alone, there were 1,336 cases of rape during the first ten days of September, out of a population of less than two million.[24] Likewise, some standard Western accounts indicate that dozens or even hundreds of rapes took place every day in the early months after the Allied takeover.[25] More recent research has suggested that these figures are overblown and partly the result of a misinterpretation of official Japanese statistics.[26] Consensus on even an approximate number of Japanese women victimized will probably never materialize, but it is highly unlikely that Japan saw anything approaching the wave of rape that the Soviet Army unleashed on Eastern Germany in 1945, or for that matter the brutal practices of the Japanese forces, especially in China beginning in 1937.

Old enmities died hard. Former Japanese soldiers were easily recognizable because most still wore the characteristic field cap and some also maintained the puttees that had been part of their footwear during the war years. "If there was a small group of them, when we went by in this jeep they would turn their backs on us," said a GI.[27] Others were more openly hostile. Marine Alvin Orsland and some of his comrades went to inspect a group of captured Japanese soldiers and were surprised by their defiant attitude. "What's a matter, Marine, you chicken?" they taunted them, and if they had not been separated by barbed wire, it would have come to blows.[28]

Little by little, relations improved. Art G. Anderson, a Marine intelligence officer, saw it with the old men first. "You'd go by and they'd give you the old 'V' sign and bow at the hip, saying 'OK', 'OK'," he said.[29] A rifleman arrived at the port of Sasebo in the middle of September and noticed the same Japanese characters being repeated again and again on signs in the city. "We finally asked the interpreter what it was. He said, 'The Emperor says honor and respect the Americans.' We had absolutely no trouble."[30] Even the most fanatic members of the former Japanese military gradually showed signs of adopting a more conciliatory attitude. Naval aviator Noel Gayler remembered "talking to a bunch of kamikaze pilots who were damned glad the war was over."[31]

At the outset, Captain Henri Smith-Hutton of the US Navy considered the presence of tens of thousands of Allied troops in Japan, alongside a similar number of their former adversaries, to be a potentially explosive situation. "There was plenty of opportunity for misunderstandings. Except for a few isolated incidents which weren't serious, all went well. We have reason to be very proud of the record."[32]

The American encounter with Japan in 1945 was similar to the encounter in 1854, when US Navy ships had appeared off the coast of the isolated island nation to pry it open for trade, in that it was much more successful than anyone had dared to hope.[33] After recovering from the initial shock of defeat, most Japanese were bent on rebuilding their country as soon as possible, and some were optimistic that the conditions were there for a speedier recovery than generally expected. Fujiyama Aiichiro, a business leader and future foreign minister, recalled that "when it was learned that the occupying power would be the US... many industrialists uncorked their champagne bottles and toasted the coming of a new industrialist era."[34]

Japan's industrial output in 1946 was only 27.6 percent of what it had been before Pearl Harbor, but by 1951 it was back at prewar levels, and in 1960 it was nearly four times as large.[35] Japan had unleashed its productive and creative powers in the pursuit of profit rather than conquest. Eventually, this would make it the world's second-largest economy and lead to a situation where former Marines, who had fought their way through the jungles of Guadalcanal and up the slopes of Mount Suribachi, would be driving Japanese-made cars in their retirement.

That was all hard to see in the mid-1940s, with Japan devastated from one end to the other, but even back then, the scene was being set for the nation's post-war economic miracle. Vice Admiral Kanazawa Masao, a jovial and smiling 53-year-old, predicted as much when he met with Western correspondents in September 1945 in the port city of Kure. "Japan will now by peaceful methods accomplish what she could not do in war," he said. "You beat us at war, but we will beat you at golf."[36]

Don L. Holmes, a US Marine sent on guard duty in China immediately after the cessation of hostilities, had been expecting to have to struggle mainly with the issue of a huge Japanese army of occupation that might be less than willing to obey the Americans, since it had not been defeated in battle, but only laid down its weapons because ordered to. The reality on the ground turned out to be completely different. "The only problem we had was the Chinese Communists were fighting the Chinese loyalist army. We kind of were caught in between in some cases. The Japanese cooperated one hundred percent."[37]

This had surprising consequences. Robert B. Luckey, a Marine artillery officer posted to China immediately after the war, found himself working with his former Japanese foes to keep order in China. "The Japs that surrendered to the division there were immediately put to work guarding the railroad against the Chinese Communists at that time, who were just getting organized and were just making themselves disagreeable along the lines of communication in North China."[38]

The end of the war against Japan did not bring peace to China. Instead, it set off fierce competition between the Nationalists and the Communists. When the Japanese surrendered in August, the two parties, led by Chiang Kai-shek in the southwest and Mao Zedong in the north, positioned themselves to benefit to the maximum extent possible, even at the cost of renewed bloodshed. The fact that Chiang and Mao met in Chongqing and toasted each other on the victory did little to change the rivalry. "The battle for control will be intense," the Communist Party's Central Committee said in mid-August in a message to regional leaders. "Our party must prepare to mobilize our military forces and deal with a civil war… on a scale that will be dictated by circumstances."[39]

The flashpoint was Manchuria. There was a bitter irony to this, since that was also the part of China where the friction with Japan had gradually escalated into open war in the early 1930s. The Manchurian provinces were as important as they had been during the previous decade, if not more so. They were rich in natural resources, and a decade and a half of Japanese quasi-colonial rule had left them with fairly sophisticated industries which could be of key importance when embarking on the gargantuan task of rebuilding the devastated Chinese economy. Finally, the Soviet Army was present with 1.5 million soldiers, in possession of all the weaponry that had been seized from the Japanese.

Within weeks of the Japanese capitulation, Nationalist and Communist troops were facing each other in large-scale battles, fighting over some of the same locations that had been contested with equal ferocity during the war with Japan in the 1930s. November 1945 saw vicious combat between Nationalists and Communists over possession of the pass of Shanhaiguan on the eastern edge of the Great Wall, the exact same spot where Chinese and Japanese forces had clashed in 1933. Shortly afterwards, the battle moved on to the city of Jinzhou, also a scene of hostilities during in 1931, at the start of Japanese expansion in Manchuria.[40]

The Soviet forces in Manchuria were highly ambivalent about allowing the Communists into the areas they occupied, and for a period prohibited them from carrying out any political activities in Soviet-occupied areas. This somewhat surprising Soviet position reflected a policy in the initial phase of the post-war period of trying to establish a modus vivendi with the Nationalists under Chiang Kai-shek.[41] In addition, Soviet dictator Joseph Stalin may have been motivated by a wish to keep China divided and weak, giving him an incentive to shift support back and forth between the Communists and the Nationalists.

Eventually, however, the Soviets agreed to hand over captured Japanese weaponry to the Chinese Communists. The list was impressive: 1,436 field artillery pieces; 8,989 machine guns; 11,052 grenade launchers; 3,078 trucks; 14,777 horses; 21,084 supply vehicles; 815 specialized vehicles, and 287 command cars.[42] As for the machinery and other industrial assets seized by the Soviet forces in Manchuria, neither the Communists nor the Nationalists benefited much. Before they pulled out of the region in the course of 1946, the Soviets made sure to dismantle up to 90 percent of the region's industrial capacity and ship it back home, treating it as spoils of war, similar to the way they had stripped Eastern Germany of most of its productive capacity.[43]

Complicating the picture in China, the Americans also got involved, allocating transport planes and ships to ferry Nationalist soldiers to parts of the country where they were not present at the time of the Japanese surrender. Large numbers of Nationalist troops were transported to Manchurian ports, triggering Soviet suspicion about American intentions. Zhang Jia, a Nationalist official involved in negotiations with the Soviet side, noted in his diary: "The Soviets are unwilling to have us rely on the United States to transport our troops. In other words, they are unwilling to have the United States acquire a foothold in the Northeast."[44]

In fact, while the United States overall demonstrated a preference for the Nationalists, there was also a lingering belief that the Communists represented a more vigorous force that should at least be co-opted. The Americans tried to mediate between the two rival sides, and hoped ideally for a coalition government that could give the vast Chinese nation a sense of unity and purpose. Even though the US government sent one of its war heroes, General George Marshall, the army chief-of-staff and proverbial architect of victory, it was all in vain. The civil war went on.

The ongoing civil war often manifested itself in brutal ways. Don Holmes, the US Marine, described a scene that he witnessed one day in the port city of Tianjin: "I saw them bring about twelve guys in roped together at the neck into the middle of [Tianjin] and kneel them down and execute them because they were communists."[45] The idea that people who could kill each other in this manner might also cooperate seemed ludicrous. Perhaps the task the Americans had set for themselves in China had been doomed from the start. "We were, in effect, seeking the reconciliation of irreconcilable differences," senior US diplomat Dean Acheson, later secretary of state, wrote in his memoirs.[46]

China's fratricidal war would continue on and off for four more years, irrespective of American attempts to bring the sides to the negotiating table, and it ended in October 1949 with Mao Zedong standing triumphant at the entrance of Beijing's Forbidden City, where shortly before a huge portrait of Chiang Kai-shek had been hanging, declaring the victory of Communism in the world's most populous country. "China has arisen," Mao would say.

For the Americans, it was to be known as "the loss of China." It was the end of their century-long "China Dream," which had begun as a vision of molding the vast Asian nation in their own image: a Christian, technologically advanced civilization in the heart of Asia. It was all a mirage, an illusion that could not be sustained because it rested on a flawed idea of what kind of nation China was. It "grew out of a century of American evangelical, educational, philanthropic and business association with China," according to US diplomat John Paton Davies. "There resulted a sentimental, condescending, proprietary love of fictional Chinese, who, Americans fancied, reciprocated with due gratitude, admiration and loyalty."[47]

Meanwhile, most Chinese just tried to get on. Holmes, the Marine, sat in a bar in Tianjin while the bar owner gave him a lecture in the Chinese art of survival amid political storms. "How did you all fare when the Japs were here? How did they treat you all?" Holmes asked. The bar owner said, "Well, you know, when you all came ashore… and all those people were down there waving American flags? When the Japanese came in they were down there waving Japanese flags. The Chinese don't care who's going to be in charge. They just go on and do their thing," he said. "They're resilient. Nobody's ever conquered China because we just absorb them."[48]

Even many years after the war, Mustapha Hussein remembered his reaction when he heard that Japan had surrendered: "I cried." A political radical in the former British colony of Malaya, he had hoped that the peninsula's separatist movement would seize the opportunity and declare independence during the brief period that offered itself while Japan was fatally weak and the Allies had not yet declared victory. Now that Japan had formally capitulated, the reimposition of British rule was just a matter of time. The chance was wasted. "I regretted the matter deeply as Malaya would once again be colonized and gripped by Western power."[49]

Elsewhere in Southeast Asia, some activists did try to exploit the brief interregnum between Japan's surrender and the arrival of the Western victors. In the East Indies on August 17, two days after the Japanese had accepted their defeat, the head of the separatist movement, Sukarno, declared independence, creating "an electrifying effect on the mass of Indonesians," according to an observer.[50] In Indochina two weeks later, on September 2, the day of the surrender ceremony on the USS *Missouri* in Tokyo Bay, the US-backed guerrilla leader Ho Chi Minh did the same for Vietnam. "Today we are determined to oppose the wicked schemes of the French imperialists, and we call upon the victorious Allies to recognize our freedom and independence," he told a jubilant crowd in Hanoi.[51]

Both attempts were squashed within weeks as the old imperialists returned, battered but determined to pick up where they had left off. It would seem that it was now back to colonial business as usual, and that the Western empires would be resurrected to their former grandeur. Nothing could be further from the truth. The European colonies, some dating back centuries, only returned for a brief interlude before evaporating forever. This also meant that the peace that was heralded by Hirohito's speech in August 1945 was not peace at all, but more war by new means. This went for virtually all of Southeast Asia. For every society in the region except Thailand, the first two decades after the war that ended in 1945 brought new mass-scale violence, whether in the form of war, civil war, or revolution, or a combination of the three.[52]

It came as completely unexpected to most Europeans. B. C. de Jonge, governor general of the Dutch East Indies in the 1930s, had confidently signaled that his country's control of the Southeast Asian archipelago was essentially for eternity. "We have ruled here for 300 years with the whip and the club and we shall still be doing it in another 300 years," he had said.[53] In fact, counting from the time they returned to the East Indies in 1945 trying to reinstate their authority, the Dutch had only four years left as colonial masters. The Dutch had shown in 1941 that they could be beaten, fast and decisively, and the aura of superiority which had enabled them to control a country many times larger than their own was gone forever.

The genie of independence was out of the bottle, and it could not be put back in. Often it had horrifically violent results. Dirk Bogarde, the future actor, was on the island of Java with British forces and saw how Dutch internees, returning from the camps and trying to start their lives anew in their looted homes, often were murdered by frenzied mobs. In one instance, an elderly Dutch couple had been hacked to death in their small villa: "The woman... had put up a desperate fight, her hands shredded by the knives, her blood sprayed in elegant arcs across the tiled walls. The man lay face downwards in the sitting room, his balding head almost severed from his body."[54]

The inability of the Western colonial powers to deal efficiently with social problems that the colonized people, left to their own devices, had occasionally proven better at solving further contributed to the Western loss of prestige in the former colonies. An example was the famine in Indochina, which was alleviated after the French authorities had been ousted in the spring of 1945 and replaced with an indigenous regime propped up by the Japanese. Immediately after assuming power, the colony's new rulers introduced new measures to reduce speculation on the pricing of scarce rice supplies while improving the transportation of grains to the hunger-stricken provinces. "Brutal measures that we ourselves would not have ventured to take bring a momentary abundance," a French writer reluctantly acknowledged, adding that the people of Indochina "have come to think very seriously that they are ripe to be a great nation."[55]

This was only reinforced when the Japanese left and handed back Indochina to the Western powers. Despite the improvement made in the spring, the food situation quickly turned desperate again. "Hanoi with a population of

200,000 inhabitants is literally dying of hunger," a foreign observer wrote. "The worst situation is that of feeding the infants."[56] This was only partly the result of Western mismanagement. More importantly, Indochina experienced devastating flooding, with river levels in Hanoi reaching a historical record, but the prestige of the colonial authorities suffered yet another blow.[57]

As in the East Indies, a protracted guerrilla campaign followed in Indochina, fueled by the population's thirst for independence, and French determination to hold onto its prized possession. If France let go of this "admirable balcony on the Pacific," it would no longer be a great power, a leading French politician said.[58] The result was long years of bloodshed which gradually evolved into a full-scale conventional war, and only ended with the withdrawal of the French colonial rulers and the division of Indochina into two in 1954.

Captain Henri Smith-Hutton of the US Navy was a naval attaché at the US Embassy in France after the war and was often informed by French officers returning from service in the East about the many challenges associated with the unconventional warfare in Indochina. He could not know it at the time, but the problems were eerily similar to the ones that the Americans would be facing themselves less than a generation into the future in what had by then become Vietnam:

"All remarked on the great difficulty in carrying on operations against guerrillas, that they used tactics that are classic in guerrilla warfare, that since very few of the French spoke the languages and couldn't disguise themselves as natives, they were at a great disadvantage in the country, that they could control the cities and main lines of communication, but as soon as they left the roads and railroads, they were at the mercy of the guerrillas who struck without warning and then disappeared into the hinterland, so that it was impossible for regular troops to fight against such tactics in a country where few of them spoke the languages and where they didn't know the land."[59]

The war did not end for everyone in 1945, For some it lasted for years longer. That was true for Oguma Kenji, one of more than half a million Japanese soldiers kept prisoner in the Soviet Union in the second part of the 1940s. "The first winter was really tough," he said. "Almost all the deaths from malnutrition happened then."[60] He himself made it through imprisonment partly with the help of older Russian women living near his camps, many of whom had lost sons and husbands in the war. "How old are you?" they would ask, and he would reply in his broken Russian: "Twenty." The women would shake their heads with a sad expression and say, "So young."[61]

For others, the war lasted for just weeks or months after the Japanese had signed the surrender documents. President Truman was eager to bring the boys home, just as most belligerent nations wished to repatriate their soldiers as soon as feasible. Yet the war was never completely over for those who lived through it, and it stayed on as a haunting memory of events on an unprecedented scale, which had taken place during their formative years. In a sense the war is still a present reality for the dwindling but still sizable number of people who experienced the conflict at first hand.

The question of how long the war in the Asia Pacific lasted can also be put to the historian. The conventional answer is that it spanned less than four years, the time that passed between Pearl Harbor and Hiroshima. A slightly more unconventional reply would argue that it began in 1937 with the onset of all-out conventional hostilities between China and Japan. Recently, the Chinese government and some Chinese historians have asserted that the actual beginning of the war with Japan was in 1931, with the Japanese occupation of Manchuria. Obviously, the further back in time the start of the war is pushed, the more central becomes the role of China.

There is less controversy about the end of the war, as most agree on 1945 as marking the natural conclusion. Still, the conflicts which harrowed the region for the next three decades could in many ways be seen as consequences of the larger conflagration of the early 1940s. The internecine war that would lay waste to Korea only five years into the future came about partly as a result of the division of the peninsula into a Soviet-backed north and a US-supported south after the end of the Japanese occupation. Likewise, the numerous struggles against the Western colonial masters might be seen as having been kindled by the examples set by the Japanese. It could, therefore, be argued that the Japanese-American war of 1941 to 1945 was part of a much larger half-century-long narrative stretching from the civil wars of China of the 1920s all the way until the evacuation of Saigon in 1975. Perhaps it will take another century of writing about the conflict, and the sobering effect of time passed, to arrive at a satisfactory conclusion.

Whether now or in the distant future, one of the main objectives of history will be to learn from it. Some of the participants in the vast conflict began learning as soon as the weapons fell silent. On August 14, 1946, the first anniversary of Japan's decision to accept unconditional surrender, emperor Hirohito met with Prime Minister Yoshida Shigeru as well as Suzuki Kantarō, who had headed the government at the end of the war. The emperor expressed regret at the way the war had developed but pointed out this had not been the first time Japan has suffered abject defeat. Events had come full circle. In the battle of the Paekchon River in 663, Japan had met China in battle for the first time in history, and it had been beaten and forced to withdraw to the home islands. "After that, political reforms were pushed forward, and the result was a major turning point in the development of Japanese civilization," Hirohito said. "If we bear this in mind, we can naturally understand the road that Japan needs to take after this new defeat."[62]

Endnotes

Chapter One

1   Charles Adair, Oral History, US Naval Institute, 265–266.
2   Whitney Jacobs, Interview, National Museum of the Pacific War, https://digitalarchive. pacificwarmuseum.org/digital/collection/p16769coll1/id/1956/rec/5, December 13, 2020.
3   Robert B. Luckey, Oral History, Marine Corps, 144.
4   Frank O. Hough and John A. Crown, *The Campaign on New Britain* (Historical Branch, Headquarters, U.S. Marine Corps, 1952), 87.
5   James W. Johnston, *The Long Road of War: A Marine's Story of Pacific Combat* (Lincoln NE: University of Nebraska Press, 1998), 49–50.
6   John P. Leonard, Oral History, Marine Corps, 77.
7   Lewis J. Fields, Oral History, Marine Corps, 111–112.
8   Hough and Crown, *New Britain*, 94; Henry I. Shaw and Douglas T. Kane, *Isolation of Rabaul [History of U.S. Marine Corps Operations in World War II, vol. 2]* (Washington DC: US Government Printing Office, 1963), 376.
9   Hough and Crown, *New Britain*, 95.
10 Shaw and Kane, *Isolation of Rabaul*, 376.
11 Ibid.
12 Asa Bordage, *Saturday Evening Post*, quoted in Kerry L. Lane, *Guadalcanal Marine* (Jackson MS: University Press of Mississippi, 2004), 303–304.
13 Ibid.
14 Shaw and Kane, *Isolation of Rabaul*, 377.
15 Lane, *Guadalcanal Marine*, 306.
16 Shaw and Kane, *Isolation of Rabaul*, 377.
17 Murlin Spencer, "Hill 660 Tough Goal for Marines," AP, January 18, 1944.
18 Romus Valton Burgin, Interview, National Museum of the Pacific War, https://digitalarchive. pacificwarmuseum.org/digital/collection/p16769coll1/id/3485/rec/4, December 13, 2020.
19 Lewis J. Fields, Oral History, Marine Corps, 102–103.
20 Murlin Spencer, "Hill 660 Tough Goal for Marines," AP, January 18, 1944.
21 Robert K. Fitts, *Banzai Babe Ruth: Baseball, Espionage, & Assassination during the 1934 Tour of Japan* (Lincoln NE: University of Nebraska Press, 2012), xiii.
22 Shaw and Kane, *Isolation of Rabaul*, 379.
23 Hough and Crown, *New Britain*, 176.
24 Robert Leckie, *Helmet for My Pillow* (New York NY: Bantam, 2010), 216.
25 Henry W. Buse, Oral History, Marine Corps, 62–63.
26 Bernard C. Nalty, Edwin T. Turnbladh, Jr., and Henry I. Shaw, *Central Pacific Drive [History of U.S. Marine Corps Operations in World War II, vol. 3]* (Washington DC: US Government Printing Office, 1966), 139.

27 United States Strategic Bombing Survey (hereafter USSBS), *Interrogations of Japanese Officials* (Washington DC: United States Government Printing Office, 1946), Vol. I, Interrogation of Commander Chikataka Nakajima, IJN, 144.
28 Edwin Layton, Oral History, US Naval Institute, 147–149.
29 E. B. Potter, *Nimitz* (Annapolis MD: Naval Institute Press, 1976), 265.
30 USSBS, Naval Analysis Division, *Interrogations of Japanese Officials* (Washington DC, 1946), Vol. I, Interrogation of Commander Nakajima Chikataka, IJN, 144.
31 Samuel Eliot Morison, *Aleutians, Gilberts and Marshalls June 1942–April 1944*, 202.
32 Brian Garfield, *Thousand-Mile War: World War II in Alaska and the Aleutians* (Fairbanks AK: University of Alaska Press, 1995), 389.
33 Nalty, Turnbladh, and Shaw, *Central Pacific Drive*, 117–141.
34 Edwin Layton, Oral History, US Naval Institute, 153.
35 USSBS, Naval Analysis Division, *Interrogations of Japanese Officials* (Washington DC, 1946), Vol. I, Interrogation of Commander Matsuura Goro, IJN, 134.
36 Morison, *Aleutians, Gilberts and Marshalls*, 214–215.
37 Ibid., 218–219.
38 Edwin Layton, Oral History, US Naval Institute, 153.
39 Richard Sorenson, Interview, National Museum of the Pacific War, https://digitalarchive.pacificwarmuseum.org/digital/collection/p16769coll1/id/3511/rec/6, December 13, 2020, 6–7.
40 Arthur Liberty, Interview, National Museum of the Pacific War, https://digitalarchive.pacificwarmuseum.org/digital/collection/p16769coll1/id/3731/rec/13, December 15, 2020, 21.
41 Ibid., 17.
42 Carl Matthews, Interview, National Museum of the Pacific War, https://digitalarchive.pacificwarmuseum.org/digital/collection/p16769coll1/id/10634/rec/5, December 15, 2020, 16.
43 Baine Kerr, Interview, National Museum of the Pacific War, https://digitalarchive.pacificwarmuseum.org/digital/collection/p16769coll1/id/4192/rec/3, December 15, 2020, 57.
44 Nalty, Turnbladh, and Shaw, *Central Pacific Drive*, 171.
45 Ibid.
46 Richard Sorenson, Interview, 10.
47 Justice M. Chambers, Oral History, US Marine Corps, 418–419.
48 Philip A. Crowl and Edmund G. Love, *Seizure of Gilberts and Marshalls [United States Army in World War II]* (Washington DC: US Government Printing Office, 1955), 232.
49 Paul Beam, "As It Looked From the Sky," *New York Times*, February 1944: 3.
50 Crowl and Love, *Seizure of Gilberts and Marshalls*, 242–243.
51 Thomas B. Buell, *The Quiet Warrior: A Biography of Admiral Raymond A. Spruance* (Annapolis MD: Naval Institute Press, 1987), 246.
52 Ernie Pyle, *Last Chapter* (New York NY: Henry Holt, 1946), 7–8.
53 Ernest J. King, *US Navy at War, 1941–1945: Official Reports to the Secretary of the Navy* (Washington DC: United States Navy Department, 1946), 171.
54 Baine Kerr, Interview, National Museum of the Pacific War, https://digitalarchive.pacificwarmuseum.org/digital/collection/p16769coll1/id/4192/rec/3, December 15, 2020, 54–55.
55 Edwin Layton, Oral History, US Naval Institute, 152.
56 Grace Person Hayes, *The History of the Joint Chiefs of Staff in World War II: The War Against Japan* (Annapolis MD: Naval Institute Press, 1982), 547–548.
57 Oliver Jensen, *Carrier War* (New York NY: Simon and Schuster, 1945), 97.

58 Fitzhugh Lee, "First Cruise of the *Essex*," in *Carrier Warfare in the Pacific: An Oral History Collection*, ed. E. T. Wooldridge (Washington DC: Smithsonian Institution Press, 1993), 114.

59 John Prados, *Combined Fleet Decoded: The Secret History of American Intelligence and the Japanese Navy in World War II* (New York NY: Random House, 1995), 533–536.

60 Ronald H. Spector, *Eagle Against the Sun: The American War With Japan* (New York NY: Vintage Books, 1985), 271.

61 Buell, *Quiet Warrior*, 256.

62 Ibid., 256.

63 Ibid., 254.

64 Edwin Layton, Oral History, US Naval Institute, 154–155.

65 James L. Day, Oral History, US Marine Corps, 77.

66 Al Adkins, Interview, National Museum of the Pacific War, https://digitalarchive.pacificwar-museum.org/digital/collection/p16769coll1/id/11030/rec/1, 33.

67 Crowl and Love, *Seizure of Gilberts and Marshalls*, 365.

68 Paul Kennedy, *The Rise and Fall of the Great Powers* (New York NY: Vintage Books, 1989), 354.

69 Potter, *Nimitz*, 228.

70 Ibid., 26–27.

71 Charles A. Lockwood and Hans C. Adamson, *Battles of the Philippine Sea* (New York NY: Crowell, 1967), 7, quoted in D. Clayton James, *The Years of MacArthur* (Boston MA: Houghton Mifflin Company, 1985), vol. 2, 398–399.

72 Henri Smith-Hutton, Oral History, US Naval Institute, 492.

73 Lockwood and Adamson, *Philippine Sea*, 7, quoted in James, *Years of MacArthur*, vol. 2, 398–399; Potter, *Nimitz*, 29.

74 Potter, *Nimitz*, 225.

75 Edwin Layton, Oral History, US Naval Institute, 149.

76 Lockwood and Adamson, *Philippine Sea*, 7, quoted in James, *Years of MacArthur*, vol. 2, 398–399.

77 Charles Adair, Oral History, US Naval Institute, 341–342.

78 Robert L. Eichelberger with Milton MacKaye, *Our Jungle Road to Tokyo* (New York NY: The Viking Press, 1950), 177.

79 Charles Adair, Oral History, US Naval Institute, 328.

80 Waldo Heinrich and Marc Gallicchio, *Implacable Foes: War in the Pacific 1944–1945* (New York NY: Oxford University Press, 2017), 41.

81 James, *Years of MacArthur*, vol. 2, 450.

82 Edwin A. Pollock, Oral History, US Marine Corps, 178.

83 Bill Filter, Interview, National Museum of the Pacific War, https://digitalarchive.pacificwar-museum.org/digital/collection/p16769coll1/id/5492/rec/7, December 23, 2020, 9.

84 William Manchester, *American Caesar* (London: Hutchinson of London, 1979), 4.

85 Maurice Matloff, *Strategic Planning for Coalition Warfare 1943–1944 [United States Army in World War II]* (Washington DC: US Government Printing Office, 1958), 319–320.

86 Douglas MacArthur, *Reminiscences* (New York NY: McGraw-Hill Book Company, 1964), 183.

87 Potter, *Nimitz*, 280.

88 Ibid., 280–282.

89 Ibid., 283.

90 Kiyosawa Kiyoshi, *A Diary of Darkness: The Wartime Diary of Kiyosawa Kiyoshi*, ed. Eugene Soviak, Princeton University Press, 1998), 131.

91 Akira Iriye, *Power and Culture: The Japanese-American War 1941–1945* (Cambridge MA: Harvard University Press, 1981), 168.

92 USSBS, *The Effects of Strategic Bombing on Japanese Morale* (Washington DC: Morale Division, 1947), 17–18.

93 Thomas R. H. Havens, *Valley of Darkness: The Japanese People and World War Two* (New York NY: W. W. Norton, 1978), 151.

94 Ugaki Matome, *Fading Victory: The Diary of Admiral Matome Ugaki 1941–1945*, ed. Donald M. Goldstein and Katherine V. Dillon (Annapolis MD: Naval Institute Press, 1991), 35.

95 Havens, *Valley of Darkness*, 150.

96 Samuel Hideo Yamashita, *Daily Life in Wartime Japan, 1940–1945* (Lawrence KS: University Press of Kansas, 2015), 40–41.

97 W. Puck Brecher, *Honored and Dishonored Guests: Westerners in Wartime Japan* (Cambridge MA: Harvard University Asia Center, 2017), 244.

98 Yamashita, *Daily Life*, 15.

99 Michael Kort, *The Columbia Guide to Hiroshima and the Bomb* (New York NY: Columbia University Press, 2007), 304.

100 Ibid., 304–305

101 Kawamura Noriko, *Emperor Hirohito and the Pacific War* (Seattle WA: University of Washington Press, 2015), 123–124; Shindo Hiroyuki, "Holding on to the Finish: The Japanese Army in the South and Southwest Pacific, 1944–45," in *Australia 1944–45: Victory in the Pacific*, ed. Peter Dean (Port Melbourne: Cambridge University Press, 2015), 52.

102 Kawamura, *Emperor Hirohito and the Pacific War*, 125.

103 Shindo, "Holding on to the Finish," 56.

104 Ibid., 55–56.

105 Kawamura, *Emperor Hirohito and the Pacific War*, 124.

106 Ibid., 126.

107 F. Spencer Chapman, *The Jungle is Neutral* (London: Chatto and Windus, 1950), 296.

Chapter Two

1 Frank Ficklin, Interview, National Museum of the Pacific War, https://digitalarchive.pacificwarmuseum.org/digital/collection/p16769coll1/id/2306/rec/2, January 5, 2021.

2 George Dennis Shanks, "Malaria-Associated Mortality in Australian and British Prisoners of War on the Thai-Burma Railway 1943–1944," *American Journal of Tropical Medicine and Hygiene*, vol. 100, no. 4 (2019): 846.

3 Ronald E. Marcello, "Lone Star POWs: Texas National Guardsmen and the Building of the Burma-Thailand Railroad, 1942–1944," *The Southwestern Historical Quarterly*, vol. 95, no. 3 (January 1992): 309.

4 Lionel Wigmore, *The Japanese Thrust [Australia in the War of 1939–1945, Series 1 (Army), vol. 4]* (Canberra: Australian War Memorial, 1957), 588.

5 Futamatsu Yoshihiko, *Across the Three Pagodas Pass: The Story of the Thai-Burma Railway* (Kent: Renaissance Books, 2013), 137.

6 Wigmore, *The Japanese Thrust*, 588.

7 Julian Thompson, *Forgotten Voices of Burma* (London: Ebury Press, 2009), 254.

8 William Slim, *Defeat into Victory* (New York NY: David McKay Co., 1961), 447.

9 Ibid., 209.

10 Norman Bowdler, Oral History (IWM SR 22342), Imperial War Museum.
11 Quoted in Kaushik Roy, *Tropical warfare in the Asia-Pacific Region, 1941–45* (London: Routledge, 2017), 217.
12 Ronald Brockman, "Mountbatten," in *The Warlords*, ed. Michael Carver (London: Weidenfeld and Nicolson, 1976), 366.
13 John Terraine, *The Life and Times of Lord Mountbatten* (London: Hutchinson, 1969), 103.
14 John Shipster, *Mist on the Rice-fields: A Soldier's Story of the Burma Campaign and the Korean War* (London: Leo Cooper, 2000), 32.
15 Louis Mountbatten, *Personal Diary of Admiral the Lord Louis Mountbatten 1943–1946*, ed. Philip Ziegler (London: Collins, 1988), 66.
16 Thompson, *Forgotten Voices*, 272.
17 Terraine, *Life and Times*, 110.
18 Louis Allen, *Burma: The Longest War 1941–45* (London: Phoenix Press, 1984), 232.
19 Bert Harwood, Oral History (IWM SR 20769), Imperial War Museum.
20 Romanus and Sunderland, *Stilwell's Command Problems [United States Army in World War II: China-Burma-India Theater]* (Washington DC: United States Army Center of Military History, 1956), 127.
21 Ibid., 125.
22 Simon J. Anglim, *Major General Orde Wingate's Chindit Operations in World War II* (Reading: University of Reading, 2009).
23 Ibid., 37.
24 Joseph W. Stilwell, *The Stilwell Papers*, ed. Theodor H. White (New York NY: William Sloane Associates Inc., 1948), 280.
25 Raymond Thorpe, Interview, National Museum of the Pacific War, https://digitalarchive.pacificwarmuseum.org/digital/collection/p16769coll1/id/5121/rec/5, 13.
26 *Crisis Fleeting: Original Reports on Military Medicine in India and Burma in the Second World War*, ed. James H. Stone (Washington DC: Government Printing Office, 1969), 303.
27 James E. T. Hopkins, Interview, National Museum of the Pacific War, https://digitalarchive.pacificwarmuseum.org/digital/collection/p16769coll1/id/3253/rec/8, 26.
28 Ibid.
29 Thomas Phillips, Interview, National Museum of the Pacific War, https://digitalarchive.pacificwarmuseum.org/digital/collection/p16769coll1/id/5389/rec/20, 4.
30 "Tampa Marauder Back From 1000-Mile March in Burma," *Tampa Sunday Tribune*, August 27, 1944: 15.
31 David Richardson, Interview, National Museum of the Pacific War, https://digitalarchive.pacificwarmuseum.org/digital/collection/p16769coll1/id/10164/rec/5, 11–12.
32 Charlton Ogburn, Jr., *The Marauders* (New York NY: Ballantine Books, 1959), 194.
33 Gavin Mortimer, *Merrill's Marauders: The Untold Story of Unit Galahad and the Toughest Special Forces Mission of World War II* (Minneapolis MN: 2013), 186.
34 Slim, *Defeat into Victory*, 238.
35 Romanus and Sunderland, *Stilwell's Command Problems*, 226.
36 David Richardson, Interview, National Museum of the Pacific War, https://digitalarchive.pacificwarmuseum.org/digital/collection/p16769coll1/id/10164/rec/5, 18.
37 *Under the Same Army Flag: Recollections of the Veterans of the World War II*, ed. Jean Pei and William W. Wang (Beijing: China Intercontinental Press, 2005), 116–118.
38 Ibid.
39 Ibid., 158.

40 Asano Toyomi, "Japanese Operations in Yunnan and North Burma," in *The Battle for China*, ed. Mark Peattie, Edward Drea and Hans van de Ven (Stanford CA: Stanford University Press, 2011), 366.

41 Zhang Yunhu, "Chinese Operations in Yunnan and Central Burma," in *The Battle for China*, ed. Mark Peattie, Edward Drea, and Hans van de Ven (Stanford CA: Stanford University Press, 2011), 389.

42 Derek Tulloch, *Wingate in Peace and War* (London: Macdonald, 1972), 161.

43 Ch'i Hsi-sheng, "The Military Dimension, 1942–1945," in *China's Better Victory: The War with Japan 1937–1945*, ed. James C. Hsiung and Steven I. Levine (Armonk NY: M.E. Sharpe, 1992), 162.

44 E. J. King and W. M. Whitehill, *Fleet Admiral King* (New York NY: Norton, 1952), 362, 419–420.

45 John Paton Davies Jr., *China Hand: An Autobiography* (Philadelphia PA: University of Pennsylvania Press, 2012), 192.

46 Alan "Buck" Saunders, Interview, National Museum of the Pacific War, https://digitalarchive.pacificwarmuseum.org/digital/collection/p16769coll1/id/1460/rec/5, January 7, 2021, 8.

47 Randy Watson, Interview, National Museum of the Pacific War, https://digitalarchive.pacificwarmuseum.org/digital/collection/p16769coll1/id/8624/rec/1, January 7, 2021, 5.

48 Evans F. Carlson, *Evans F. Carlson on China at War, 1937–1941* (New York NY: China and Us Publication, 1993), 111.

49 Edward L. Dreyer, *China at War 1901–1949* (London: Longman, 1995), 292.

50 Peck, *Two Kinds of Time*, 571–572.

51 Li Tsung-jen and Tong Te-kong, *The Memoirs of Li Tsung-jen* (Boulder CO: Westview Press, 1979), 417.

52 Erleen Christensen, *In War and Famine: Missionaries in China's Honan Province in the 1940s* (Montreal and Kingston: McGill-Queen's University Press, 2005), 146.

53 *Foreign Relations of the United States: Diplomatic Papers, 1944, China, Volume VI* (Washington DC: United States Government Printing Office, 1967), 58.

54 Ch'i Hsi-sheng, *Nationalist China at War: Military Defeats and Political Collapse, 1937–45* (Ann Arbor MI: University of Michigan Press, 1982), 74.

55 Hans van de Ven, *China at War: Triumph and Tragedy in the Emergence of the New China 1937–1945* (London: Profile Books, 2017), 179; Bōeichō Bōeikenshūjo, *Senshi sōsho. Ichigō sakusen. 2: Kōnan no sakusen [War History. Operation Ichigō. 2: The Battle for Hunan]* (Tokyo: Asagumo shimbunsha, 1968), 48.

56 Chen Zhenfeng, "Zhuanzhan Yuzhong" ["Shifting the Battle to Central Henan"], in *Zhongyuan Kangzhan: Yuan Guomindang jiangling Kangri Zhanzheng qinliji [The War of Resistance in the Central Plain: Personal Recollections from the War of Resistance against Japan by Former Nationalist Commanders]* (Beijing: Zhongguo Wenshi Chubanshe, 1995), 276.

57 Fujiwara Akira, "Taipingyang zhanzheng baofahou de Riji zhanzheng" ["The Sino-Japanese War after the Outbreak of the Pacific War"], transl. Xie Lili, *Zhonggongdang shi yanjiu*, no. 1 (1989): 83.

58 Hara Takeshi, "The Ichigō Offensive," in *The Battle for China*, ed. Mark Peattie, Edward Drea, and Hans van de Ven (Stanford CA: Stanford University Press, 2011), 398.

59 Romanus and Sunderland, *Stilwell's Command Problems*, 316.

60 van de Ven, *China at War*, 181.

61 Fujiwara Akira, "Taipingyang zhanzheng baofahou de Riji zhanzheng" ["The Sino-Japanese War after the Outbreak of the Pacific War"], transl. Xie Lili, *Zhonggongdang shi yanjiu*, no. 1 (1989): 83.

62 Ibid.

63 Hara, "The Ichigō Offensive," 397.

64 Hsi-sheng Ch'i, *Nationalist China at War: Military Defeats and Political Collapse, 1937–45* (Ann Arbor MI: University of Michigan Press, 1982), 74.

65 Chiang Kai-shek's diary, April 22, 1944. Hoover Institution, Stanford University.

66 Chen, "Zhuanzhan Yuzhong," 278.

67 John Toland, *The Rising Sun: The Decline and Fall of the Japanese Empire 1936–1945* (New York NY: Random House, 1970), 618–619.

68 Christensen, *In War and Famine*, 149–150.

69 Ibid., 149.

70 Chiang Kai-shek's diary, April 28, 1944. Hoover Institution, Stanford University.

71 van de Ven, *China at War*, 183.

72 Christensen, *In War and Famine*, 150.

73 Liu Yaxian, "Luoyang zhanyi huiyi" ["Reminiscences about the Battle of Luoyang"], in *Zhongyuan Kangzhan: Yuan Guomindang jiangling Kangri Zhanzheng qinliji [The War of Resistance in the Central Plain: Personal Recollections from the War of Resistance against Japan by Former Nationalist Commanders]* (Beijing: Zhongguo Wenshi Chubanshe, 1995), 373.

74 Xing Jutian, "Luoyang zhandou jishi" ["A Factual Account of the Luoyang Battle"], in *Zhongyuan Kangzhan: Yuan Guomindang jiangling Kangri Zhanzheng qinliji [The War of Resistance in the Central Plain: Personal Recollections from the War of Resistance against Japan by Former Nationalist Commanders]* (Beijing: Zhongguo Wenshi Chubanshe, 1995), 367; Liu, "Luoyang zhanyi," 373–374.

75 James, *Years of MacArthur*, 380.

76 Ibid., 368–369.

77 Courtney Whitney, *MacArthur: His Rendezvous with History* (New York NY: Alfred A. Knopf, 1956), 107–108.

78 John Miller, *Cartwheel: The Reduction of Rabaul [United States Army in World War II: The War in the Pacific]* (Washington DC: Office of the Chief of Military History, Department of the Army 1959), 326–328.

79 William C. Frierson, *The Admiralties: Operations of the 1st Cavalry Division, 29 February–18 May 1944* (Washington DC: United States Army Center of Military History, 1946), 28.

80 James, *Years of MacArthur*, vol. 2, 384.

81 Fred Faiz, Interview, National Museum of the Pacific War, https://digitalarchive.pacificwarmuseum.org/digital/collection/p16769coll1/id/8569/rec/3, December 27, 2020.

82 Charles H. Walker, *Combat Officer: A Memoir of War in the South Pacific* (New York NY: Ballantine Books, 2004), 123.

83 Martin Gonzales, Interview, National Museum of the Pacific War, https://digitalarchive.pacificwarmuseum.org/digital/collection/p16769coll1/id/9227/rec/2, December 27, 2020.

84 Frierson, *Admiralties*, 133.

85 Robert L. Eichelberger, *Our Jungle Road to Tokyo* (New York NY: The Viking Press, 1950), 247.

86 Robert Ross Smith, *The Approach to the Philippines* [United States Army in World War II: The War in the Pacific] (Washington DC: United States Army Center of Military History, 1952), 208

87 Frank Futrell, "Hollandia," in *The Pacific: Guadalcanal to Saipan: August 1942 to July 1944 [The Army Air Forces in World War II, vol. 4]*, ed. Wesley Frank Craven and James Lea Cate (Chicago IL: University of Chicago Press, 1950), 609.

88 Edward J. Drea, *MacArthur's Ultra: Codebreaking and the War against Japan, 1942–1945* (Lawrence KS: University of Kansas Press, 1992), 120–121.

89 *Reports of General MacArthur. The Campaigns of MacArthur in the Pacific*, vol. 1, prepared by his General Staff. (Washington DC: Government Printing Office, 1966), 148.

Chapter Three

1 Hans van de Ven, *China at War: Triumph and Tragedy in the Emergence of the New China 1937–1945* (London: Profile Books, 2017), 185–187; Chen Yong-fa, "Guanjian de yinian: Jiang Zhongheng yu Yu Xiang Gui kuibai ["The Pivotal Year: Chiang Kai-shek and the Rout of Henan, Hunan and Guangxi"] in *Zhongguo lishi de zaisikao [A Reassessment of Chinese History]*, ed. Liu Cuirong (Taipei: Linking Books, 2015), 376–377.

2 Wang Qisheng, "The Battle of Hunan and the Chinese Military's Response to Operation Ichigō," in *The Battle for China*, ed. Mark Peattie, Edward Drea, and Hans van de Ven (Stanford CA: Stanford University Press, 2011), 409.

3 Ibid., 408.

4 Chen, "Chiang Kai-shek," 49.

5 Ibid.

6 Zhang Wenjia, "Disi Jun qishou Changsha jingguo" ["How the Fourth Army Surrendered Changsha"], in *Hunan sida huizhan: Yuan Guomindang jiangling Kangri Zhanzheng qinliji [The Four Major Battles of Hunan: Personal Recollections from the War of Resistance against Japan by Former Nationalist Commanders]* (Beijing: Zhongguo Wenshi Chubanshe, 1995), 471.

7 Wang Qisheng, "The Battle of Hunan," 410.

8 Chiang Kai-shek's diary, June 20, 1944. Hoover Institution, Stanford University.

9 Hara, "Ichigo Offensive," 399.

10 van de Wen, *China at War*, 186; Wang, "The Battle of Hunan," 410.

11 Graham Peck, *Two Kinds of Time* (Seattle: University of Washington Press, 2008), 571.

12 Wang, "The Battle of Hunan," 411.

13 Zeng Jing, "Huigu Hengyang baoweizhan" ["A Look Back at the Battle to Defend Hengyang"] in *Hunan sida huizhan: Yuan Guomindang jiangling Kangri Zhanzheng qinliji [The Four Major Battles of Hunan: Personal Recollections from the War of Resistance against Japan by Former Nationalist Commanders]* (Beijing: Zhongguo Wenshi Chubanshe, 1995), 503.

14 Gan Yinsen, "Hengyang zhanyi huiyi" ["A Memoir of the Battle of Hengyang"] in *Hunan sida huizhan: Yuan Guomindang jiangling Kangri Zhanzheng qinliji [The Four Major Battles of Hunan: Personal Recollections from the War of Resistance against Japan by Former Nationalist Commanders]* (Beijing: Zhongguo Wenshi Chubanshe, 1995), 500.

15 Wang, "The Battle of Hunan," 412.

16 Ibid., 418.

17 Chiang Kai-shek, *Zongtong Jianggong sixiang yanlun zongji [General Collection of President Chiang Kai-shek's Thoughts and Speeches]*, vol. 20 (Taipei: Zhongguo Guomindang zhongyang weiyuanhui dangshi weiyuanhui, 1985), 445–446.

18 Kurasawa Aiko, "Forced Delivery of Paddy and Peasant Uprising in Indramayu: Japanese Occupation and Social Change," *Developing Economies*, vol. 21, no. 1 (March 1983): 65–66.

19 Ibid.," 60–65, 67.

20 Akira Iriye, *Power and Culture: The Japanese-American War 1941–1945* (Cambridge MA: Harvard University Press, 1981), 162.

21 Kanahele, "The Japanese Occupation of Indonesia," 151.

22 Nakamura Mitsuo, "General Imamura and the Early Period of Japanese Occupation," *Indonesia*, no. 10 (October 1970): 7.

23 J. Thomas Lindblad, "The eclipse of the Indonesian economy under Japanese Occupation," in *Economies under Occupation: The hegemony of Nazi Germany and Imperial Japan in World War II*, eds. Marcel Boldorf and Okazaki Tetsuji (London: Routledge, 2015), 211.

24 Ibid., 212.

25 Sintha Melati, "In the Service of the Underground," in *Local Opposition and Underground Resistance to the Japanese in Java 1942–1945*, ed. Anton Lucas (Clayton: Monash Papers on Southeast Asia, no. 13, Centre of Southeast Asian Studies, Monash University, 1986), 200.

26 Nugroho Notosusanto, "The Revolt of a PETA-Battalion in Blitar," *Asian Studies*, vol. 7, no. 1 (1969): 114.

27 Paul H. Kratoska and Ken'ichi Goto, "Japanese Occupation of Southeast Asia, 1941–1945," in *The Cambridge History of the Second World War, Volume II: Politics and Ideology*, ed. B. Bosworth and Joseph A. Maiolo (Cambridge: Cambridge University Press, 2015), 552–553.

28 Nakano Satoshi, "Appeasement and Coercion," in *The Philippines under Japan: Occupation Policy and Reaction*, ed. Ikehata Setsuho and Ricardo Trota Jose, (Quezon City: ADMU Press, 1999), 50–51.

29 Claro M. Recto, *The Complete Works of Claro M. Recto*, edited by Isagani R. Medina and Myrna S. Feliciano (Manila: Claro M. Recto Memorial Foundation, 1990), vol. 5, 383.

30 Mountbatten, *Personal Diary*, 110.

31 Field Marshal Lord Alanbrooke, *War Diaries, 1939–1945*, eds. Alex Danchev and Daniel Todman (London: Phoenix Press, 2003), 553.

32 Allen, *Burma*, 289.

33 Slim, *Defeat into Victory*, 266.

34 Allen, *Burma*, 264.

35 Ibid.

36 Thompson, *Forgotten Voices*, 293.

37 Ibid.

38 Romanus and Sunderland, *Stilwell's Command Problems*, 253–254.

39 Michael Calvert, *Prisoner of Hope* (London: Leo Cooper, 1971), 189.

40 George J. Giffard, "Operations in Assam and Burma from 23 June 1944 to 12 November 1944," *Supplement to the London Gazette* (March 30, 1951): 1711.

41 Keith Park, "Air Operations in South East Asia from 1 June 1944 to the Occupation of Rangoon 2 May 1945," *Third Supplement to the London Gazette* (6 April 1951): 1966.

42 USSBS, Naval Analysis Division, *Interrogations of Japanese Officials* (Washington DC, 1946), vol. 1, 6.

43 A. Sunderland Brown, "Burma Banzai: The Air War in Burma through Japanese Eyes," *Canadian Military History*, vol. 11, no. 2 (Spring 2002): 57.

44 Eichelberger, *Jungle Road*, 137.

45 Raymond Arcuna, Interview, National Museum of the Pacific War, https://digitalarchive.pacificwarmuseum.org/digital/collection/p16769coll1/id/1309, 9–10.

46 Smith, *Approach to the Philippines*, 271.

47 Spencer Davis, "Enemy on Biak Cut an Awful Swath," *New York Times*, June 1, 1944: 8.

48 Ibid.

49 Calvin Stowell, Interview, National Museum of the Pacific War, https://digitalarchive.pacificwarmuseum.org/digital/collection/p16769coll1/id/11930, 10.

50 Ibid., 12.

51 Charles A. Lindbergh, *The Wartime Journals of Charles A. Lindbergh* (New York NY: Harcourt Brace Jovanovich Inc., 1970), 879–880.

52 Ibid., 880.

53 Peter Schrijvers, *Bloody Pacific: American Soldiers at War with Japan* (Basingstoke: Palgrave Macmillan, 2010), 209.

54 Tanaka Yukiko, *Hidden Horrors: Japanese War Crimes in World War II* (Boulder CO: Westview Press, 1996), 114.

55 Ibid., 144.

56 Charles Adair, Oral History, US Naval Institute, 339–340.

57 Samuel Eliot Morison, *New Guinea and the Marianas March 1944–August 1944 [History of the United States Naval Operations in World War II, vol. 8]* (Boston MA: Little, Brown and Co., 1953), 160.

58 Holland M. Smith, *Coral and Brass* (New York NY: Charles Scribner's Sons, 1949), 181–182.

59 Robert Ellinger, Interview, National Museum of the Pacific War, https://digitalarchive.pacificwarmuseum.org/digital/collection/p16769coll1/id/10411/rec/42, 5.

60 Baine Kerr, Interview, National Museum of the Pacific War, https://digitalarchive.pacificwarmuseum.org/digital/collection/p16769coll1/id/4192/rec/3, 87.

61 Carl W. Hoffman, Oral History, US Marine Corps, 32–33.

62 Ibid., 36–38.

63 Raymond L. Murray, Oral History, US Marine Corps, 157–159.

64 Carl Matthews, Interview, National Museum of the Pacific War, https://digitalarchive.pacificwarmuseum.org/digital/collection/p16769coll1/id/10634/rec/5, 41.

65 Arthur Liberty, Interview, National Museum of the Pacific War, https://digitalarchive.pacificwarmuseum.org/digital/collection/p16769coll1/id/3731/rec/13, 25–26.

66 Carl W. Hoffman, Oral History, US Marine Corps, 39–40.

67 Philip A. Crowl, *Campaign in the Marianas [United States Army in World War II: The War in the Pacific]* (Washington DC: Office of the Chief of Military History, Department of the Army, 1960), 93.

68 Carl Matthews, Interview, National Museum of the Pacific War, https://digitalarchive.pacificwarmuseum.org/digital/collection/p16769coll1/id/10634/rec/5, 42–43.

69 Henry I. Shaw, Bernard C. Nalty, and Edwin T. Turnbladh, *Central Pacific Drive [History of U.S. Marine Corps Operations in World War II, vol. 3]* (Washington DC: US Government Printing Office, 1966), 278–279.

70 Kawamura, *Emperor Hirohito and the Pacific War*, 128.

71 W. D. Dickson, *The Battle of the Philippine Sea, June 1944* (London: Ian Allan, 1975), 63.

72 Paul S. Dull, *A Battle History of the Imperial Japanese Navy (1941–1945)* (Annapolis MD: Naval Institute Press, 1978), 303.

73 USSBS, *Interrogations of Japanese Officials*, vol. 1, 145.

74 Dull, *Imperial Japanese Navy*, 303–304.

75 Ibid., 330.

76 Michael Bak, Oral History, US Naval Institute, 143–144

77 *Reports of General MacArthur, Japanese Operations in the Southwest Pacific Area*, vol. 2, part 2, 292.

78 Ugaki Matome, *Fading Victory: The Diary of Admiral Matome Ugaki 1941–1945* (Annapolis MD: Naval Institute Press, 1991), 407.

79 Clark G. Reynolds, *The Fast Carriers: The Forging of an Air Navy* (New York NY: McGraw-Hill, 1968), 184.

80 Thomas B. Buell, *The Quiet Warrior: A Biography of Admiral Raymond A. Spruance* (Annapolis MD: Naval Institute Press, 1987), 293–295.

81 James Ramage, Interview, National Museum of the Pacific War, https://digitalarchive.pacificwarmuseum.org/digital/collection/p16769coll1/id/10256, 4.

82 Edwin Layton, Oral History, US Naval Institute, 161.

83 Dull, *Imperial Japanese Navy*, 305.

84 Alex Vraciu, Interview, National Museum of the Pacific War, https://digitalarchive.pacificwar-museum.org/digital/collection/p16769coll1/id/4230/rec/3.

85 James Ramage, Interview, National Museum of the Pacific War, https://digitalarchive.pacificwarmuseum.org/digital/collection/p16769coll1/id/10256, 5.

86 Dull, *Imperial Japanese Navy*, 305.

87 Abe Zenji, *The Emperor's Sea Eagle* (Honolulu HI: Arizona Memorial Museum Association, 2006), 160.

88 Morison, *New Guinea and the Marianas*, 277.

89 Theodore Taylor, *The Magnificent Mitscher* (New York NY: Norton, 1954), 227; Alex Vraciu, Interview, National Museum of the Pacific War, https://digitalarchive.pacificwarmuseum.org/digital/collection/p16769coll1/id/4230/rec/3, 68.

90 Morison, *New Guinea and the Marianas*, 278–282.

91 Arleigh Burke, Interview, National Museum of the Pacific War, https://digitalarchive.pacificwarmuseum.org/digital/collection/p16769coll1/id/9466, 1.

92 Nomura Minoru, "Ozawa in the Pacific: A Junior Officer's Experience," in *The Japanese Navy in World War Two*, ed. David C. Evans (Annapolis MD: Naval Institute Press, 2017), 327.

93 James Ramage, Interview, National Museum of the Pacific War, https://digitalarchive.pacificwarmuseum.org/digital/collection/p16769coll1/id/10256, 7–8.

94 Cecil S. King, Oral History, US Naval Institute, 239.

95 Morison, *New Guinea and the Marianas*, 302.

96 James Ramage, Interview, National Museum of the Pacific War, https://digitalarchive.pacificwarmuseum.org/digital/collection/p16769coll1/id/10256, 10.

97 John Prados, *Combined Fleet Decoded: The Secret History of American Intelligence and the Japanese Navy in World War II* (New York NY: Random House, 1995), 562.

98 Crowl, *Campaign in the Marianas*, 178–179.

99 Carl Matthews, Interview, National Museum of the Pacific War, https://digitalarchive.pacificwarmuseum.org/digital/collection/p16769coll1/id/10634/rec/5, 51.

100 Ibid., 71.

101 Ibid., 52–53.

102 Ibid., 45.

103 Wood B. Kyle, Oral History, US Marine Corps, 90–91.

104 Robert Sherrod, "The Nature of the Enemy," *Time*, August 7, 1944: 27.

105 Wood B. Kyle, Oral History, US Marine Corps, 91.

106 Justice M. Chambers, Oral History, US Marine Corps, 495–496.

107 Prados, *Combined Fleet Decoded*, 578.

108 Justice M. Chambers, Oral History, US Marine Corps, 485.

Chapter Four

1 Ugaki, *Fading Victory*, 416.

2 Kawamura, *Emperor Hirohito and the Pacific War*, 129.

3 Ibid., 128.

4 Assistant Chief of Staff-Intelligence, Headquarters Army Air Forces, *Mission Accomplished. Interrogations of Japanese Industrial Military, and Civil Leaders of World War II* (Washington DC: US Government Printing Office, 1946), 19.

5   Assistant Chief of Staff-Intelligence, Headquarters Army Air Forces, *Mission Accomplished. Interrogations of Japanese Industrial Military, and Civil Leaders of World War II* (Washington DC: US Government Printing Office, 1946), 19.

6   Crowl, *Campaign in the Marianas*, 1; USSBS, *Interrogations of Japanese Officials*, vol. 2, 356.

7   Assistant Chief of Staff-Intelligence, Headquarters Army Air Forces, *Mission Accomplished. Interrogations of Japanese Industrial Military, and Civil Leaders of World War II* (Washington DC: US Government Printing Office, 1946), 19.

8   "Grave Days in Tokyo," *New York Times*, July 23, 1944: 78.

9   Kawamura, *Emperor Hirohito and the Pacific War*, 130.

10   Robert J. C. Butow, *Tojo and the Coming of the War* (Stanford CA: Stanford University Press, 1961), 435.

11   Edward J. Drea, *In the Service of the Emperor: Essays on the Imperial Japanese Army* (Lincoln NE: University of Nebraska Press, 1998), 192.

12   Toland, *Rising Sun*, 524.

13   Herbert P. Bix, *Hirohito and the Making of Modern Japan* (New York NY: Perennial, 2001), 477–478.

14   Toland, *Rising Sun*, 526.

15   Kawamura, *Emperor Hirohito and the Pacific War*, 137.

16   Edwin Layton, Oral History, US Naval Institute, 151.

17   *How the Guam Operation Was Conducted* (Tokyo: Ground Self Defense Forces Staff School, 1962), 117.

18   Crowl, *Campaign in the Marianas*, 337.

19   Ralph Ketcham, Interview, National Museum of the Pacific War, https://digitalarchive. pacificwarmuseum.org/digital/collection/p16769coll1/id/2367/rec/4, 22.

20   Schrijvers, *Bloody Pacific*, 172.

21   Ralph Ketcham, Interview, National Museum of the Pacific War, https://digitalarchive. pacificwarmuseum.org/digital/collection/p16769coll1/id/2367/rec/4, 22–23.

22   Ibid., 25.

23   Raymond Strohmeyer, Interview, National Museum of the Pacific War, https://digitalarchive. pacificwarmuseum.org/digital/collection/p16769coll1/id/5034/rec/3, 50–51.

24   *How the Guam Operation Was Conducted*, 175–176.

25   Alpha L. Bowser, making comment in interview with Carl W. Hoffman, Oral History, US Marine Corps, 54–55.

26   R. O. Lodge, *The Recapture of Guam* (Washington DC: Historical Branch, United States US Marine Corps, 1954), 78.

27   Frank Hough, *The Island War* (New York NY: J. B. Lippincott Company, 1947), 279.

28   Raymond Strohmeyer, Interview, National Museum of the Pacific War, https://digitalarchive. pacificwarmuseum.org/digital/collection/p16769coll1/id/5034/rec/3, 50.

29   Lodge, *Recapture of Guam*, 130.

30   James L. Day, Oral History, US Marine Corps, 11.

31   Raymond Strohmeyer, Interview, National Museum of the Pacific War, https://digitalarchive. pacificwarmuseum.org/digital/collection/p16769coll1/id/5034/rec/3, 74–75.

32   *Guam: Operations of the 77th Division 21 July–10 August 1944* (Washington DC: US Government Printing Office, 1990), 111–113.

33   Carl W. Hoffman, Oral History, US Marine Corps, 32, 47–48.

34   Ibid., 49.

35   Robert M. Neiman and Kenneth W. Estes, *Tanks on the Beaches: A Marine Tanker in the Great Pacific War* (College Station TX: Texas A&M University Press, 2002), 109.

36 Arthur Liberty, Interview, National Museum of the Pacific War, https://digitalarchive. pacificwarmuseum.org/digital/collection/p16769coll1/id/3731/rec/13, 35.

37 Ibid., 51.

38 Baine Kerr, Interview, National Museum of the Pacific War, https://digitalarchive.pacificwar-museum.org/digital/collection/p16769coll1/id/4192/rec/3, 93.

39 Alfred L. Castle, "President Roosevelt and General MacArthur at the Honolulu Conference of 1944," *Hawaiian Journal of History* (2004): 169–171.

40 Grace Person Hayes, *The History of the Joint Chiefs of Staff in World War II: The War against Japan* (Annapolis MD: Naval Institute Press, 1982), 616–617.

41 D. Clayton James, *The Years of MacArthur, vol. 2* (Boston MA: Houghton Mifflin Company, 1975), 523.

42 Ibid.

43 James MacGregor Burns, *Roosevelt: The Soldier of Freedom, 1940–1945* (London: Weidenfeld and Nicolson, 1971), 489.

44 Samuel Eliot Morison, *Victory in the Pacific 1945 [History of the United States Naval Operations in World War II, vol. 14]* (Boston MA: Little, Brown and Co., 1960), 4.

45 James, *Years of MacArthur*, 534.

46 Richard Toye, *Churchill's Empire: The World That Made Him and the World He Made* (New York NY: Henry Holt and Company, 2010), 250.

47 Hastings Lionel Ismay, *The Memoirs of Lord Ismay* (London: Heinemann, 1960), 375.

48 "Aide-Memoire Initialed by President Roosevelt and Prime Minister Churchill," *Foreign Relations of the United States: The Conference at Quebec 1944* (Washington DC: United States Government Printing Office, 1972), 492.

49 M. Hamlin Cannon, *Leyte: The Return to the Philippines [United States Army in World War II: The War in the Pacific]* (Washington DC: United States Army Center of Military History, 1954), 8.

50 Potter, *Nimitz*, 325.

51 Remark made while interviewing Jonas M. Platt, Jonas M. Platt, Oral History, US Marine Corps, 69.

52 Jonas M. Platt, Oral History, US Marine Corps, 69.

53 Ibid., 68.

54 R. V. Burgin, Interview, National Museum of the Pacific War, https://digitalarchive.pacificwar-museum.org/digital/collection/p16769coll1/id/3485/rec/4, 10.

55 Raymond G. Davis, Oral History, US Marine Corps, 131–132.

56 Jonas M. Platt, Oral History, US Marine Corps, 72.

57 Tom Lea, "Peleliu Landing," in *Reporting World War II: American Journalism 1938–1946*, eds. Samuel Hynes, Nancy Caldwell Sorel, Anne Matthews, and Roger J Spiller (New York NY: Literary Classics of the United States, Inc., 1995), vol. 2, 504.

58 Clifton La Bree, *The Gentle Warrior: General Oliver Prince Smith, USMC* (Kent OH: Kent State University Press, 2001), 60.

59 Jonas M. Platt, Oral History, US Marine Corps, 72–73.

60 *Central Pacific Operations Record Part II, April–November 1944 [Japanese Monograph no. 49]* (Washington DC: Department of the Army, 1949), 85.

61 George W. Garand and Truman R. Strobridge, *Western Pacific Operations [History of U.S. Marine Corps Operations in World War II, vol. 4]*, Washington DC: US Government Printing Office, 1971), 131.

62 Garand and Strobridge, *Western Pacific Operations*, 71.

63 Joseph H. Alexander, "Peleliu 1944," *Marine Corps Gazette* (November 1996): 20.

64 Robert Leckie, *Strong Men Armed: The United States Marines Against Japan* (New York NY: Random House, 1962), 391.
65 R. V. Burgin, Interview, National Museum of the Pacific War, https://digitalarchive.pacificwarmuseum.org/digital/collection/p16769coll1/id/3485/rec/4, 11.
66 Lewis J. Fields, Oral History, US Marine Corps, 120.
67 Ibid., 126.
68 R. V. Burgin, Interview, National Museum of the Pacific War, https://digitalarchive.pacificwarmuseum.org/digital/collection/p16769coll1/id/3485/rec/4, 12.
69 Martin Clayton, Interview, National Museum of the Pacific War, https://digitalarchive.pacificwarmuseum.org/digital/collection/p16769coll1/id/3715, 13.
70 Ibid., 14.
71 Kenneth Harrell, Interview, National Museum of the Pacific War, https://digitalarchive.pacificwarmuseum.org/digital/collection/p16769coll1/id/8518/rec/3, 13.
72 Maurice Matloff, *Strategic Planning for Coalition Warfare 1943–1944 [United States Army in World War II]* (Washington DC: US Government Printing Office, 1958), 396–397.
73 Alvin P. Stauffer, *The Quartermaster Corps: Operations in the War Against Japan [United States Army in World War II]* (Washington DC: US Government Printing Office, 1956), 88.
74 Charles Furey, *Going Back: A Navy Airman in the Pacific War* (Lincoln NE: University of Nebraska Press, 2004), 111.
75 Samuel Eliot Morison, *Leyte June 1944–January 1945 [History of the United States Naval Operations in World War II, vol. 12]* (Boston MA: Little, Brown and Co., 1958), 49.
76 Samuel Eliot Morison, *Victory in the Pacific 1945 [History of the United States Naval Operations in World War II, vol. 14]* (Boston MA: Little, Brown and Co., 1960), 110.
77 Michael Bak, Oral History, US Naval Institute, 152.
78 Ibid., 152–153.
79 Paul H. Kratoska and Ken'ichi Goto, "Japanese Occupation of Southeast Asia, 1941–1945" in *The Cambridge History of the Second World War, Vol. 2: Politics and Ideology*, eds. Richard Bosworth and Joseph Maiolo (Cambridge: Cambridge University Press, 2015), 546.
80 Paul Kratoska, *The Japanese Occupation of Malaya and Singapore, 1941–45: A Social and Economic History* (Singapore: NUS Press, 2018), 170–171.
81 Ibid., 171.
82 Wang, "The Battle of Hunan," 403.
83 Peck, *Two Kind of Time*, 588–590.
84 Chen Yung-fa, "Chiang Kai-shek and the Japanese Ichigo Offensive, 1944," in *Chiang Kai-shek and His Time: New Historical and Historiographical Perspectives*, eds. Laura De Giorgi and Guido Samarani (Venice: Edizioni Ca' Foscari, 2017), 64 n4.
85 Wang, "The Battle of Hunan," 417.
86 Li Tsung-jen, *Memoirs*, 399–400.
87 Ibid., 428.
88 Ibid., 399–400.
89 Owen Lattimore, *China Memoirs: Chiang Kai-shek and the War Against Japan* (Tokyo: University of Tokyo Press, 1990), 187–188.
90 Romanus and Sunderland, *Stilwell's Command Problems*, 362.
91 David Richardson, Interview, National Museum of the Pacific War, https://digitalarchive.pacificwarmuseum.org/digital/collection/p16769coll1/id/10164/rec/5, 19.
92 Slim, *Defeat into Victory*, 319.
93 Li Tsung-jen, *Memoirs*, 412.

94 David Richardson, Interview, National Museum of the Pacific War, https://digitalarchive.pacificwarmuseum.org/digital/collection/p16769coll1/id/9333/rec/4, 15.

95 Hans van de Ven, *War and Nationalism in China 1925–1945* (Abingdon: RoutledgeCurzon, 2003), 56.

96 van de Ven, *China at War*, 192.

97 *Foreign Relations of the United States: Diplomatic Papers, 1944, China, Volume VI* (Washington DC: United States Government Printing Office, 1967), 166.

98 van de Ven, *China at War*, 192–193.

99 Romanus and Sunderland, *Stilwell's Command Problems*, 363.

100 Tan Geming. "Guilin fangshou ji lunxian jingguo" ["The Defense and Fall of Guilin"], in *Yue Gui Qian Dian Kangzhan: Yuan Guomindang jiangling Kangri Zhanzheng qinliji [The War of Resistance in Guangdong, Guangxi, Guizhou and Yunnan: Personal Recollections from the War of Resistance against Japan by Former Nationalist Commanders]* (Beijing: Zhongguo Wenshi Chubanshe, 1995), 334.

101 Ibid., 340.

102 Roger B. Jeans, ed., *The Marshall Mission to China, 1945–1947: The Letters and Diary of Colonel John Hart Caughey* (Lanham MD: Rowman and Littlefield, 2011), 52.

103 van de Ven, *China at War*, 190.

104 Charles F. Romanus and Riley Sunderland, *Time Runs Out in CBI [United States Army in World War II: China-Burma-India Theater]* (Washington DC: United States Army Center of Military History, 1959), 50–51.

Chapter Five

1 Michael Bak, Oral History, US Naval Institute, 152.

2 Eichelberger, *Jungle Road*, 166.

3 Charles Adair, Oral History, US Naval Institute, 390–391.

4 Samuel Eliot Morison, *Leyte June 1944–January 1945 [History of the United States Naval Operations in World War II, vol. 12]* (Boston MA: Little, Brown and Co., 1958), 92.

5 Fukudome Shigeru, "The Air Battle off Taiwan," in *The Japanese Navy in World War II*, ed. David C. Evans (Annapolis MD: Naval Institute Press, 2017), 347.

6 Ibid., 352.

7 Ibid., 353.

8 Morison, *Leyte*, 113.

9 Charles Adair, Oral History, US Naval Institute, 272.

10 George C. Kenney, *General Kenney Reports: A Personal History of the Pacific War* (New York NY: Duell, Sloane, and Pearce, 1949), 448.

11 James, *Years of MacArthur*, vol. 2, 557.

12 Bill Filter, Oral History, National Museum of the Pacific War, https://digitalarchive.pacificwarmuseum.org/digital/collection/p16769coll1/id/5492/rec/7, 9–10.

13 A. Frank Reel, *The Case of General Yamashita* (Chicago IL: University of Chicago Press, 1949), 19.

14 Cannon, *Leyte*, 50.

15 Ibid., 50–51.

16 Toland, *Rising Sun*, 547.

17 *Interrogations of Japanese Officials*, vol. 2, 317.

18 Morison, *Leyte*, 188–192.

19 David McClintock, Oral History, National Museum of the Pacific War, https://digitalarchive.pacificwarmuseum.org/digital/collection/p16769coll1/id/6978, 8.

20 Morison, *Leyte*, 169–174; David McClintock, Oral History, National Museum of the Pacific War, https://digitalarchive.pacificwarmuseum.org/digital/collection/p16769coll1/id/6978, 10.

21 Thomas J. Cutler, *The Battle of Leyte Gulf* (Annapolis MD: Naval Institute Press, 1994), 152.

22 Morison, *Leyte*, 58.

23 Ibid., 58–59.

24 Ibid., 203–211.

25 Richard Rowe, Oral History, National Museum of the Pacific War, https://digitalarchive.pacificwarmuseum.org/digital/collection/p16769coll1/id/1549/rec/3, 4.

26 Morison, *Leyte*, 228.

27 Michael Bak, Oral History, US Naval Institute, 154–155.

28 *Interrogations of Japanese Officials*, vol. 1, 149.

29 James D. Hornfischer, *The Last Stand of the Tin Can Sailors* (New York NY: Bantam Books, 2004), 150.

30 Bill Wilson, Oral History, National Museum of the Pacific War, https://digitalarchive.pacificwarmuseum.org/digital/collection/p16769coll1/id/6988/rec/8, 4.

31 Alfonso Perez, Oral History, National Museum of the Pacific War, https://digitalarchive.pacificwarmuseum.org/digital/collection/p16769coll1/id/3869/rec/10, 8.

32 Michael Bak, Oral History, US Naval Institute, 160.

33 Ibid., 157–158.

34 Alfonso Perez, Oral History, National Museum of the Pacific War, https://digitalarchive.pacificwarmuseum.org/digital/collection/p16769coll1/id/3869/rec/10, 11.

35 Richard K. Rohde, Oral History, National Museum of the Pacific War, https://digitalarchive.pacificwarmuseum.org/digital/collection/p16769coll1/id/8264/rec/38, 43.

36 William McDowell, Oral History, National Museum of the Pacific War, https://digitalarchive.pacificwarmuseum.org/digital/collection/p16769coll1/id/9997/rec/24, 15.

37 Koyanagi Tomiji, "The Battle of Leyte Gulf," in *The Japanese Navy in World War Two*, ed. David C. Evans (Annapolis MD: Naval Institute Press, 2017), 379.

38 Cutler, *Leyte Gulf*, 269.

39 Joseph Mika, Oral History, National Museum of the Pacific War, https://digitalarchive.pacificwarmuseum.org/digital/collection/p16769coll1/id/7299/rec/20, 15.

40 Cutler, *Leyte Gulf*, 269.

41 Clive Howard and Joe Whitley, *One Damned Island After Another: The Saga of the Seventh* (Chapel Hill NC: University of North Carolina Press, 1946), 355.

42 Richard Rowe, Oral History, National Museum of the Pacific War, https://digitalarchive.pacificwarmuseum.org/digital/collection/p16769coll1/id/1549/rec/3, 10–11.

43 Inoguchi Rikihei and Nakajima Tadashi, "The Kamikaze Attack Corps," in *The Japanese Navy in World War Two*, ed. David C. Evans (Annapolis MD: Naval Institute Press, 2017), 422.

44 Robert Ellinger, Oral History, National Museum of the Pacific War, https://digitalarchive.pacificwarmuseum.org/digital/collection/p16769coll1/id/10411/rec/42, 12.

45 Francis J. McHugh, *Fundamentals of Wargaming* (Newport RI: US Naval War College Press, 1966), 64.

46 Yokoi Toshiyuki, "Kamikazes in the Okinawa Campaign," in *The Japanese Navy in World War Two*, ed. David C. Evans (Annapolis MD: Naval Institute Press, 2017), 455.

47 Emiko Ohnuki-Tierney, *Kamikaze Diaries: Reflections of Japanese Student Soldiers* (Chicago IL: University of Chicago Press, 2006), 90.

48 Ibid., 96.

49 "Last Letters of Kamikaze Pilots," *Mānoa*, vol. 13, no. 1 (summer 2001): 123.

50 Cannon, *Leyte*, 94.

51 Ibid., 102.

52 Ronald H. Spector, *Eagle Against the Sun* (New York NY: Vintage Books, 1985), 511–517.

53 Eichelberger, *Jungle Road*, 178–179.

54 *Biennial Reports of the Chief of Staff of the United States Army to the Secretary of War, 1 July 1939–30 June 1945* (Washington DC: Center of Military History United States Army, 1996), 173.

55 James, *Years of MacArthur*, vol. 2, 602.

56 Eichelberger, *Jungle Road*, 182.

57 Edward M. Flanagan, *The Angels: A History of the 11th Airborne Division 1943–1946* (Washington DC: Infantry Journal Press, 1948), 3.

58 Cannon, *Leyte*, 359.

59 James O'Donnel, Interview, National Museum of the Pacific War, https://digitalarchive. pacificwarmuseum.org/digital/collection/p16769coll1/id/5393/rec/4, 33–35.

60 S. A. Ayer, *Unto Him a Witness: The Story of Netaji Subhas Chandra Bose in East Asia* (Bombay: Thacker & Co., 1951), 265–266.

61 Sugata Bose, *His Majesty's Opponent: Subhas Chandra Bose and India's Struggle against Empire* (Cambridge MA: The Belknap Press of Harvard University Press, 2011), 285.

62 Ibid., 286.

63 Joyce C. Lebra, *Japanese-Trained Armies in Southeast Asia* (Singapore: Institute of Southeast Asian Studies, 2010), 36.

64 Jeremy E. Taylor, *Iconographies of Occupation: Visual Cultures in Wang Jingwei's China, 1939–1945* (Honolulu HI: University of Hawaii Press, 2021), 82.

65 Ch'en Li-fu, *The Storm Clouds Clear over China: The Memoir of Ch'en Li-fu 1900–1993* (Stanford CA: Hoover Institution Press, 1994), 141.

66 Frederic Wakeman Jr., "Hanjian (Traitor)! Collaboration and Retribution in Wartime Shanghai," in *Becoming Chinese: Passages to Modernity and Beyond*, ed. Yeh Wen-hsin (Berkeley CA: University of California Press, 2000), 312.

67 Ibid.

68 Jeremy E. Taylor, "From Traitor to Martyr: Drawing Lessons from the Death and Burial of Wang Jingwei 1944," *Journal of Chinese History*, vol. 3 no. 1 (2019): 148–149.

69 David P. Barrett, "The Wang Jingwei Regime, 1940–1945: Continuities and Disjunctures with Nationalist China," in *Chinese Collaboration with Japan, 1932–1945: The Limits of Accommodation*, eds. David P. Barrett and Larry N. Shyu (Palo Alto CA: Stanford University Press, 2002), 104–105.

70 Barrett, "Wang Jingwei Regime," 105–107.

71 Chan Cheong-choo, *Memoirs of a Citizen of Early XX Century China* (Willowdale: n. p., 1978), 133–34.

72 James Lea Cate and James C. Olson, "Precision Bombardment Campaign," in *The Pacific: Matterhorn to Nagasaki [The Army Air Forces in World War II, vol. 5]*, eds. Wesley Frank Craven and James Lea Cate (Chicago IL: University of Chicago Press, 1953), 557–558.

73 "B-29s Fill Air at Saipan As They Leave to Hit Tokyo," *New York Times*, November 29, 1944: 1.

74 Cate and Olson, "Precision Bombardment Campaign," 554–555.

75 Ibid., 558.

76 Ibid., 558–560.

77 Anthony G. Williams and Emmanuel Gustin, *Flying Guns World War II: Development of Aircraft Guns, Ammunition and Installations 1933–45* (Ramsbury: Crowood Press, 2003), 165.

78 Assistant Chief of Staff-Intelligence, Headquarters Army Air Forces, *Mission Accomplished. Interrogations of Japanese Industrial Military, and Civil Leaders of World War II* (Washington DC: US Government Printing Office, 1946), 18.

79 Alvin D. Coox, "Air War Against Japan," in *Case Studies in the Achievement of Air Superiority*, ed. Benjamin Franklin Cooling (Washington DC: Center for Air Force History, 1994), 411.

80 Herman S. Wolk, *Cataclysm: General Hap Arnold and the Defeat of Japan* (Denton TX: University of North Texas Press, 2010), 112–113.

81 Richard B. Frank, *Downfall: The End of the Imperial Japanese Empire* (New York NY: Random House, 1999), 335.

82 USSBS Military Analysis Division, *Report 67: Air Operations in China, Burma, India* (Washington DC: n. p., 1947), 90.

83 Claire Lee Chennault, *Way of a Fighter* (New York NY: G.P. Putnam's Sons, 1949), 329–330.

84 Ibid.

85 USSBS Military Analysis Division, *Report 67: Air Operations in China, Burma, India* (Washington DC: n. p., 1947), 90.

86 Stephen R. MacKinnon, "The US Firebombing of Wuhan, Part 2," http://www.chinaww2.com/2015/09/16/the-us-firebombing-of-wuhan-part-2/.

87 Bob Wilbanks, *Last Man Out: Glenn McDole, USMC, Survivor of the Palawan Massacre in World War II* (Jefferson NC: McFarland & Co., 2004), 112–115.

88 Dick Camp, "Survivor: Corporal Glenn McDole And the Palawan Massacre," *Leatherneck*, vol. 92, no. 6 (June 2009): 26.

89 Wilbanks, *Last Man Out*, 116–123.

90 "United States and Others v. Sadao Araki and Others. International Military Tribunal for the Far East (IMTFE), 4–12 November 1948," *International Law Studies*, vol. 60 (1979): 445.

91 Jay Rye, Interview, National Museum of the Pacific War, https://digitalarchive.pacificwarmuseum.org/digital/collection/p16769coll1/id/2010/rec/4.

92 Ibid.

93 Futamatsu Yoshihiko, *Across the Three Pagodas Pass: The Story of the Thai-Burma Railway* (Kent: Renaissance Books, 2013), 107–108.

94 Sarah Kovner, *Prisoners of the Japanese: Inside Japanese POW Camps* (Cambridge MA: Harvard University Press, 2020), 126.

95 Joan Beaumont, "The Long Silence: Australian Prisoners of the Japanese," in *Australia 1944–45: Victory in the Pacific*, ed. Peter Dean (Port Melbourne: Cambridge University Press, 2015), 79.

96 *Nippon Times*, February 11, 1944, quoted in A. Hamish Ion, "'Much Ado About Too Few': Aspects of the Treatment of Canadian and Commonwealth POWs and Civilian Internees in Metropolitan Japan 1941–1945," *Defence Studies*, vol. 6, no. 3 (September 2006): 292.

97 Shibutani Tamotsu, *The Derelicts of Company K: A Sociological Study of Demoralization* (Berkeley CA: University of California Press, 1978), 355.

98 "Praises Prisoner Camps," *New York Times*, April 5, 1944: 10.

99 Arnold Krammer, "Japanese Prisoners of War in America," *Pacific Historical Review*, vol. 52, no. 1 (February 1983): 78.

100 Ruth Benedict, *The Chrysanthemum and the Sword* (London: Secker & Warburg, 1947), 41.

101 Krammer, "Japanese Prisoners," 79.

102 E. V. Timms, "The Blood Bath at Cowra," in *As You Were*. Quoted in Gavin Long, *The Final Campaigns [Australia in the War of 1939–1945, Series I (Army), vol. 7]* (Canberra: Australian War Memorial, 1963), 623.

103 James O'Donnel, Interview, National Museum of the Pacific War, https://digitalarchive.pacificwarmuseum.org/digital/collection/p16769coll1/id/2973/rec/6.

104 Charles A. Lindbergh, *The Wartime Journals of Charles A. Lindbergh* (New York NY: Harcourt Brace Jovanovich Inc., 1970), 881.

Chapter Six

1   Buell, *Quiet Warrior*, 347.
2   George Horne, "Nimitz Promises Blockade of Japan," *New York Times*, January 2, 1945: 10.
3   "Forecast for 1945," *MacLean's*, January 1, 1945:44.
4   Eichelberger, *Jungle Road*, 186.
5   Michael Bak, Oral History, US Naval Institute, 170.
6   Halsey and Bryan, *Admiral Halsey's Story*, 242.
7   "Fiery Victory Call Issued Home Front in Koiso Broadcast," *Nippon Times*, January 3, 1945: 1–2.
8   Samuel Hideo Yamashita, *Daily Life in Wartime Japan, 1940–1945* (Lawrence KS: University Press of Kansas, 2015), 75.
9   Kase Toshikazu, *Journey to the Missouri* (New Haven CT: Yale University Press, 1950), 99.
10 MacArthur, *Reminiscences*, 198.
11 James, *The Years of MacArthur*, vol. 2, 617.
12 Morison, *Leyte*, 113.
13 Manchester, *American Caesar*, 406.
14 Samuel Eliot Morison, *The Liberation of the Philippines: Luzon, Mindanao, the Visayas 1944–1945 [History of the United States Naval Operations in World War II, vol. 13]* (Boston MA: Little, Brown and Co., 1959), 108.
15 Robert Ross Smith, *Triumph in the Philippines [United States Army in World War II: The War in the Pacific]* (Washington DC: United States Army Center of Military History, 1963), 78.
16 "Japanese Urges His Navy to Fight," *New York Times*, January 11, 1945: 1, 3.
17 Kawamura, *Emperor Hirohito and the Pacific War*, 140.
18 *Biennial Reports of the Chief of Staff of the United States Army*, 176.
19 Walter Krueger, *From Down Under to Nippon* (Nashville TN: Battery Press, 1989), 244.
20 Eichelberger, *Jungle Road*, 189.
21 Ibid., 195.
22 Frazier Hunt, *The Untold Story of Douglas MacArthur* (New York NY: Manor Books, 1977), 365.
23 Fred Faiz, Interview, National Museum of the Pacific War, https://digitalarchive.pacificwar-museum.org/digital/collection/p16769coll1/id/8567/rec/1, 21.
24 Hunt, *Untold Story*, 365–366.
25 Fred Faiz, Interview, National Museum of the Pacific War, https://digitalarchive.pacificwar-museum.org/digital/collection/p16769coll1/id/8567/rec/1, 22–23.
26 A. V. H. Hartendorp, *The Japanese Occupation of the Philippines, vol. 2* (Manila: Bookmark, 1967), 525.
27 *Philippine Area Naval Operations Part IV, January 1945–August 1945 [Japanese Monograph, no. 114]* (Washington DC: Department of the Army, 1952), 18.
28 James L. Halsema, *The Diary of James J. Halsema*, unpublished manuscript.
29 Frank F. Mathias, *GI Jive: An Army Bandsman in World War II* (Lexington KY: University Press of Kentucky, 1982), 132.
30 Eichelberger, *Jungle Road*, 197.
31 Krueger, *From Down Under to Nippon*, 250.
32 Eichelberger, *Jungle Road*, 194–195.

33   James, *The Years of MacArthur*, vol. 2, 635.

34   Robert L. Eichelberger, *Dear Miss Em: General Eichelberger's War in the Pacific, 1942–1945*, (Westport CT: Greenwood Press, 1972), 230.

35   Kenney, *General Kenney Reports*, 517.

36   Resident Commissioner of the Philippines to the United States, *Report on the Destruction of Manila and Japanese Atrocities* (Washington DC, 1945), 35–36.

37   Pascal Lottaz, "Neutral States and Wartime Japan: The Diplomacy of Sweden, Spain, and Switzerland towards the Empire," (PhD diss., National Graduate Institute for Policy Studies, 2018), 306–307.

38   Edward T. Imparato, *General MacArthur: Speeches and Reports 1908–1964* (Paducah KY: Turner Pub., 2000), 132–133.

39   Eichelberger, *Jungle Road*, 200.

40   Jan Valtin, *Children of Yesterday* (New York NY: The Readers' Press, 1946), 270.

41   Morison, *Victory*, 4.

42   Robert S. Burrell, *The Ghosts of Iwo Jima* (College Station, TX: Texas A&M University Press, 2006), 40.

43   Edwin A. Pollock, Oral History, US Marine Corps, 190.

44   Morison, *Victory*, 33.

45   Joseph H. Alexander, *Closing In: Marines in the Seizure of Iwo Jima* (Washington DC: Marine Corps Historical Center, 1994), 11.

46   Norman T. Hatch, Oral History, US Marine Corps, 179.

47   Arthur Talmadge, Interview, National Museum of the Pacific War, https://digitalarchive. pacificwarmuseum.org/digital/collection/p16769coll1/id/7872/rec/16, 24.

48   Ralph Simoneau, Interview, National Museum of the Pacific War, https://digitalarchive. pacificwarmuseum.org/digital/collection/p16769coll1/id/1625/rec/18, 43.

49   Ibid., 47–48.

50   Robert Amstutz, Interview, National Museum of the Pacific War, https://digitalarchive. pacificwarmuseum.org/digital/collection/p16769coll1/id/7501/rec/40, 29.

51   Ralph Ketcham, Interview, National Museum of the Pacific War, https://digitalarchive. pacificwarmuseum.org/digital/collection/p16769coll1/id/2367/rec/4, 28.

52   Robert Sherrod, "The First Three Days," *Life*, March 5, 1945: 44.

53   Ralph Simoneau, Interview, National Museum of the Pacific War, https://digitalarchive. pacificwarmuseum.org/digital/collection/p16769coll1/id/1625/rec/18, 46, 49.

54   Edwin A. Pollock, Oral History, US Marine Corps, 190–191.

55   Alvin Orsland, Interview, National Museum of the Pacific War, https://digitalarchive. pacificwarmuseum.org/digital/collection/p16769coll1/id/9279/rec/5, 12.

56   Ibid., 13.

57   Art G. Anderson, Interview, National Museum of the Pacific War, https://digitalarchive. pacificwarmuseum.org/digital/collection/p16769coll1/id/2882/rec/36, 16–17.

58   Robert Amstutz, Interview, National Museum of the Pacific War, https://digitalarchive. pacificwarmuseum.org/digital/collection/p16769coll1/id/7501/rec/40, 36–37.

59   Alvin Orsland, Interview, National Museum of the Pacific War, https://digitalarchive. pacificwarmuseum.org/digital/collection/p16769coll1/id/9279/rec/5, 17–18.

60   Michael Long, Interview, National Museum of the Pacific War, https://digitalarchive. pacificwarmuseum.org/digital/collection/p16769coll1/id/7056/rec/26, 14.

61   Charles Adair, Oral History, US Naval Institute, 354–355.

62   Duong Van Mai Ellliott, *The Sacred Willow: Four Generations in the Life of a Vietnamese Family* (Oxford: Oxford University Press, 1999), 108.

63 David G. Marr, *Vietnam 1945: The Quest for Power* (Berkeley CA: University of California Press, 1999), 96.

64 Marr, *Vietnam 1945*, 99–100.

65 Ibid., 104.

66 Motoo Furuta, "A Survey of Village Conditions during the 1945 Famine in Vietnam," in *Food Supplies and the Japanese Occupation of South-East Asia*, ed. Paul H. Kratoska (Basingstoke: Macmillan, 1998), 229, 232.

67 Nguyên Thê Anh, "Japanese Food Policies and the 1945 Great Famine in Indochina," in *Food Supplies and the Japanese Occupation of South-East Asia*, ed. Paul H. Kratoska (Basingstoke: Macmillan, 1998), 217.

68 Marr, *Vietnam 1945*, 101.

69 Ibid., 87.

70 Ibid., 90–91.

71 Fredrik Logevall, *Embers of War: The Fall of an Empire and the Making of America's Vietnam* (New York NY: Random House, 2015), 69–70.

72 Marr, *Vietnam 1945*, 109.

73 Fredrik Logevall, *Embers of War: The Fall of an Empire and the Making of America's Vietnam* (New York NY: Random House, 2015), 69–70.

74 Elliott, *Sacred Willow*, 103–104.

75 Marr, *Vietnam 1945*, 106.

76 Ibid., 112.

77 L. de Jong, *The Collapse of a Colonial Society: The Dutch in Indonesia during the Second World War* (Leiden: KITLV Press, 2002), 279.

78 Ibid., 280.

79 Ibid., 232.

80 Aiko Kurasawa, "Transportation and Rice Distribution in South-East Asia during the Second World War," in *Food Supplies and the Japanese Occupation in South-East Asia*, ed. Paul H. Kratoska (Basingstoke: Macmillan, 1998), 42.

81 Shigeru Sato, "Oppression and Romanticism: The Food Supply of Java during the Japanese Occupation," in *Food Supplies and the Japanese Occupation in South-East Asia*, ed. Paul H. Kratoska (Basingstoke: Macmillan, 1998), 177.

82 Kurasawa, "Transportation," 45–48.

83 de Jong, *Collapse*, 281.

84 George Sanford Kanahele, "The Japanese Occupation of Indonesia: Prelude to Independence" (PhD diss., Cornell University, 1967), 140–141.

85 Nugroho Notosusanto, "The Revolt of a PETA-Battalion in Blitar," *Asian Studies*, vol. 7, no. 1 (1969): 117.

86 Sintha Melati, "In the Service of the Underground," in *Local Opposition and Underground Resistance to the Japanese in Java 1942–1945*, ed. Anton Lucas (Clayton: Monash Papers on Southeast Asia, no. 13, Centre of Southeast Asian Studies, Monash University, 1986), 200.

87 Kanahele, "The Japanese Occupation of Indonesia," 185–187; Notosusanto, "Revolt of a PETA-Battalion," 116–122.

88 Michael Bak, Oral History, US Naval Institute, 191.

89 Kiyosawa Kiyoshi, *A Diary of Darkness: The Wartime Diary of Kiyosawa Kiyoshi*, ed. Eugene Soviak (Princeton NJ: Princeton University Press, 1998), 131.

90 Koji Takai and Henry Sakaida, *B-29 Hunters of the JAAF* (Oxford: Osprey, 2001), 96.

91 *USSBS: Summary Report (Pacific War)* (Washington DC: US Government Printing Office, 1946), 17.

92 Philip D. Webster, *Thirty-Five Missions over Japan* (Bluebird Books, 2017), 113.

93 "Tokyo's Burning," radio documentary, ABC, 1995.

94 Haruko Taya Cook and Theodore F. Cook, *Japan at War: An Oral History* (New York NY: The New Press, 1992), 345.

95 Raymond Francis "Hap" Halloran, Interview, National Museum of the Pacific War, https://digitalarchive.pacificwarmuseum.org/digital/collection/p16769coll1/id/5234/rec/13, 23.

96 James Lea Cate and James C. Olson, "Urban Area Attacks," in *The Army Air Forces in World War II, vol. 5: The Pacific: Matterhorn to Nagasaki, June 1944 to August 1945*, eds. Wesley Frank Craven and James Lea Cate (Chicago IL: University of Chicago Press, 1953), 617.

97 Cook and Cook, *Japan at War*, 348.

98 Cate and Olson, "Urban Area Attacks," 617.

99 Ibid.

100 Assistant Chief of Staff-Intelligence, Headquarters Army Air Forces, *Mission Accomplished. Interrogations of Japanese Industrial Military, and Civil Leaders of World War II* (Washington DC: US Government Printing Office, 1946), 26.

101 Curtis LeMay, *Mission with LeMay: My Story* (Garden City NY: Doubleday, 1965), 387.

102 Michael Sherry, *The Rise of American Air Power: The Creation of Armageddon* (New Haven, CT: Yale University Press), 287.

103 Raymond Francis "Hap" Halloran Interview, National Museum of the Pacific War, https://digitalarchive.pacificwarmuseum.org/digital/collection/p16769coll1/id/5234/rec/13, 24.

104 USSBS, *The Effects of Strategic Bombing on Japanese Morale*, 40.

105 Thomas R.H. Havens, *Valley of Darkness: The Japanese People and World War Two* (New York NY: W. W. Norton and Company, 1978), 161.

106 Kawamura, *Emperor Hirohito and the Pacific War*, 142.

107 Toshiaki Kawahara, *Hirohito and His Times: A Japanese Perspective* (Tokyo: Kodansha International, 1990) 119.

108 Kawamura, *Emperor Hirohito and the Pacific War*, 146.

Chapter Seven

1 Yoshida Mitsuru, "The Sinking of the *Yamato*," in *The Japanese Navy in World War Two*, ed. David C. Evans (Annapolis MD: Naval Institute Press, 2017), 475–476.

2 Dyer, *Amphibians*, vol. 2, 1104.

3 Buell, *Quiet Warrior*, 371.

4 Morison, *Victory*, 108–109.

5 Dyer, *Amphibians*, vol. 2, 1094.

6 Roy E. Appleman, James M. Burns, Russell A. Gugeler and John Stevens, *Okinawa: The Last Battle [United States Army in World War II: The War in the Pacific]* (Washington DC: United States Army Center of Military History, 1948), 46.

7 Al Adkins, Interview, National Museum of the Pacific War, https://digitalarchive.pacificwarmuseum.org/digital/collection/p16769coll1/id/11032/rec/51, 60.

8 Buell, *Quiet Warrior*, 379.

9 Bill Filter, Interview, National Museum of the Pacific War, https://digitalarchive.pacificwarmuseum.org/digital/collection/p16769coll1/id/5492/rec/7, 15–16.

10 Joseph H. Alexander, *The Final Campaign: Marines in the Victory on Okinawa* (Washington DC: Marine Corps Historical Center, 1994), 35.

11 Kenneth Harrell, Interview, National Museum of the Pacific War, https://digitalarchive.pacificwarmuseum.org/digital/collection/p16769coll1/id/8518/rec/3, 19.

12 Bill Filter, Interview, National Museum of the Pacific War, https://digitalarchive.pacificwar-museum.org/digital/collection/p16769coll1/id/5492/rec/7, 21–22.

13 Halsey and Bryan, *Admiral Halsey's Story*, 255.

14 Benis M. Frank and Henry I. Shaw, *Victory and Occupation [History of U.S. Marine Corps Operations in World War II, vol. 5]* (Washington DC: US Government Printing Office, 1968), 324.

15 Robert M. Neiman and Kenneth W. Estes, *Tanks on the Beaches: A Marine Tanker in the Great Pacific War* (College Station TX: Texas A&M University Press, 2002), 150.

16 Arthur Aicklen, Interview, National Museum of the Pacific War, https://digitalarchive.pacificwarmuseum.org/digital/collection/p16769coll1/id/4633/rec/9, 130–134.

17 Morison, *Victory*, 282.

18 Dyer, *Amphibians*, vol. 2, 1101.

19 Morison, *Victory*, 282.

20 Noel A. M. Gayler, Oral History, US Naval Institute, 133.

21 William F. Halsey and J. Bryan III, *Admiral Halsey's Story* (New York NY: Da Capo Press, 1976), 253.

22 Frank and Shaw, *Victory and Occupation*, 37.

23 Schrijvers, *Bloody Pacific*, 179.

24 George R. Nelson, *I Company: The First and Last to Fight on Okinawa* (Bloomington IN: Authorhouse, 2003), 229.

25 Elbert Dixon, Interview, National Museum of the Pacific War, https://digitalarchive.pacificwar-museum.org/digital/collection/p16769coll1/id/10093/rec/23, 8.

26 Schrijvers, *Bloody Pacific*, 211.

27 Morison, *Victory*, 203.

28 Prados, *Combined Fleet Decoded*, 710–711.

29 Morison, *Victory*, 203.

30 Ibid., 205–206.

31 Yoshida, "Sinking," 492.

32 Morison, *Victory*, 208.

33 Joseph Muse Worthington, Oral History, US Naval Institute, 306.

34 Halsey and Bryan, *Admiral Halsey's Story*, 249–250.

35 Lawson P. Ramage, Oral History, US Naval Institute.

36 Ralph Simoneau, Interview, National Museum of the Pacific War, https://digitalarchive.pacificwarmuseum.org/digital/collection/p16769coll1/id/1625/rec/18, 68.

37 Raymond Strohmeyer, Interview, National Museum of the Pacific War, https://digitalarchive.pacificwarmuseum.org/digital/collection/p16769coll1/id/5034/rec/3, 69.

38 *Public Papers of the Presidents of the United States: Harry S. Truman, Containing the Public Messages, Speeches, and Statements of the President, April 12 to December 1945* (Washington DC: United States Government Printing Office, 1961), 27.

39 "Japanese Premier Voices 'Sympathy'," *New York Times*, April 15, 1945: 3.

40 "International: The Enemy Speaks," *Time*, April 23, 1945.

41 "Japanese Premier Voices 'Sympathy'," *New York Times*, April 15, 1945: 3.

42 Ibid.

43 James Fallows, "Yasukuni, Yūshūkan: Yes, There Is More," *The Atlantic*, January 3, 2014.

44 Appleman et al., *Okinawa*, 125.

45 Neiman and Estes, *Tanks on the Beaches*, 98–99.

46 Michael Bak, Oral History, US Naval Institute, 187.

47 Noel A. M. Gayler, Oral History, Naval Institute, 138.

48 Ibid., 130.

49 Roy S. Benson, Oral History, Naval Institute, 306.
50 Gustavo Vázquez Lozano, *201st Squadron: The Aztec Eagles* (n. p.: Libros de México), 83.
51 Lozano, *201st Squadron*, 75–76.
52 Kiyosawa, *Diary of Darkness*, 327.
53 Aleksei A. Kirichenko and Sergey V. Grishachev "The 'Manchurian Blitzkrieg' of 1945 and Japanese Prisoners of War in the Soviet Union, in *A History of Russo-Japanese Relations: Over Two Centuries of Cooperation and Competition*, eds. Dmitry Streltsov and Nobuo Shimotomai (Leiden: Brill, 2019), 336.
54 USSBS, *The Effects of Strategic Bombing on Japanese Morale*, 19.
55 Ibid., 25.
56 Ibid., 22.
57 Erwin Wickert, *Mut und Übermut. Geschichten aus meinem Leben*, (Stuttgart: Deutsche Verlags-Anstalt, 1992), 427.
58 Kawamura, *Hirohito*, 155.
59 Drea, *In the Service of the Emperor*, 201.
60 Miles Smeeton, *A Change of Jungles* (London: Rupert Hart-Davis, 1962), 91.
61 Mountbatten, *Personal Diary*, 181.
62 Thompson, *Forgotten Voices*, 333.
63 Slim, *Defeat into Victory*, 374–375.
64 Ibid., 375.
65 Thompson, *Forgotten Voices*, 351.
66 Ibid., 331–332.
67 Allen, *Burma*, 482.
68 Gerhard L. Weinberg, *A World at Arms: A Global History of World War II* (Cambridge: Cambridge University Press, 1994), 860.
69 Mountbatten, *Personal Diary*, 211.
70 Thompson, *Forgotten Voices*, 352.
71 Lee Bowen, "Victory in China," in *The Pacific: Matterhorn to Nagasaki: June 1944 to August 1945. [The Army Air Forces in World War II, vol. 5]*, ed. Wesley Frank Craven and James Lea Cate (Chicago IL: University of Chicago Press, 1953), 267.
72 Albert C. Wedemeyer, *Wedemeyer Reports!* (New York NY: Henry Holt and Co., 1958), 331.
73 Theresa L. Kraus, *China Offensive* (Washington DC: Department of the Army, 1996), 8.
74 Ibid, 15.
75 Bowen, "Victory in China," 266.
76 Romanus and Sunderland, *Time Runs Out*, 288.
77 Hara, "Ichigō Offensive," 401.
78 van de Ven, *China at War*, 197.
79 Ibid., 198.
80 Lyman P. Van Slyke, "The Chinese Communist movement during the Sino-Japanese War, 1937–1945," in *The Nationalist Era in China, 1927–1949*, ed. Lloyd E. Eastman, Jerome Ch'en, Suzanne Pepper and Lyman P. Van Slyke (Cambridge: Cambridge University Press, 1991), 277.
81 Hara, "Ichigō Offensive," 402.
82 Davies, *China Hand*, 216.
83 "Report by the Second Secretary of Embassy in China (Service)," *Foreign Relations of the United States: Diplomatic Papers 1944, vol. VI: China* (Washington DC: United States Government Printing Office, 1967), 518.

84 Chen Jian, *Mao's China and the Cold War* (Chapel Hill NC: University of North Carolina Press, 2001), 22; Rana Mitter, *China's War With Japan, 1937–1945: The Struggle For Survival* (London: Allen Lane, 2013), 354.

85 David Richardson, Interview, National Museum of the Pacific War, https://digitalarchive. pacificwarmuseum.org/digital/collection/p16769coll1/id/10164/rec/5 8.

86 David Horner, "Advancing National Interests: Deciding Australia's War Strategy, 1944–45," in *Australia 1944–45: Victory in the Pacific*, ed. Peter Dean (Port Melbourne: Cambridge University Press, 2015), 13. Horner argues that Australian overseas deployments after 1945 have also been motivated by political concerns, rather than military necessity.

87 Ibid., 9.

88 Ibid., 14.

89 Ibid., 16–18.

90 Margaret Barter, *Far Above Battle: The Experiences and Memory of Australian Soldiers in War* (Sydney: Allen & Unwin, 1994), 235.

91 Michael John Pyne, "Relationships between Officers and Other Ranks in the Australian Army in the Second World War" (PhD diss., University of Western Sydney, 2016), 103–104.

92 Yoshihara Kane, "Southern Cross: memories of the war in eastern New Guinea," [manuscript MSS0725] (Canberra: Australian War Memorial, 1955), Chapter 20.

93 Peter J. Dean and Kevin Holzimmer, "The Southwest Pacific Area: Military Strategy and Operations, 1944–45," in *Australia 1944–45: Victory in the Pacific*, ed. Peter Dean (Port Melbourne: Cambridge University Press, 2015), 43.

94 Dean and Holzimmer, "Southwest Pacific Area," 45.

95 USSBS, *Interrogations of Japanese Officials*, vol. 1, 88–89.

96 Ibid.

Chapter Eight

1 Dyer, *Amphibians*, vol. 2, 1108.

2 United States Department of State, *Foreign relations of the United States: Diplomatic papers. The Conference of Berlin (the Potsdam Conference), 1945*, vol. 1 (Washington DC: Government Printing Office, 1960), 909.

3 "He Wishes There Were," *Washington Post*, 17 March 1945: 1.

4 Art G. Anderson, Interview, National Museum of the Pacific War, https://digitalarchive. pacificwarmuseum.org/digital/collection/p16769coll1/id/2882/rec/36, 22.

5 USSBS, *The Effects of Strategic Bombing on Japanese Morale*, 29.

6 General Headquarters United States Army Forces in the Pacific, *"Downfall": Strategic Plan for Operations in the Japanese Archipelago* (n.p.: United States Army, 1945), 2.

7 USSBS, *The Effects of Strategic Bombing on Japanese Morale*, 23.

8 Ibid., 22.

9 Yamashita, *Daily Life*, 87.

10 Assistant Chief of Staff-Intelligence, Headquarters Army Air Forces, *Mission Accomplished. Interrogations of Japanese Industrial Military, and Civil Leaders of World War II* (Washington DC: US Government Printing Office, 1946), 19.

11 USSBS, *Japanese Air Power* (Washington DC: Military Analysis Division, 1946), 69–70.

12 Noel A. M. Gayler, Oral History, US Naval Institute, 140.

13 Halsey and Bryan, *Admiral Halsey's Story*, 266.

14 Morison, *Victory*, 310–311.

15 Ibid., 312.
16 Halsey and Bryan, *Admiral Halsey's Story*, 260.
17 Morison, *Victory*, 314.
18 Halsey and Bryan, *Admiral Halsey's Story*, 260.
19 Noel A. M. Gayler, Oral History, US Naval Institute, 131–132.
20 Eugene B. Fluckey, *Thunder Below! The USS Barb Revolutionizes Submarine Warfare in World War II* (Urbana and Chicago IL: University of Illinois Press, 1997), 383.
21 Clay Blair Jr., *Silent Victory: The U.S. Submarine War against Japan* (Philadelphia PA and New York NY: J.B. Lippincott Co., 1975), 867.
22 Morison, *Victory*, 294–297.
23 Roy S. Benson, Oral History, US Naval Institute, 306–307.
24 Blair, *Silent Victory*, 860.
25 USSBS, *Interrogations of Japanese Officials*, vol. 1, 144.
26 Morison, *Victory*, 322–324.
27 Doug Stanton, *In Harm's Way* (New York NY: Henry Holt and Company, 2001), 163.
28 Morison, *Victory*, 327.
29 USSBS, *The Effects of Strategic Bombing on Japanese Morale*, 91.
30 James Lea Cate and Wesley Frank Craven, "Victory," in *The Pacific: Matterhorn to Nagasaki [The Army Air Forces in World War II, vol. 5]*, eds. Wesley Frank Craven and James Lea Cate (Chicago IL: University of Chicago Press, 1953), 716–717.
31 Ray Monk, *Inside the Centre: The Life of J. Robert Oppenheimer* (London: Jonathan Cape, 2012), 445.
32 Deidre Carmody, "Hiroshima A-Bomb Log Nets $37,000," *New York Times*, November 24, 1971: 37.
33 Wickert, *Mut*, 387.
34 USSBS, *The Effects of the Atomic Bombings of Hiroshima and Nagasaki* (Washington DC: US Government Printing Office, 1946), 15.
35 USSBS, *The Effects of Strategic Bombing on Japanese Morale*, 92–93.
36 Ibid., 93.
37 Ibid.
38 Aaron Barlow (ed.), *The Manhattan Project and the Dropping of the Atomic Bomb* (Santa Barbara CA: ABC-CLIO, 2020), 225.
39 Michael Bak, Oral History, US Naval Institute, 219.
40 Buckner Fanning, Interview, National Museum of the Pacific War, https://digitalarchive.pacificwarmuseum.org/digital/collection/p16769coll1/id/1427/rec/2, 7–8.
41 William L. Laurence, "Atomic Bombing of Nagasaki Told by Flight Member, *New York Times*, September 9, 1945: 35.
42 Cook and Cook, *Japan at War*, 479.
43 "Memorandum on the Use of S-1 Bomb," War Department, June 1945.
44 Michael Bak, Oral History, US Naval Institute, 219.
45 Garold Weasmer, Interview, National Museum of the Pacific War, https://digitalarchive.pacificwarmuseum.org/digital/collection/p16769coll1/id/4795/rec/1, 24.
46 Dyer, *Amphibians*, vol. 2, 1108.
47 Halsey and Bryan, *Admiral Halsey's Story*, 261.
48 David M. Glantz and Jonathan M. House, *When Titans Clashed: How the Red Army Stopped Hitler* (Lawrence KS: University Press of Kansas, 2015), 351–352.
49 Edward J. Drea, "Missing Intentions: Japanese Intelligence and the Soviet Invasion of Manchuria, 1945," *Military Affairs*, vol. 48, no. 2, (April 1984): 70.

50 Hatano Sumio, "Wartime Relations between Japan and the Soviet Union, 1941–1945," in *A History of Russo-Japanese Relations: Over Two Centuries of Cooperation and Competition*, eds. Dmitry Streltsov and Nobuo Shimotomai (Leiden: Brill, 2019), 249.

51 Glantz and House, *When Titans Clashed*, 353.

52 Lori Watt, *When Empire Comes Home: Repatriation and Reintegration in Postwar Japan* (Cambridge MA: Harvard University Asia Center, 2009), 39.

53 Oguma, Eiji, *Return from Siberia: A Japanese Life in War and Peace, 1925–2015* (Tokyo: LTCB International library Trust, 2018), 63.

54 Chan Yeeshan, *Abandoned Japanese in Postwar Manchuria: The Lives of War Orphans and Wives in Two Countries* (Abingdon: Taylor & Francis Group, 2011), 19–20.

55 Chan, *Abandoned Japanese*, 20–21.

56 Itoh Mayumi, *Japanese War Orphans in Manchuria: Forgotten Victims of World War II* (New York NY: Palgrave Macmillan, 2010), 35–36.

57 Ibid., 30.

58 Ibid., 32.

59 Chan, *Abandoned Japanese*, 17–20.

60 Richard A. Russell, *Project Hula: Secret Soviet-American Cooperation in the War Against Japan* (Washington DC: Naval Historical Center, 1997), 8.

61 Russell, *Project Hula*, 1, 39–40.

62 D. M. Giangreco, "The Hokkaido Myth," *Journal of Strategy and Politics*, vol. 2 (2015): 148–164.

63 Kawamura, *Hirohito and the Pacific War*, 162.

64 Alvin D. Coox, "The Enola Gay and Japan's Struggle to Surrender," *The Journal of American-East Asian Relations*, vol. 4, no. 2 (Summer 1995): 166–167.

65 Ugaki, *Fading Victory*, 655, 659.

66 Alvin D. Coox, "The Enola Gay and Japan's Struggle to Surrender," *The Journal of American-East Asian Relations*, vol. 4, no. 2 (Summer 1995): 167.

67 Edward J. Drea, "Intelligence Forecasting for the Invasion of Japan: Previews of Hell," in *Hiroshima in History: The Myths of Revisionism*, ed. Robert James Maddox (Columbus MO: University of Missouri Press, 2007), 70; Barton Bernstein, "Eclipsed by Hiroshima and Nagasaki: Early Thinking about Tactical Nuclear Weapons," *International Security*, vol. 15, no. 4 (Spring 1991): 164.

68 Tomita Takeshi, "The Reality of the Siberian Internment: Japanese Captives in the Soviet Union and Their Movements after Repatriation," in *A History of Russo-Japanese Relations: Over Two Centuries of Cooperation and Competition*, eds. Dmitry Streltsov and Nobuo Shimotomai (Leiden: Brill, 2019), 306.

69 Sadao Asada, "The Shock of the Atomic Bomb and Japan's Decision to Surrender—A Reconsideration," in *Hiroshima in History: The Myths of Revisionism*, ed. Robert James Maddox (Columbus MO: University of Missouri Press, 2007), 44.

70 Kawamura, *Hirohito and the Pacific War*, 164.

71 Ibid., 166.

72 Kazuo Kawai, "Militarist Activity between Japan's Two Surrender Decisions," *Pacific Historical Review*, vol. 22, no. 4 (1953): 383–384.

73 Barton J. Bernstein, "The Perils and Politics of Surrender: Ending the War with Japan and Avoiding the Third Atomic Bomb," *Pacific Historical Review*, vol. 46, no. 1 (February 1977): 3.

74 Bernstein, "Perils and Politics," 4–5.

75 Robert J. C. Butow, *Japan's Decision to Surrender* (Stanford CA: Stanford University Press, 1954), 245.

76 Bernstein, "Perils and Politics," 7–8.
77 Kawamura, *Hirohito and the Pacific War*, 167–168.
78 Ibid., 175–176.
79 Ibid.
80 Kawahara, *Hirohito and His Times*, 134; Toland, *Rising Sun*, 837–848.
81 Ibid.
82 USSBS, *The Effects of Strategic Bombing on Japanese Morale*, 24.
83 Kawamura, *Hirohito and the Pacific War*, 182.
84 Ugaki, *Fading Victory*, 664.
85 Cook and Cook, *Japan at War*, 419.
86 Oguma, *Return from Siberia*, 65.
87 F. Spencer Chapman, *The Jungle Is Neutral* (London: Chatto and Windus, 1950), 420.
88 John J. A. Michel, *Mr. Michel's War: From Manila to Mukden: an American Navy Officer's War with the Japanese, 1941–1945* (Novato CA: Presidio, 1998), 263–264.
89 Peter Dennis, *Troubled Days of Peace: Mountbatten and South East Asia Command, 1945–46* (Manchester: Manchester University Press, 1987), 226.
90 Michael Bak, Oral History, US Naval Institute, 218.
91 Karl James, *The Hard Slog: Australians in the Bougainville Campaign, 1944–45* (Cambridge: Cambridge University Press, 2012), 246.
92 Peter Medcalf, *War in the Shadows: Bougainville 1944–45* (Canberra: Australian War Memorial, 1986), 115.
93 Bose, *His Majesty's Opponent*, 299–300.
94 Ibid., 300.
95 Joyce Chapman Lebra, *The Indian National Army and Japan* (Singapore: Institute of Southeast Asian Studies, 2008), 197.
96 Edwin Layton, Oral History, US Naval Institute, 168–169.
97 Noel A. M. Gayler, Oral History, Naval Institute, 140–141.
98 Eichelberger, *Jungle Road*, 264.
99 Noel A. M. Gayler, Oral History, Naval Institute, 138.
100 Homer Bigart, "Japan Signs, Second World War Is Ended," in *Reporting World War II: American Journalism 1938–1946*, eds. Samuel Hynes, Nancy Caldwell Sorel, Anne Matthews, and Roger J Spiller (New York NY: Literary Classics of the United States, Inc., 1995), vol. 2, 773.
101 Halsey and Bryan, *Admiral Halsey's Story*, 282.
102 Henri Smith-Hutton, Oral History, Naval Institute, 502.
103 MacArthur, *Reminiscences*, 275–276.

Chapter Nine

1 *Inaugural Addresses of the Presidents of the United States from George Washington 1789 to Richard Mulhouse Nixon 1969* (Washington DC: Government Printing Office, 1969), 248.
2 Cecil S. King, Oral History, US Naval Institute Oral History Program, 259–260.
3 MacArthur, *Reminiscences*, 295.
4 Jim Sansom, Interview, National Museum of the Pacific War, https://digitalarchive.pacificwarmuseum.org/digital/collection/p16769coll1/id/1457/rec/3, 23.
5 Arthur Liberty, Interview, National Museum of the Pacific War, https://digitalarchive.pacificwarmuseum.org/digital/collection/p16769coll1/id/3731/rec/13, 48.

6   Robert Ellinger, Interview, National Museum of the Pacific War, https://digitalarchive. pacificwarmuseum.org/digital/collection/p16769coll1/id/10411/rec/42, 17.

7   Michael Bak, Oral History, 211.

8   Ralph Simoneau, Interview, National Museum of the Pacific War, https://digitalarchive. pacificwarmuseum.org/digital/collection/p16769coll1/id/1625/rec/18, 49–51.

9   John Ellis, Interview, National Museum of the Pacific War, https://digitalarchive.pacificwar-museum.org/digital/collection/p16769coll1/id/4307/rec/1, 22.

10 Keith W. Olson, "The G. I. Bill and Higher Education: Success and Surprise," *American Quarterly*, vol. 25, no. 5 (December 1973): 598

11 Bill Filter, Interview, National Museum of the Pacific War, https://digitalarchive.pacificwar-museum.org/digital/collection/p16769coll1/id/5492/rec/7, 22–23.

12 Andrew E. Barshay, "Postwar Social and Political Thought, 1945–90," in *Modern Japanese Thought*, ed. Bob T. Wakabayashi (Cambridge: Cambridge University Press, 2012), 277.

13 Louis Morton, *Strategy and Command: The First Two Years [United States Army in World War II: The War in the Pacific]* (Washington DC: Office of the Chief of Military History, Department of the Army, 1962), 125.

14 H. P. Wilmott, *The Barrier and the Javelin: Japanese and Allied Pacific Strategies, February to June 1942* (Annapolis MD: Naval Institute Press, 1983), 3.

15 John W. Dower, *War Without Mercy* (New York NY: W. W. Norton and Co., 1986), 297–299.

16 United States Department of State, *Foreign relations of the United States: Diplomatic papers. The Conference of Berlin (the Potsdam Conference), 1945*, vol. 1 (Washington DC: Government Printing Office, 1960), 905.

17 Dower, *War Without Mercy*, 297–299.

18 Michael Bak, Oral History, 225.

19 Art G. Anderson, Interview, National Museum of the Pacific War, https://digitalarchive. pacificwarmuseum.org/digital/collection/p16769coll1/id/2882/rec/36, 23.

20 Brian Walsh, "Sexual Violence During the Occupation of Japan," *The Journal of Military History*, no. 82 (October 2018): 1206.

21 Yuki Tanaka, *Japan's Comfort Women: Sexual Slavery and Prostitution During World War II and the US Occupation* (London and New York NY: Routledge, 2001), 121.

22 Allan Stephen Clifton, *Time of Fallen Blossoms* (New York NY: A. A. Knopf 1951), 167.

23 Walsh, "Sexual Violence," 1206 n27.

24 Ibid., 1217–1219.

25 Ian Buruma, *Year Zero: A History of 1945* (New York NY: Penguin Press, 2013), 38.; John W. Dower, *Embracing Defeat: Japan in the Wake of World War II* (New York NY: W. W. Norton and Co., 1999), 579 n16.

26 Walsh, "Sexual Violence," esp. 1218–1220.

27 Ralph Simoneau, Interview, National Museum of the Pacific War, https://digitalarchive. pacificwarmuseum.org/digital/collection/p16769coll1/id/1625/rec/18, 59.

28 Alvin Orsland, Interview, National Museum of the Pacific War, https://digitalarchive. pacificwarmuseum.org/digital/collection/p16769coll1/id/9279/rec/5, 26.

29 Art G. Anderson, Interview, National Museum of the Pacific War, https://digitalarchive. pacificwarmuseum.org/digital/collection/p16769coll1/id/2882/rec/36, 23.

30 Alvin Orsland, Interview, National Museum of the Pacific War, https://digitalarchive. pacificwarmuseum.org/digital/collection/p16769coll1/id/9279/rec/5, 25.

31 Noel A. M. Gayler, Oral History, US Naval Institute, 133.

32 Henri Smith-Hutton, Oral History, US Naval Institute Oral History Program, 501–502.

33 Foster Rhea Dulles, *Yankees and Samurai: America's Role in the Emergence of Modern Japan* (New York NY: Harper and Row, 1965), 68.

34 John D. Montgomery, *Forced to Be Free: The Artificial Revolution in Germany and Japan* (Chicago IL: University of Chicago Press, 1957), 106–107.

35 Nakayama Ichirō, *Industrialization of Japan* (Tokyo: Centre for East Asian Cultural Studies, 1964), 7.

36 Antony Whitlock, "Japan Will Still Win, Smiles Kanazawa," *The Sydney Morning Herald,* September 14, 1945: 3.

37 Don L. Holmes, Interview, National Museum of the Pacific War, https://digitalarchive. pacificwarmuseum.org/digital/collection/p16769coll1/id/1337/rec/35, 4.

38 Robert B. Luckey, Oral History, US Marine Corps, 184.

39 Shen Zhihua, *Mao, Stalin and the Korean War: Trilateral Communist Relations in the 1950s* (Abingdon: Taylor & Francis Group, 2012), 48.

40 Peter Harmsen, *Storm Clouds over the Pacific 1931–1941* (Havertown PA: Casemate, 2018), 30–31, 36–37.

41 Shen, *Mao, Stalin and the Korean War*, 52.

42 S. C. M. Paine, *The Wars for Asia* (Cambridge: Cambridge University Press, 2012), 245.

43 Paine, *The Wars for Asia*, 240–241.

44 Shen, *Mao, Stalin and the Korean War*, 53.

45 Don L. Holmes, Interview, National Museum of the Pacific War, https://digitalarchive. pacificwarmuseum.org/digital/collection/p16769coll1/id/1337/rec/35, 6.

46 Dean Acheson, *Present at the Creation: My Years in the State Department* (New York NY: W. W. Norton, 1969), 140.

47 Davies, *China Hand*, 266.

48 Don L. Holmes, Interview, National Museum of the Pacific War, https://digitalarchive. pacificwarmuseum.org/digital/collection/p16769coll1/id/1337/rec/35, 5–6.

49 Christopher Bayly and Tim Harper, *Forgotten Armies: The Fall of British Asia, 1941–1945* (Cambridge MA: The Belknap Press of Harvard University Press, 2004), 455.

50 Benedict Richard O'Gorman Anderson, *Some Aspects of Indonesian Politics Under the Japanese Occupation: 1944–1945* (Ithaca NY: Cornell University, 1961), 98.

51 Logevall, *Embers of War*, 97–98.

52 Gregg Huff, *World War II and Southeast Asia: Economy and Society under Japanese Occupation* (Cambridge: Cambridge University Press, 2020), 399.

53 Herbert Feith, *The Decline of Constitutional Democracy in Indonesia* (Ithaca NY: Cornell University Press, 1962), 5.

54 Dirk Bogarde, *Backcloth: A Memoir* (London: Bloomsbury, 2013), 175.

55 Nguyên, "Japanese Food Policies," 218–220.

56 Ibid., 221.

57 Ibid., 220.

58 Logevall, *Embers of War*, 181.

59 Henri Smith-Hutton, Oral History, US Naval Institute, 647.

60 Oguma, *Return from Siberia*, 87.

61 Ibid., 81.

62 Guo Daijun, *Chongtan Kangrishi [Revisiting the Second Sino-Japanese War, 1931–1945], vol. 1* (Taipei: Linking Book, 2015), 19.

Bibliography

Abe Zenji. *The Emperor's Sea Eagle*. Honolulu HI: Arizona Memorial Museum Association, 2006.

Acheson, Dean. *Present at the Creation: My Years in the State Department*. New York NY: W. W. Norton, 1969.

Alanbrooke, Field Marshal Lord. *War Diaries, 1939–1945*. Edited by Alex Danchev and Daniel Todman. London: Phoenix Press, 2003.

Alexander, Joseph H. *Closing In: Marines in the Seizure of Iwo Jima*. Washington DC: Marine Corps Historical Center, 1994.

———, *The Final Campaign: Marines in the Victory on Okinawa*. Washington DC: Marine Corps Historical Center, 1996.

Allen, Louis. *Burma: The Longest War 1941–45*. London: Phoenix Press, 1984.

Anderson, Benedict Richard O'Gorman. *Some Aspects of Indonesian Politics Under the Japanese Occupation: 1944–1945*. Ithaca NY: Cornell University, 1961.

Anglim, Simon J. *Major General Orde Wingate's Chindit Operations in World War II*. Reading: University of Reading, 2009.

Appleman, Roy E., James M. Burns, Russell A. Gugeler, and John Stevens. *Okinawa: The Last Battle [United States Army in World War II: The War in the Pacific]*. Washington DC: United States Army Center of Military History, 1948.

Asano Toyomi. "Japanese Operations in Yunnan and North Burma." In *The Battle for China*, edited by Mark Peattie, Edward Drea, and Hans van de Ven, 361–385. Stanford CA: Stanford University Press, 2011.

Assistant Chief of Staff-Intelligence, Headquarters Army Air Forces. *Mission Accomplished. Interrogations of Japanese Industrial Military, and Civil Leaders of World War II*. Washington DC: US Government Printing Office, 1946.

Ayer, S. A. *Unto Him a Witness: The Story of Netaji Subhas Chandra Bose in East Asia*. Bombay: Thacker & Co., 1951.

Barlow, Aaron. *The Manhattan Project and the Dropping of the Atomic Bomb*. Santa Barbara CA: ABC-CLIO, 2020.

Barrett, David P. "The Wang Jingwei Regime, 1940–1945: Continuities and Disjunctures with Nationalist China." In *Chinese Collaboration with Japan, 1932–1945: The Limits of Accommodation*, edited by David P. Barrett and Larry N. Shyu, 102–115. Palo Alto CA: Stanford University Press, 2002.

Barter, Margaret. *Far Above Battle: The Experiences and Memory of Australian Soldiers in War*. Sydney: Allen & Unwin, 1994.

Bayly, Christopher and Tim Harper. *Forgotten Armies: The Fall of British Asia, 1941–1945*. Cambridge MA: The Belknap Press of Harvard University Press, 2004.

Beaumont, Joan. "The Long Silence: Australian Prisoners of the Japanese." In *Australia 1944–45: Victory in the Pacific*, edited by Peter Dean, 79–97. Port Melbourne: Cambridge University Press, 2015.

Benedict, Ruth. *The Chrysanthemum and the Sword.* London: Secker & Warburg, 1947.

Barton J. Bernstein. "The Perils and Politics of Surrender: Ending the War with Japan and Avoiding the Third Atomic Bomb." *Pacific Historical Review,* vol. 46, no. 1 (February 1977): 1–27.

Biennial Reports of the Chief of Staff of the United States Army to the Secretary of War, 1 July 1939–30 June 1945. Washington DC: Center of Military History United States Army, 1996.

Bix, Herbert P. *Hirohito and the Making of Modern Japan.* New York NY: Perennial, 2001.

Blair, Blair Jr. *Silent Victory: The U.S. Submarine War against Japan.* Philadelphia PA and New York NY: J.B. Lippincott Co., 1975.

Bōeichō Bōeikenshūjo *[Japanese Defense Agency's Research Institute]. Senshi sōsho. Ichigō sakusen.* 2: *Kōnan no sakusen [War History. Operation Ichigō. 2: The Battle for Hunan].* Tokyo: Asagumo shimbunsha, 1968.

Bogarde, Dirk. *Backcloth: A Memoir.* London: Bloomsbury, 2013.

Bose, Sugata. *His Majesty's Opponent: Subhas Chandra Bose and India's Struggle against Empire.* Cambridge MA: The Belknap Press of Harvard University Press, 2011.

Bowen, Lee. "Victory in China." In *The Pacific: Matterhorn to Nagasaki: June 1944 to August 1945 [The Army Air Forces in World War II, vol. 5],* edited by Wesley Frank Craven and James Lea Cate, 252–272. Chicago IL: University of Chicago Press, 1953.

Brecher, W. Puck. *Honored and Dishonored Guests: Westerners in Wartime Japan.* Cambridge MA: Harvard University Asia Center, 2017.

Brockman, Ronald. "Mountbatten." In *The Warlords,* edited by Michael Carver, 357–374. London: Weidenfeld and Nicolson, 1976.

Brown, A. Sunderland. "Burma Banzai: The Air War in Burma through Japanese Eyes," *Canadian Military History,* vol. 11, no. 2 (Spring 2002): 53–59.

Buell, Thomas B. *The Quiet Warrior: A Biography of Admiral Raymond A. Spruance.* Annapolis MD: Naval Institute Press, 1987.

Burns, James MacGregor. *Roosevelt: The Soldier of Freedom, 1940–1945.* London: Weidenfeld and Nicolson, 1971.

Buruma, Ian. *Year Zero: A History of 1945.* New York NY: Penguin Press, 2013.

Butow, Robert J. C. *Japan's Decision to Surrender.* Stanford CA: Stanford University Press, 1954.

————, *Tojo and the Coming of the War.* Stanford CA: Stanford University Press, 1961.

Calvert, Michael. *Prisoner of Hope.* London: Leo Cooper, 1971.

Camp, Dick. "Survivor: Corporal Glenn McDole And the Palawan Massacre." *Leatherneck,* vol. 92, no. 6 (June 2009): 26–29.

Cannon, M. Hamlin. *Leyte: The Return to the Philippines [United States Army in World War II: The War in the Pacific].* Washington DC: United States Army Center of Military History, 1954.

Carlson, Evans F. *Evans F. Carlson on China at War, 1937–1941.* New York NY: China and Us Publication, 1993.

Castle, Alfred L. "President Roosevelt and General MacArthur at the Honolulu Conference of 1944." *Hawaiian Journal of History* (2004): 165–173.

Cate, James Lea and James C. Olson. "Precision Bombardment Campaign." In *The Pacific: Matterhorn to Nagasaki: June 1944 to August 1945. [The Army Air Forces in World War II, vol. 5],* edited by Wesley Frank Craven and James Lea Cate, 546–576. Chicago IL: University of Chicago Press, 1953.

Cate, James Lea and Wesley Frank Craven. "Victory." In *The Pacific: Matterhorn to Nagasaki: June 1944 to August 1945 [The Army Air Forces in World War II, vol. 5],* edited by Wesley Frank Craven and James Lea Cate, 703–756. Chicago IL: University of Chicago Press, 1953.

Central Pacific Operations Record Part II, April–November 1944 [Japanese Monograph no. 49]. Washington, DC: Department of the Army, 1949.

Chan Cheong-choo. *Memoirs of a Citizen of Early XX Century China.* Willowdale: n. p., 1978.

Chan Yeeshan. *Abandoned Japanese in Postwar Manchuria: The Lives of War Orphans and Wives in Two Countries.* Abingdon: Taylor & Francis Group, 2011.

Chapman, F. Spencer. *The Jungle Is Neutral.* London: Chatto and Windus, 1950.

Chen Jian. *Mao's China and the Cold War.* Chapel Hill NC: University of North Carolina Press, 2001.

Ch'en Li-fu. *The Storm Clouds Clear over China: The Memoir of Ch'en Li-fu 1900–1993.* Stanford CA: Hoover Institution Press, 1994.

Chen Yung-fa. "Guanjian de yinian: Jiang Zhongheng yu Yu Xiang Gui kuibai" ["The Pivotal Year: Chiang Kai-shek and the Rout of Henan, Hunan and Guangxi"]. In *Zhongguo lishi de zaisikao [A Reassessment of Chinese History]* edited by Liu Cuirong, 347–431. Taipei: Linking Books, 2015.

———, "Chiang Kai-shek and the Japanese Ichigo Offensive, 1944." In *Chiang Kai-shek and His Time: New Historical and Historiographical Perspectives,* edited by Laura De Giorgi and Guido Samarani, 37–74. Venice: Edizioni Ca' Foscari, 2017.

Chen Zhenfeng. "Zhuanzhan Yuzhong" ["Shifting the Battle to Central Henan"]. In *Zhongyuan Kangzhan: Yuan Guomindang jiangling Kangri Zhanzheng qinliji [The War of Resistance in the Central Plain: Personal Recollections from the War of Resistance against Japan by Former Nationalist Commanders],* 273–296. Beijing: Zhongguo Wenshi Chubanshe, 1995.

Chennault, Claire Lee. *Way of a Fighter.* New York NY: G. P. Putnam's Sons, 1949.

Ch'i Hsi-sheng. *Nationalist China at War: Military Defeats and Political Collapse, 1937–45.* Ann Arbor MI: University of Michigan Press, 1982.

———, "The Military Dimension, 1942–1945." In *China's Better Victory: The War with Japan 1937–1945,* edited by James C. Hsiung and Steven I. Levine, 157–184. Armonk NY: M. E. Sharpe, 1992.

Chiang Kai-shek. *Zongtong Jianggong sixiang yanlun zongji [General Collection of President Chiang Kai-shek's Thoughts and Speeches].* Taipei: Zhongguo Guomindang zhongyang weiyuanhui dangshi weiyuanhui, 1985.

Christensen, Erleen. *In War and Famine: Missionaries in China's Honan Province in the 1940s.* Montreal and Kingston: McGill-Queen's University Press, 2005.

Clifton, Allan Stephen. *Time of Fallen Blossoms.* New York NY: A. A. Knopf 1951.

Cook, Haruko Taya and Theodore F. Cook. *Japan at War: An Oral History.* New York NY: The New Press, 1992.

Coox, Alvin D. "Air War Against Japan." In *Case Studies in the Achievement of Air Superiority,* edited by Benjamin Franklin Cooling. Washington DC: Center for Air Force History, 1994, 383–452.

Crisis Fleeting: Original Reports on Military Medicine in India and Burma in the Second World War, edited by James H. Stone. Washington DC: Government Printing Office, 1969.

Crowl, Philip A. *Campaign in the Marianas [United States Army in World War II: The War in the Pacific].* Washington DC: Office of the Chief of Military History, Department of the Army, 1960.

Crowl, Philip A. and Edmund G. Love. *Seizure of Gilberts and Marshalls [United States Army in World War II].* Washington DC: US Government Printing Office, 1955.

Cutler, Thomas J. *The Battle of Leyte Gulf.* Annapolis MD: Naval Institute Press, 1994.

Davies, John Paton Jr. *China Hand: An Autobiography.* Philadelphia PA: University of Pennsylvania Press, 2012.

Dean, Peter J. and Kevin Holzimmer. "The Southwest Pacific Area: Military Strategy and Operations, 1944–45." In *Australia 1944–45: Victory in the Pacific,* ed. Peter Dean, 28–50. Port Melbourne: Cambridge University Press, 2015.

Dennis, Peter. *Troubled Days of Peace: Mountbatten and South East Asia Command, 1945–46.* Manchester: Manchester University Press, 1987.

Dick, Philip K. *The Man in the High Castle.* London: Penguin, 2010.

Dickson, W. D. *The Battle of the Philippine Sea, June 1944*. London: Ian Allan, 1975.

Dower, John W. *War Without Mercy*. New York NY: W. W. Norton and Co. 1986.

———, *Embracing Defeat: Japan in the Wake of World War II*. New York NY: W. W. Norton and Co., 1999.

Drea, Edward J. "Missing Intentions: Japanese Intelligence and the Soviet Invasion of Manchuria, 1945." *Military Affairs*, vol. 48, no. 2, (April 1984): 66–73.

———, *MacArthur's Ultra: Codebreaking and the War against Japan, 1942–1945*. Lawrence KS: University of Kansas Press, 1992.

———, *In the Service of the Emperor: Essays on the Imperial Japanese Army*. Lincoln NE: University of Nebraska Press, 1998.

Dreyer, Edward L. *China at War 1901–1949*. London: Longman, 1995.

Dull, Paul S. *A Battle History of the Imperial Japanese Navy (1941–1945)*. Annapolis MD: Naval Institute Press, 1978.

Dulles, Foster Rhea. *Yankees and Samurai: America's Role in the Emergence of Modern Japan*. New York NY: Harper and Row, 1965.

Dyer, George Carroll. *The Amphibians Came to Conquer: The Story of Admiral Richmond Kelly Turner*. Washington DC: Department of the Navy, 1972.

Eichelberger, Robert L. *Our Jungle Road to Tokyo*. New York NY: The Viking Press, 1950.

———, *Dear Miss Em: General Eichelberger's War in the Pacific, 1942–1945*. Westport CT: Greenwood Press, 1972.

Elliott, Duong Van Mai. *The Sacred Willow: Four Generations in the Life of a Vietnamese Family*. Oxford: Oxford University Press, 1999.

Feith, Herbert. The *Decline of Constitutional Democracy in Indonesia*. Ithaca NY: Cornell University Press, 1962.

Fitts, Robert K. *Banzai Babe Ruth: Baseball, Espionage, & Assassination during the 1934 Tour of Japan*. Lincoln NE: University of Nebraska Press, 2012.

Flanagan, Edward M. *The Angels: A History of the 11th Airborne Division 1943–1946*. Washington DC: Infantry Journal Press, 1948.

Fluckey, Eugene B. *Thunder Below! The USS Barb Revolutionizes Submarine Warfare in World War II*. Urbana and Chicago IL: University of Illinois Press, 1997.

Foreign Relations of the United States. Washington DC: United States Government Printing Office.

Frank, Benis M. and Henry I. Shaw. *Victory and Occupation [History of U.S. Marine Corps Operations in World War II, vol. 5]*. Washington DC: US Government Printing Office, 1968.

Frank, Richard B. *Downfall: The End of the Imperial Japanese Empire*. New York NY: Random House, 1999.

Frierson, William C. *The Admiralties: Operations of the 1st Cavalry Division, 29 February – 18 May 1944*. Washington, DC: United States Army Center of Military History, 1946.

Fujiwara Akira. "Taipingyang zhanzheng baofahou de Riji zhanzheng" ["The Sino-Japanese War after the Outbreak of the Pacific War"]. Translated by Xie Lili. *Zhonggongdang shi yanjiu*, no. 1 (1989): 79–85.

Fukudome Shigeru. "The Air Battle off Taiwan." In *The Japanese Navy in World War Two*, edited by David C. Evans, 334–354. Annapolis MD: Naval Institute Press, 2017.

Futamatsu Yoshihiko. *Across the Three Pagodas Pass: The Story of the Thai-Burma Railway*. Kent: Renaissance Books, 2013.

Futrell, Frank. "Hollandia." In *The Pacific: Guadalcanal to Saipan: August 1942 to July 1944 [The Army Air Forces in World War II, vol. 4]*. Edited by Wesley Frank Craven and James Lea Cate, 575–614. Chicago IL: University of Chicago Press, 1950.

Gan Yinsen. "Hengyang zhanyi huiyi" ["A Memoir of the Battle of Hengyang"]. In *Hunan sida huizhan: Yuan Guomindang jiangling Kangri Zhanzheng qinliji [The Four Major Battles of Hunan: Personal Recollections from the War of Resistance against Japan by Former Nationalist Commanders]*, 499–501. Beijing: Zhongguo Wenshi Chubanshe, 1995.

Garand, George W. and Truman R. Strobridge. *Western Pacific Operations [History of U.S. Marine Corps Operations in World War II, vol. 4]*. Washington DC: US Government Printing Office, 1971.

Garfield, Brian. *Thousand-Mile War: World War II in Alaska and the Aleutians*. Fairbanks AK: University of Alaska Press, 1995.

General Headquarters United States Army Forces in the Pacific. *"Downfall": Strategic Plan for Operations in the Japanese Archipelago*. n. p.: United States Army, 1945.

Giangreco, D. M. "The Hokkaido Myth." *Journal of Strategy and Politics*, vol. 2 (2015): 148–164.

Giffard, George J. "Operations in Assam and Burma from 23 June 1944 to 12 November 1944." *Supplement to the London Gazette* (March 30, 1951): 1711–1737.

Glantz, David M. and Jonathan M. House. *When Titans Clashed: How the Red Army Stopped Hitler*. Lawrence KS: University Press of Kansas, 2015.

Guam: Operations of the 77th Division 21 July–10 August 1944. Washington DC: US Government Printing Office, 1990.

Guo Daijun, *Chongtan Kangrishi [Revisiting the Second Sino-Japanese War, 1931–1945], vol. 1*. Taipei: Linking Book, 2015.

Halsey, William F. and J. Bryan III. *Admiral Halsey's Story*. New York NY: Da Capo Press, 1976.

Hara Takeshi. "The Ichigō Offensive." In *The Battle for China*. Edited by Mark Peattie, Edward Drea and Hans van de Ven, 392–402. Stanford CA: Stanford University Press, 2011.

Harmsen, Peter. *Storm Clouds over the Pacific 1931–1941*. Havertown PA: Casemate, 2018.

Hartendorp, A. V. H. *The Japanese Occupation of the Philippines, vol. 1–2*. Manila: Bookmark, 1967.

Hatano Sumio. "Wartime Relations between Japan and the Soviet Union, 1941–1945." In *A History of Russo-Japanese Relations: Over Two Centuries of Cooperation and Competition*, edited by Dmitry Streltsov and Nobuo Shimotomai, 241–258. Leiden: Brill, 2019.

Havens, Thomas R. H. *Valley of Darkness: The Japanese People and World War Two*. New York NY: W. W. Norton and Company, 1978.

Hayes, Grace Person. *The History of the Joint Chiefs of Staff in World War II: The War against Japan*. Annapolis MD: Naval Institute Press, 1982.

Heinrich, Waldo and Marc Gallicchio. *Implacable Foes: War in the Pacific 1944–1945*. New York NY: Oxford University Press, 2017.

Horner, David. "Advancing National Interests: Deciding Australia's War Strategy, 1944–45." In *Australia 1944–45: Victory in the Pacific*, edited by Peter Dean, 9–27. Port Melbourne: Cambridge University Press, 2015.

Hornfischer, James D. *The Last Stand of the Tin Can Sailors*. New York NY: Bantam Books, 2004.

Hough, Frank O. *The Island War*. New York NY: J. B. Lippincott Company, 1947.

Hough, Frank O. and John A. Crown. *The Campaign on New Britain*. Historical Branch, Headquarters, U.S. Marine Corps, 1952.

How the Guam Operation Was Conducted. Tokyo: Ground Self Defense Forces Staff School, 1962.

Huff, Gregg. *World War II and Southeast Asia: Economy and Society under Japanese Occupation*. Cambridge: Cambridge University Press, 2020.

Hunt, Frazier. *The Untold Story of Douglas MacArthur*. New York NY: Manor Books, 1977.

Imparato, Edward T. *General MacArthur: Speeches and Reports 1908–1964*. Paducah KY: Turner Pub., 2000.

Inaugural Addresses of the Presidents of the United States from George Washington 1789 to Richard Mulhouse Nixon 1969. Washington DC: Government Printing Office, 1969.

Inoguchi Rikihei and Nakajima Tadashi. "The Kamikaze Attack Corps." In *The Japanese Navy in World War Two*, edited by David C. Evans, 415–439. Annapolis MD: Naval Institute Press, 2017.

Ion, A. Hamish. "'Much Ado About Too Few': Aspects of the Treatment of Canadian and Commonwealth POWs and Civilian Internees in Metropolitan Japan 1941–1945." *Defence Studies*, vol. 6, no. 3 (September 2006): 292–317.

Iriye Akira. *Power and Culture: The Japanese-American War 1941–1945*. Cambridge MA: Harvard University Press, 1981.

Ismay, Hastings Lionel. *The Memoirs of Lord Ismay*. London: Heinemann, 1960.

Itoh Mayumi. *Japanese War Orphans in Manchuria: Forgotten Victims of World War II*. New York NY: Palgrave Macmillan, 2010.

James, D. Clayton. *The Years of MacArthur*. Boston MA: Houghton Mifflin Company, 1970–1985.

James, Karl. *The Hard Slog: Australians in the Bougainville Campaign, 1944–45*. Cambridge: Cambridge University Press, 2012.

Jeans, Roger B. ed. *The Marshall Mission to China, 1945–1947: The Letters and Diary of Colonel John Hart Caughey*. Lanham MD: Rowman and Littlefield, 2011.

Jensen, Oliver. *Carrier War*. New York NY: Simon and Schuster, 1945.

Johnston, James W. *The Long Road of War: A Marine's Story of Pacific Combat*. Lincoln NE: University of Nebraska Press, 1998.

de Jong, L. *The Collapse of a Colonial Society: The Dutch in Indonesia during the Second World War*. Leiden: KITLV Press, 2002.

Kanahele, George Sanford. "The Japanese Occupation of Indonesia: Prelude to Independence." PhD diss., Cornell University, 1967.

Kase Toshikazu. *Journey to the Missouri*. New Haven CT: Yale University Press, 1950.

Kawahara, Toshiaki. *Hirohito and His Times: A Japanese Perspective*. Tokyo: Kodansha International, 1990.

Kawai Kazuo. "Militarist Activity between Japan's Two Surrender Decisions." *Pacific Historical Review*, vol. 22, no. 4 (1953): 383–389.

Kawamura Noriko. *Emperor Hirohito and the Pacific War*. Seattle WA: University of Washington Press, 2015.

Kennedy, Paul. *The Rise and Fall of the Great Powers*. New York NY: Vintage Books, 1989.

Kenney, George C. *General Kenney Reports: A Personal History of the Pacific War*. New York NY: Duell, Sloane, and Pearce, 1949.

King, Ernest J. *US Navy at War, 1941–1945: Official Reports to the Secretary of the Navy*. Washington DC: United States Navy Department, 1946.

King, Ernest J. and W. M. Whitehill. *Fleet Admiral King*. New York NY: Norton, 1952.

Kirichenko, Aleksei A. and Sergey V. Grishachev. "The 'Manchurian Blitzkrieg' of 1945 and Japanese Prisoners of War in the Soviet Union." In *A History of Russo-Japanese Relations: Over Two Centuries of Cooperation and Competition*, edited by Dmitry Streltsov and Nobuo Shimotomai, 334–351. Leiden: Brill, 2019.

Kiyosawa Kiyoshi. *A Diary of Darkness: The Wartime Diary of Kiyosawa Kiyoshi*, edited by Eugene Soviak. Princeton NJ: Princeton University Press, 1998.

Kort, Michael. *The Columbia Guide to Hiroshima and the Bomb*. New York NY: Columbia University Press, 2007.

Kovner, Sarah. *Prisoners of the Japanese: Inside Japanese POW Camps*. Cambridge MA: Harvard University Press, 2020.

Koyanagi Tomiji. "The Battle of Leyte Gulf." In *The Japanese Navy in World War Two*, edited by David C. Evans, 355–384. Annapolis MD: Naval Institute Press, 2017.

Krammer, Arnold. "Japanese Prisoners of War in America." *Pacific Historical Review*, vol. 52, no. 1 (February 1983): 67–91.

Kratoska, Paul H. *The Japanese Occupation of Malaya and Singapore, 1941–45: A Social and Economic History*. Singapore: NUS Press, 2018.

Kratoska, Paul H. and Ken'ichi Goto. "Japanese Occupation of Southeast Asia, 1941–1945." In *The Cambridge History of the Second World War, Vol. 2: Politics and Ideology*, edited by Richard Bosworth and Joseph Maiolo, 533–557. Cambridge: Cambridge University Press, 2015.

Kraus, Theresa L. *China Offensive*. Washington DC: Department of the Army, 1996.

Krueger, Walther. *From Down Under to Nippon*. Nashville TN: Battery Press, 1989.

Kurasawa Aiko. "Transportation and Rice Distribution in South-East Asia during the Second World War." In *Food Supplies and the Japanese Occupation in South-East Asia*, edited by Paul H. Kratoska, 32–66. Basingstoke: Macmillan, 1998.

Lane, Kerry L. *Guadalcanal Marine*. Jackson MS: University Press of Mississippi, 2004.

"Last Letters of Kamikaze Pilots." *Mānoa*, vol. 13, no. 1 (summer 2001): 120–123.

Lattimore, Owen. *China Memoirs: Chiang Kai-shek and the War Against Japan*. Tokyo: University of Tokyo Press, 1990.

Lea, Tom. "Peleliu Landing." In *Reporting World War II: American Journalism 1938–1946*, vol. 2, edited by Samuel Hynes, Nancy Caldwell Sorel, Anne Matthews, and Roger J. Spiller, 498–535. New York NY: Literary Classics of the United States, Inc., 1995.

Lebra, Joyce C. *The Indian National Army and Japan*. Singapore: Institute of Southeast Asian Studies, 2008.

———, *Japanese-Trained Armies in Southeast Asia*. Singapore: Institute of Southeast Asian Studies, 2010.

Leckie, Robert. *Strong Men Armed: The United States Marines Against Japan*. New York NY: Random House, 1962.

———, *Helmet for My Pillow*. New York NY: Bantam, 2010.

Lee, Fitzhugh. "First Cruise of the *Essex*." In *Carrier Warfare in the Pacific: An Oral History Collection*, edited by E. T. Wooldridge, 106–114. Washington DC: Smithsonian Institution Press, 1993.

LeMay, Curtis. *Mission with LeMay: My Story*. Garden City NY: Doubleday, 1965.

Li Tsung-jen and Tong Te-kong. *The Memoirs of Li Tsung-jen*. Boulder CO: Westview Press, 1979.

Lindbergh, Charles A. *The Wartime Journals of Charles A. Lindbergh*. New York NY: Harcourt Brace Jovanovich Inc., 1970.

Lindblad, Thomas J. "The eclipse of the Indonesian economy under Japanese Occupation." In *Economies under Occupation: The hegemony of Nazi Germany and Imperial Japan in World War II*, edited by Marcel Boldorf and Okazaki Tetsuji, 205–217. London: Routledge, 2015.

Liu Yaxian. "Luoyang zhanyi huiyi" ["Reminiscences about the Battle of Luoyang"]. In *Zhongyuan Kangzhan: Yuan Guomindang jiangling Kangri Zhanzheng qinliji [The War of Resistance in the Central Plain: Personal Recollections from the War of Resistance against Japan by Former Nationalist Commanders]*, 369–376. Beijing: Zhongguo Wenshi Chubanshe, 1995.

Lockwood, Charles A. and Hans C. Adamson. *Battles of the Philippine Sea*. New York NY: Crowell, 1967.

Lodge, R. O. *The Recapture of Guam*. Washington DC: Historical Branch, United States Marine Corps, 1954.

Logevall, Fredrik. *Embers of War: The Fall of an Empire and the Making of America's Vietnam*. New York NY: Random House, 2015.

Long, Gavin. *The Final Campaigns [Australia in the War of 1939–1945, Series I (Army), vol. 7]*. Canberra: Australian War Memorial, 1963.

Lottaz, Pascal. "Neutral States and Wartime Japan: The Diplomacy of Sweden, Spain, and Switzerland towards the Empire." PhD diss., National Graduate Institute for Policy Studies, 2018.

Lozano, Gustavo Vázquez. *201st Squadron: The Aztec Eagles.* n. p.: Libros de México, 2019.

MacArthur, Douglas. *Reminiscences.* New York NY: McGraw-Hill Book Company, 1964.

Manchester, William. *American Caesar.* London: Hutchinson of London, 1979.

Marcello, Ronald E. "Lone Star POWs: Texas National Guardsmen and the Building of the Burma-Thailand Railroad, 1942–1944." *The Southwestern Historical Quarterly,* vol. 95, no. 3 (January 1992): 293–321.

Marr, David G. *Vietnam 1945: The Quest for Power.* Berkeley CA: University of California Press, 1999.

Matloff, Maurice. *Strategic Planning for Coalition Warfare 1943–1944 [United States Army in World War II].* Washington DC: US Government Printing Office, 1958.

Mathias, Frank F. *GI Jive: An Army Bandsman in World War II.* Lexington KY: University Press of Kentucky, 1982.

Medcalf, Peter. *War in the Shadows: Bougainville 1944–45.* Canberra: Australian War Memorial, 1986.

Melati, Sintha. "In the Service of the Underground." In *Local Opposition and Underground Resistance to the Japanese in Java 1942–1945,* edited by Anton Lucas, 123–164. Clayton: Monash Papers on Southeast Asia, no. 13, Centre of Southeast Asian Studies, Monash University, 1986.

Michel, John J. A. *Mr. Michel's War: From Manila to Mukden: an American Navy Officer's War with the Japanese, 1941–1945.* Novato CA: Presidio, 1998.

Miller, John. *Cartwheel: The Reduction of Rabaul [United States Army in World War II: The War in the Pacific].* Washington DC: Office of the Chief of Military History, Department of the Army 1959.

Mitter, Rana. *China's War With Japan, 1937–1945: The Struggle For Survival.* London: Allen Lane, 2013.

Monk, Ray. *Inside the Centre: The Life of J. Robert Oppenheimer.* London: Jonathan Cape, 2012.

Montgomery, John D. *Forced to Be Free: The Artificial Revolution in Germany and Japan.* Chicago, IL: University of Chicago Press, 1957.

Morison, Samuel Eliot. *Aleutians, Gilberts and Marshalls June 1942–April 1944 [History of the United States Naval Operations in World War II, vol. 7].* Boston MA: Little, Brown and Co., 1951.

———, *New Guinea and the Marianas March 1944–August 1944 [History of the United States Naval Operations in World War II, vol. 8].* Boston MA: Little, Brown and Co., 1953.

———, *Leyte June 1944–January 1945 [History of the United States Naval Operations in World War II, vol. 12].* Boston MA: Little, Brown and Co., 1958.

———, *The Liberation of the Philippines: Luzon, Mindanao, the Visayas 1944–1945 [History of the United States Naval Operations in World War II, vol. 13].* Boston MA: Little, Brown and Co., 1959.

———, *Victory in the Pacific 1945 [History of the United States Naval Operations in World War II, vol. 14].* Boston MA: Little, Brown and Co., 1960.

Mortimer, Gavin. *Merrill's Marauders: The Untold Story of Unit Galahad and the Toughest Special Forces Mission of World War II.* Minneapolis MN: 2013.

Morton, Louis. *Strategy and Command: The First Two Years [United States Army in World War II: The War in the Pacific].* Washington DC: Office of the Chief of Military History, Department of the Army, 1962.

Mountbatten, Louis. *Personal Diary of Admiral the Lord Louis Mountbatten 1943–1946,* edited by Philip Ziegler. London: Collins, 1988.

Nakano Satoshi. "Appeasement and Coercion." In *The Philippines under Japan: Occupation Policy and Reaction,* edited by Ikehata Setsuho and Ricardo Trota Jose, 21–58. Quezon City: ADMU Press, 1999.

Nakayama Ichirō. *Industrialization of Japan.* Tokyo: Centre for East Asian Cultural Studies, 1964.

Neiman, Robert M. and Kenneth W. Estes. *Tanks on the Beaches: A Marine Tanker in the Great Pacific War*. College Station TX: Texas A&M University Press, 2002.

Nelson, George R. *I Company: The First and Last to Fight on Okinawa*. Bloomington IN: Authorhouse, 2003.

Nomura Minoru. "Ozawa in the Pacific: A Junior Officer's Experience." In *The Japanese Navy in World War Two*, edited by David C. Evans, 278–333. Annapolis MD: Naval Institute Press, 2017.

Notosusanto, Nugroho. "The Revolt of a PETA-Battalion in Blitar." *Asian Studies*, vol. 7, no. 1 (1969): 111–123.

Ogburn, Charlton, Jr. *The Marauders*. New York NY: Ballantine Books, 1959.

Oguma Eiji. *Return from Siberia: A Japanese Life in War and Peace, 1925–2015*. Tokyo: LTCB International Library Trust, 2018.

Ohnuki-Tierney, Emiko. *Kamikaze Diaries: Reflections of Japanese Student Soldiers*. Chicago IL: University of Chicago Press, 2006.

Olson, Keith W. "The G. I. Bill and Higher Education: Success and Surprise." *American Quarterly*, vol. 25, no. 5 (December 1973): 596–610.

Paine, S. C. M. *The Wars for Asia*. Cambridge: Cambridge University Press, 2012.

Park, Keith. "Air Operations in South East Asia from 1 June 1944 to the Occupation of Rangoon 2 May 1945." *Third Supplement to the London Gazette* (April 6, 1951): 1965–1992.

Paz, María Emilia. *Strategy, Security and Spies: Mexico and the U.S. as Allies in World War II*. University Park PA: Pennsylvania State University Press, 1997.

Peck, Graham. *Two Kinds of Time*. Seattle: University of Washington Press, 2008.

Philippine Area Naval Operations Part IV, January 1945–August 1945 [Japanese Monograph, no. 114]. Washington DC: Department of the Army, 1952.

Potter, E. B. *Nimitz*. Annapolis, MD: Naval Institute Press, 1976.

Prados, John. *Combined Fleet Decoded: The Secret History of American Intelligence and the Japanese Navy in World War II*. New York NY: Random House, 1995.

Public Papers of the Presidents of the United States: Harry S. Truman, Containing the Public Messages, Speeches, and Statements of the President, April 12 to December 1945. Washington DC: United States Government Printing Office, 1961.

Pyle, Ernie. *Last Chapter*. New York NY: Henry Holt, 1946.

Pyne, Michael John. "Relationships between Officers and Other Ranks in the Australian Army in the Second World War." PhD diss., University of Western Sydney, 2016.

Recto, Claro M. *The Complete Works of Claro M. Recto*, edited by Isagani R. Medina and Myrna S. Feliciano. Manila: Claro M. Recto Memorial Foundation, 1990.

Reel, A. Frank. *The Case of General Yamashita*. Chicago IL: University of Chicago Press, 1949.

Reports of General MacArthur. The Campaigns of MacArthur in the Pacific. Prepared by his General Staff. Washington DC: Government Printing Office, 1966.

Resident Commissioner of the Philippines to the United States. *Report on the Destruction of Manila and Japanese Atrocities*. Washington DC, 1945.

Romanus, Charles F. and Riley Sunderland. *Stilwell's Command Problems [United States Army in World War II: China-Burma-India Theater]*. Washington DC: United States Army Center of Military History, 1956.

———, *Time Runs Out in CBI [United States Army in World War II: China-Burma-India Theater]*. Washington DC: United States Army Center of Military History, 1959.

Roy, Kaushik. *Tropical warfare in the Asia-Pacific Region, 1941–45*. London: Routledge, 2017.

Russell, Richard A. *Project Hula: Secret Soviet-American Cooperation in the War Against Japan*. Washington, DC: Naval Historical Center, 1997.

Sato Shigeru. "Oppression and Romanticism: The Food Supply of Java during the Japanese Occupation." In *Food Supplies and the Japanese Occupation in South-East Asia*, edited by Paul H. Kratoska, 167–186. Basingstoke: Macmillan, 1998.

Schrijvers, Peter. *Bloody Pacific: American Soldiers at War with Japan*. Basingstoke: Palgrave Macmillan, 2010.

Shanks, George Dennis. "Malaria-Associated Mortality in Australian and British Prisoners of War on the Thai–Burma Railway 1943–1944." *American Journal of Tropical Medicine and Hygiene*, vol. 100, no. 4 (2019): 846–850.

Shaw, Henry I. and Douglas T. Kane, *Isolation of Rabaul [History of U.S. Marine Corps Operations in World War II, vol. 2]*. Washington DC: US Government Printing Office, 1963.

Shaw, Henry I., Bernard C. Nalty and Edwin T. Turnbladh. *Central Pacific Drive [History of U.S. Marine Corps Operations in World War II, vol. 3]*. Washington DC: US Government Printing Office, 1966.

Shen Zhihua. *Mao, Stalin and the Korean War: Trilateral Communist Relations in the 1950s*. Abingdon: Taylor & Francis Group, 2012.

Sherry, Michael. *The Rise of American Air Power: The Creation of Armageddon*. New Haven, CT: Yale University Press.

Shibutani Tamotsu. *The Derelicts of Company K: A Sociological Study of Demoralization*. Berkeley CA: University of California Press, 1978.

Shindo Hiroyuki. "Holding on to the Finish: The Japanese Army in the South and Southwest Pacific, 1944–45." In *Australia 1944–45: Victory in the Pacific*, edited by Peter Dean, Port Melbourne: Cambridge University Press, 2015.

Shipster, John. *Mist on the Rice-fields: A Soldier's Story of the Burma Campaign and the Korean War*. London: Leo Cooper, 2000.

Slim, William. *Defeat into Victory*. New York NY: David McKay Co., 1961.

Smeeton, Miles. *A Change of Jungles*. London: Rupert Hart-Davis, 1962.

Smith, Holland M. *Coral and Brass*. New York NY: Charles Scribner's Sons, 1949.

Smith, Robert Ross. *The Approach to the Philippines [United States Army in World War II: The War in the Pacific]*. Washington DC: United States Army Center of Military History, 1952.

———, *Triumph in the Philippines [United States Army in World War II: The War in the Pacific]*. Washington DC: United States Army Center of Military History, 1963.

Spector, Ronald H. *Eagle Against the Sun*. New York NY: Vintage Books, 1985.

Stanton, Doug. *In Harm's Way*. New York NY: Henry Holt and Company, 2001.

Stauffer, Alvin P. *The Quartermaster Corps: Operations in the War Against Japan [United States Army in World War II]*. Washington DC: US Government Printing Office, 1956.

Stilwell, Joseph W. *The Stilwell Papers*, edited by Theodor H. White. New York NY: William Sloane Associates Inc., 1948.

Takai Koji and Henry Sakaida. *B-29 Hunters of the JAAF*. Oxford: Osprey, 2001.

Tan Geming. "Guilin fangshou ji lunxian jingguo" ["The Defense and Fall of Guilin"]. In *Yue Gui Qian Dian Kangzhan: Yuan Guomindang jiangling Kangri Zhanzheng qinliji [The War of Resistance in Guangdong, Guangxi, Guizhou and Yunnan: Personal Recollections from the War of Resistance against Japan by Former Nationalist Commanders]*, 325–352. Beijing: Zhongguo Wenshi Chubanshe, 1995.

Tanaka Yukiko. *Hidden Horrors: Japanese War Crimes in World War II*. Boulder CO: Westview Press, 1996.

———, *Japan's Comfort Women: Sexual Slavery and Prostitution During World War II and the US Occupation*. London and New York NY: Routledge, 2001.

Taylor, Jeremy E. "From Traitor to Martyr: Drawing Lessons from the Death and Burial of Wang Jingwei 1944." *Journal of Chinese History*, vol. 3 no. 1 (2019): 137–158.

———, *Iconographies of Occupation: Visual Cultures in Wang Jingwei's China, 1939–1945*. Honolulu HI: University of Hawaii Press, 2021.

Taylor, Theodore. *The Magnificent Mitscher*. New York NY: Norton, 1954.

Terraine, John. *The Life and Times of Lord Mountbatten*. London: Hutchinson, 1969.

Thompson, Julian. *Forgotten Voices of Burma*. London: Ebury Press, 2009.

Toland, John. *The Rising Sun: The Decline and Fall of the Japanese Empire 1936–1945*. New York NY: Random House, 1970.

Tomita Takeshi. "The Reality of the Siberian Internment: Japanese Captives in the Soviet Union and Their Movements after Repatriation." In *A History of Russo-Japanese Relations: Over Two Centuries of Cooperation and Competition*, edited by Dmitry Streltsov and Nobuo Shimotomai, 305–333. Leiden: Brill, 2019.

Toye, Richard. *Churchill's Empire: The World That Made Him and the World He Made*. New York NY: Henry Holt and Company, 2010.

Tulloch, Derek. *Wingate in Peace and War*. London: Macdonald, 1972.

Ugaki Matome. *Fading Victory: The Diary of Admiral Matome Ugaki 1941–1945*, edited by Donald M. Goldstein and Katherine V. Dillon. Annapolis MD: Naval Institute Press, 1991.

Under the Same Army Flag: Recollections of the Veterans of the World War II, edited by Jean Pei and William W. Wang. Beijing: China Intercontinental Press, 2005.

United States Strategic Bombing Survey. The Effects of the Atomic Bombings of Hiroshima and Nagasaki (Washington DC: US Government Printing Office, 1946.

———, *Interrogations of Japanese Officials*. Washington DC: US Government Printing Office, 1946.

———, *Summary Report (Pacific War)*. Washington DC: US Government Printing Office, 1946.

———, *The Effects of Strategic Bombing on Japanese Morale*. Washington DC: US Government Printing Office, 1947.

Valtin, Jan. *Children of Yesterday*. New York NY: The Readers' Press, 1946.

van de Ven, Hans. *War and Nationalism in China 1925–1945*. Abingdon: RoutledgeCurzon, 2003.

———, *China at War: Triumph and Tragedy in the Emergence of the New China 1937–1945*. London: Profile Books, 2017.

Lyman P. Van Slyke. "The Chinese Communist movement during the Sino-Japanese War, 1937–1945." In *The Nationalist Era in China, 1927–1949*, edited by Lloyd E. Eastman, Jerome Ch'en, Suzanne Pepper, and Lyman P. Van Slyke, 177–290. Cambridge: Cambridge University Press, 1991.

Wakeman, Frederic Jr. "Hanjian (Traitor)! Collaboration and Retribution in Wartime Shanghai." In *Becoming Chinese: Passages to Modernity and Beyond*, edited by Yeh Wen-hsin, 298–341. Berkeley CA: University of California Press, 2000.

Walker, Charles H. *Combat Officer: A Memoir of War in the South Pacific*. New York NY: Ballantine Books, 2004.

Walsh, Brian. "Sexual Violence During the Occupation of Japan." *The Journal of Military History*, no. 82 (October 2018): 1199–1230.

Wang Qisheng. "The Battle of Hunan and the Chinese Military's Response to Operation Ichigō." In *The Battle for China*, edited by Mark Peattie, Edward Drea, and Hans van de Ven, 403–418. Stanford CA: Stanford University Press, 2011.

Watt, Lori. *When Empire Comes Home: Repatriation and Reintegration in Postwar Japan*. Cambridge MA: Harvard University Asia Center, 2009.

Webster, Philip D. *Thirty-Five Missions over Japan*. Bluebird Books, 2017.

Wedemeyer, Albert C. *Wedemeyer Reports!* New York NY: Henry Holt and Co., 1958.

Weinberg, Gerhard L. *A World at Arms: A Global History of World War II.* Cambridge: Cambridge University Press, 1994.

Whitney, Courtney. *MacArthur: His Rendezvous with History.* New York NY: Alfred A. Knopf, 1956.

Wickert, Erwin. *Mut und Übermut. Geschichten aus meinem Leben.* Stuttgart: Deutsche Verlags-Anstalt, 1992.

Wigmore, Lionel. *The Japanese Thrust [Australia in the War of 1939–1945, Series 1 (Army), vol. 4].* Canberra: Australian War Memorial, 1957.

Wilbanks, Bob. *Last Man Out: Glenn McDole, USMC, Survivor of the Palawan Massacre in World War II.* Jefferson NC: McFarland & Co., 2004.

Wilmott, H. P. *The Barrier and the Javelin: Japanese and Allied Pacific Strategies, February to June 1942.* Annapolis MD: Naval Institute Press, 1983.

Wolk, Herman S. *Cataclysm: General Hap Arnold and the Defeat of Japan.* Denton TX: University of North Texas Press, 2010.

Xing Jutian. "Luoyang zhandou jishi" ["A Factual Account of the Luoyang Battle"]. In *Zhongyuan Kangzhan: Yuan Guomindang jiangling Kangri Zhanzheng qinliji [The War of Resistance in the Central Plain: Personal Recollections from the War of Resistance against Japan by Former Nationalist Commanders]*, 364–368. Beijing: Zhongguo Wenshi Chubanshe, 1995.

Yamashita, Samuel Hideo. *Daily Life in Wartime Japan, 1940–1945.* Lawrence KS: University Press of Kansas, 2015.

Yokoi Toshiyuki. "Kamikazes in the Okinawa Campaign." In *The Japanese Navy in World War Two*, edited by David C. Evans, 453–473. Annapolis MD: Naval Institute Press, 2017.

Yoshida Mitsuru. "The Sinking of the *Yamato*." In *The Japanese Navy in World War Two*, edited by David C. Evans, 474–498. Annapolis MD: Naval Institute Press, 2017.

Yoshihara Kane. "Southern Cross: memories of the war in eastern New Guinea," [manuscript MSS0725]. Canberra: Australian War Memorial, 1955.

Zeng Jing. "Huigu Hengyang baoweizhan" ["A Look Back at the Battle to Defend Hengyang"]. In *Hunan sida huizhan: Yuan Guomindang jiangling Kangri Zhanzheng qinliji [The Four Major Battles of Hunan: Personal Recollections from the War of Resistance against Japan by Former Nationalist Commanders]*, 502–505. Beijing: Zhongguo Wenshi Chubanshe, 1995.

Zhang Wenjia. "Disi Jun qishou Changsha jingguo" ["How the Fourth Army Surrendered Changsha"]. In *Hunan sida huizhan: Yuan Guomindang jiangling Kangri Zhanzheng qinliji [The Four Major Battles of Hunan: Personal Recollections from the War of Resistance against Japan by Former Nationalist Commanders]*, 466–473. Beijing: Zhongguo Wenshi Chubanshe, 1995.

Zhang Yunhu. "Chinese Operations in Yunnan and Central Burma." In *The Battle for China*, edited by Mark Peattie, Edward Drea, and Hans van de Ven, 386–391. Stanford CA: Stanford University Press, 2011.

Newspapers, magazines

Atlantic.
Life.
Nippon Times.
New York Times.
Sydney Morning Herald.
Tampa Sunday Tribune.
Time.

Index